UNFINISHED BUSINESS

Screening the Italian Mafia in the New Millennium

The Italian Mafia is a deadly, pervasive national problem that cannot actually be classified as a cultural trauma precisely because of its seemingly endless nature. *Unfinished Business* provides insightful analyses of popular Italian Mafia cinema, exploring how representations of gender reflect on the unfinished process of mourning and healing of Mafia-related trauma.

Dana Renga discusses eleven recent films in which vestiges of Mafia-related trauma emerge in the various forms of abuse that women in, against, or around the Mafia undergo. While focusing on films that sensationalize violence and scapegoat women, Renga also examines those in which the homosexuality of male protagonists is repressed or rewritten.

Unfinished Business looks at the mechanics of film identification and spectatorship and proposes that trauma that has yet to be worked through on the national level is displaced onto the characters in the films under consideration. In a Mafia context, female characters are sacrificed, and non-normative sexual identities are suppressed in order to solidify traditional modes of viewer identification and assure narrative closure so that the image of the nation is left undisturbed.

DANA RENGA is an assistant professor in the Department of French and Italian at the Ohio State University, and editor of *Mafia Movies: A Reader*.

DANA RENGA

Unfinished Business

Screening the Italian Mafia in the New Millennium

UNIVERSITY OF TORONTO PRESS
Toronto Buffalo London

© University of Toronto Press 2013
Toronto Buffalo London
www.utppublishing.com

ISBN 978-1-4426-4748-0 (cloth)
ISBN 978-1-4426-1558-8 (paper)

Library and Archives Canada Cataloguing in Publication

Renga, Dana, 1971–, author
Unfinished business : screening the Italian Mafia in the new millennium / Dana Renga.

(Toronto Italian studies)
Includes bibliographical references and index.
ISBN 978-1-4426-4748-0 (bound).   ISBN 978-1-4426-1558-8 (pbk.)

1. Gangster films – Italy – History and criticism.   2. Mafia in motion pictures.   3. Psychic trauma in motion pictures.   4. Motion pictures and women.   I. Title.   II. Series: Toronto Italian studies

PN1995.9.M23R454 2013   791.43'6556   C2013-902696-7

University of Toronto Press acknowledges the financial assistance to its publishing program of the Canada Council for the Arts and the Ontario Arts Council.

University of Toronto Press acknowledges the financial support of the Government of Canada through the Canada Book Fund for its publishing activities.

Contents

Acknowledgments vii

Introduction: Trauma, Gender, and Recent Italian Mafia Cinema 3

1 Oedipal Conflicts in Marco Tullio Giordana's *I cento passi* 21

2 Honour, Shame, and Vendetta: Pasquale Scimeca's *Placido Rizzotto* 36

3 Mafia Woman in a Man's World: Roberta Torre's *Angela* 51

4 The Mafia Noir: Paolo Sorrentino's *Le conseguenze dell'amore* 65

5 Men of Honour, Man of Glass: Stefano Incerti's *L'uomo di vetro* 80

6 The Female Mob Boss: Edoardo Winspeare's *Galantuomini* 99

7 Melancholia and the Mob Weepie: Davide Barletti and Lorenzo Conte's *Fine pena mai: Paradiso perduto* 116

8 Mourning Disavowed: Matteo Garrone's *Gomorra* 134

9 Recasting Rita Atria in Marco Amenta's *La siciliana ribelle* 150

10 Trauma Postponed: Claudio Cupellini's *Una vita tranquilla* 165

Epilogue: Why Must Caesar Die? 181

Notes 191
Works Cited 223
Index 245

Acknowledgments

This project was only possible thanks to the incredible support of my colleagues in the Department of French and Italian and the Film Studies Program at The Ohio State University. I am touched by the enthusiasm and friendship of Janice Aski, Diane Birckbichler, John Davidson, Sarah-Grace Heller, Charles Klopp, Danielle Marx-Scouras, Judith Mayne, Louisa Shea, Cheikh Thiam, and Jennifer Willging, among others. I cannot imagine a more supportive environment for the study of Italian cinema. I am grateful to the Department of French and Italian and the Division of Arts and Humanities at The Ohio State University for their generous research funds and for their support of the publication of this book.

A version of chapter 1 appeared as "Oedipal Conflicts in Marco Tullio Giordano's *The Hundred Steps*," in *Annali d'italianistica* 30 (2012): 197–212, and revised sections of chapters 6, 9, and 10 appeared as "Screening the Italian Mafia: Bystanders, Perpetrators and Pentite," in *Journal of Italian Cinema and Media Studies* 1, no. 1 (2012): 55–70. I thank *Annali d'italianistica* and *Journal of Italian Cinema and Media Studies* for their permission to republish.

I would like to offer my sincere thanks to all those who provided me with invaluable insight throughout the project. My research assistant David Crane deserves praise for his wonderful work and I extend thanks to all my graduate students for exciting exchanges in several seminars. Stimulating conversations with Mia Fuller, Thomas Harrison, Dominic Holdaway, Tania Modleski, Alan O'Leary, and Heather Webb helped me shape the book. To Amy Boylan, David Filipi, Ruth Glynn, Danielle Hipkins, John Hellman, Judith Mayne, Elena Past, Robin Pickering-Iazzi, Louisa Shea, and Laura Wittman, I extend my appreciation for generous and smart feedback on several of the book's chapters. I owe a special debt of gratitude to Allison Cooper, Elizabeth Leake, Julia Nelson Hawkins, and Catherine O'Rawe, who read the manuscript in nearly its entirety (some chapters more than once) and provided me with astute suggestions for revisions. I remain amazed and humbled by their generosity.

It has been an absolute honour and pleasure working with Ron Schoeffel and Anne Laughlin at the University of Toronto Press, whom I thank, along with my wonderful copyeditor, John St James, for their encouragement, professionalism, and commitment to the project. This is truly a wonderful place for Italian Studies.

To my families in California and Columbus: Brigid Butler, Elaine Espeleta, Sarah Fairchild, Vijaya Iyer, Nicolette Jaworski, Michael Powers, Patricia Powers, Alan Renga, LaDonna Renga, Todd Rensi, Jeff Smith, and Laura Wittman, I thank you for your support. I am beyond grateful to my dearest friends Allison Cooper, Elizabeth Leake, and Genny Love for their undying friendship, intellectual engagement, and humour. And I extend infinite thanks to my partner, David Filipi, for his unwavering encouragement and boundless love.

UNFINISHED BUSINESS

Screening the Italian Mafia in the New Millennium

Introduction: Trauma, Gender, and Recent Italian Mafia Cinema

As they say in the world of fashion journalism, is the Camorra the new Mafia?
Cosmo Landesman, "Gomorra"

In order for traumas to emerge at the level of the collectivity, social crises must become cultural crises.
Jeffrey C. Alexander, "Toward a Theory of Cultural Trauma," 10

In repeating the traumas of both class and gender struggle, melodrama would, in its very generic formation, constitute a traumatic cultural symptom ... The repetition of certain stories may betray a traumatic cultural symptom, while the mode's adherence to realism, and thus to closure, seals over the traumatic ruptures and breaks that the culture endured. The style reassures the viewer, who leaves the cinema believing she is safe and that all is well in her world.
E. Ann Kaplan, "Melodrama, Cinema, and Trauma," 203

The object of love and of hatred for whose defence and for whose possession the brotherhood was born, in conflict with the law of the father, is the mother, who symbolically represents possession of the earth. The secret which unites the fraternal members of the association, the *omertà* in effect, is the weapon turned against the father, the law, the state, the outside world, in defense of the world inside, in defense of a mother fantasized as uniquely good, a holyholy-mother.
Renate Siebert, *Secrets of Life and Death*, 26

Mafia as the New Italian Terrorism

Unfinished Business: Screening the Italian Mafia in the New Millennium looks at recent Italian Mafia cinema through the lens of gender and trauma theory. I am particularly interested in how representations of gender in these films dialogue with the unfinished or delayed process of grieving, mourning, and healing of Mafia-related trauma. The Italian Mafia is an ongoing, deadly, and national problem that, as of yet, cannot be classified as a cultural trauma precisely because of its seemingly endless nature. Furthermore, the Mafia is considered a "men only society," but women are a constant presence in, around, and against it.[1] Essentially, Mafia women connote a problem for those both within and outside of the organization: the trauma of the Mafia that hangs over Italy but is often disregarded. They embody the "unfinished business" that is the unresolved conflict between the Mafia and Italians. In this book, I look at a selection of filmmakers whose films sensationalize violence and scapegoat women, or rewrite or repress the homosexuality of male protagonists. In a Mafia context, female characters are sacrificed and non-normative sexual identities are elided in order to solidify traditional modes of viewer identification and assure narrative closure so that the image of the nation is left unblemished.

The phenomenon of the *piovra* or "octopus," as the Mafia is called in Italy, is unlike other contemporaneous national traumas that have specific beginning and end points, such as the First World War, the *ventennio nero* or "black twenty years" of the fascist dictatorship, the deportation and extermination of Jews during the Second World War, and the period of intense terrorism in Italy lasting from 1968 until the early 1980s known as the *anni di piombo* ("the leaden years," which date roughly from the bombing of Piazza della fontana in Milan in 1969 through the early 1980s, at which time the members of many Italian terrorist groups were arrested). In these cases, a trauma discourse has been created in the public sphere that allows for the psychological impact of traumatizing events to be understood and articulated. This is not the way things stand, however, for the Italian Mafia. We can position, with a good deal of certainty, the birth of the Mafia with the birth of the Italian state in the 1860s, and we can list the myriad social, economic, and political factors that allowed for it to come into existence and to flourish for more than 150 years.[2] Unlike most other national traumas of the twentieth and twenty-first centuries, however, with the Mafia there is no end in sight. And if it has no end, how does one properly understand, make sense of, articulate, mourn, and overcome it? Will mourning always be disavowed or deferred? It is in fact ironic that in the new millennium, instead of looking towards the future, Italy is experiencing a period of delayed mourning and national melancholia with regards to the Mafia.

The Mafia in Italy, which is composed of the Sicilian Cosa Nostra, the Camorra of Campania, the Calabrian 'Ndrangheta, and the Sacra Corona Unita of Puglia, has pervaded almost every facet of cultural life, and has left thousands of victims in its wake. A look at Italian newspapers reveals stories of corruption, clan wars, homicides, drug busts, and raids, all Mafia-related. The Mafia is endemic to Italy, and, as described by Roberto Saviano in *Gomorra* (*Gomorrah*), is an intricate "system" of both corrupt and legitimate connections into national and international commerce, industry, and politics.[3] The Mafia has killed tens of thousands of people, the majority of whom are members of the organization, but victims also include anti-Mafia activists, judges, members of the police force, bystanders, and collaborators of justice known as "pentiti," or those who were once involved with the Mafia but then turned state's evidence. Mafia power, as Renate Siebert points out, is "based on terror," and many surrender to the organization out of "mortal anxiety."[4] In short, the Mafia's extensive reach into and disruption of Italian society qualify it as a form of domestic terrorism. And yet, the Mafia has terrorized the Italian populace in a much more long-term, widespread, and systematic manner than, say, Italian terrorist organizations did some thirty to forty years ago during the *anni di piombo*. Moreover, unlike terrorism during the *anni di piombo*, which was arguably overcome, Mafia terrorism has transcended the historical boundaries that customarily delineate national traumas.[5] Thus, its ongoing effect might constitute the Mafia as a cultural trauma comparable with or even more extensive than that of terrorism in Italy during the *anni di piombo*. In this way, paradoxically, it is the newest and the oldest form of Italian terrorism.[6]

Take, for example, the case of the Camorra, the Mafia of Naples and the Campania region, which is responsible for more than 4000 deaths over the last three decades. Just some years ago, accounts of Mafia violence in Naples went largely unnoticed in the international community. Naples today, however, recalls Palermo during the 1980s, when one Mafia-related death took place every three days.[7] Contemporary news coverage of the assassination of politician and activist Angelo Vassallo, arrests, drug busts, clan wars, extortion scandals, rotting or burning garbage, attacks on the group of Africans in Castelvolturno and subsequent rioting, corpses in the streets, or troops occupying various Campanian cities evokes descriptions of Palermo in the 1980s in which the city was likened to a war zone.[8] Thirty years later, however, various media in and outside of Italy have created a business out of the

Sicilian Cosa Nostra and softened its rough edges, therefore aiding to return it underground, where it has always preferred to be.[9] In contrast, the Camorra is capturing the international imaginary, no doubt in part due to the mammoth success of the film, book, and play *Gomorra*. Yet, it is doubtful that engaged art will influence the battle against the Mafia. One reviewer asks: "As they say in the world of fashion journalism, is the Camorra the new Mafia?"[10] In today, out tomorrow, around for hundreds of years. Although Italy is frequently imagined at home and abroad as unscathed by Mafia violence, the truth is that the social order is repeatedly disrupted, reconstructed, and then overturned anew.

The Italian Mafia: A Cultural Trauma?

Throughout the organization's long history, the Mafia has had and indeed still has a traumatic impact on many Italians: for example, entire communities live in fear as they learn of the assassinations and kidnappings of those who stand up to the organization; individuals experience profound anxiety at the deaths of friends and family either involved therein or innocently standing by; tens of thousands of businesses and public officials are intimidated into paying substantial bribes to avoid misfortune; inhabitants of Campania compare the region to Chernobyl, feeling that they are being poisoned, and talk of the dramatic increase in cancer rates in the area;[11] thousands of family members of Mafiosi dwell in the shadow of routine violence, many too intimidated or desensitized to resist. These actions confirm Judith Herman's contention that traumatic events are distinguishable from other routine setbacks as they "generally involve threat to life or bodily injury, or a close personal encounter with violence and death. They confront human beings with the extremities of terror."[12]

The Mafia undoubtedly has the potential to traumatize individuals and groups alike, and mourning is important and necessary in the wake of traumatizing events. What is unclear, however, is the extent to which the Mafia can be called a collective or a cultural trauma, as the very nature of its duration problematizes the traditional epistemology of trauma studies. Or, might we say that the Mafia points to a critical limit of trauma theory, and uncovers a need, in the case of ongoing trauma, to redefine its epistemological framework? Trauma theory generally insists upon a requisite period of latency between the now of the event and the then of the realization of its traumatic impact.[13]

Trauma, as Freud tells us, involves a temporal delay. Ruth Leys explains the import of a post-traumatic "incubation" period to the notion of *Nachträglichkeit*, or "deferred action." For Freud, Leys argues, "trauma was constituted by a dialectic between two events, neither of which was intrinsically traumatic, and a temporal delay or latency through which the past was available only by a deferred act of understanding and interpretation."[14] Thus, the first event takes the individual by surprise and results in what Freud calls "fright," which is "the state a person gets into when he has run into danger without being prepared for it; it emphasizes the factor of surprise."[15] The event is then repressed until another incident, innocuous or otherwise, triggers the earlier memory that returns to haunt the individual in the guise of a variety of symptoms (dissociation, dreams, hallucinations, flashbacks, nightmares, anxiety, depression, amnesia, mania). Trauma formation, then, is contextual and involves a process; it is not "a thing in itself."[16] In other words, the originary event itself does not produce the traumatic effect, but the memory of it and its acting out, as Cathy Caruth points out in her discussion of trauma, memory, and survival: "the fact that, for those who undergo trauma, it is not only the moment of the event, but of the passing out of it that is traumatic; that *survival itself*, in other words, *can be a crisis*."[17] Thus, reacting to, working through, moving on, or surviving makes the event implicitly traumatic. Paradoxically, then, one must return to, make sense of, and give voice to the past in order to leave it behind, which is particularly challenging in the case of the Mafia, as it remains, as of yet, without a conclusion. Essentially, the Mafia certainly causes individuals and groups injury, but does not allow them to articulate traumatic responses and create a discourse of trauma in a way that recovers memory and enables the critical process of mourning to take place.

A collective trauma, however, plays out differently in its affecting not an individual psyche but an entire community. In his ground-breaking work on trauma, community, and loss in the aftermath of the 1972 Buffalo Creek (West Virginia) flood, Kai Erikson defines an individual trauma as an unexpected and brutal blow to the psyche that "breaks through one's defences" so as to impede an effective reaction. Like individual trauma, a critical component to collective trauma is delayed response. However, a collective trauma is distinct, as it entails a complete alteration of communal identity, and of bonds between members thereof. Erikson defines a collective trauma as a blow to the basic tissues of social life that damages the bonds attaching people together and impairs the prevailing sense of communality. The collective trauma works its way slowly and even insidiously into the awareness of those who suffer from it, so it does not have the quality of suddenness normally associated with "trauma." But it is a form of shock all the same, a gradual realization that the community no longer exists as an effective support and that an important part of the self has disappeared … "I" continue to exist, though damaged and maybe even permanently changed. "You" continue to exist, though distant and hard to relate to. But "we" no longer exist as a connected pair or as linked cells in a larger communal body.[18]

With an individual trauma, scars are searched for in the survivor's mind, while the experience of recovery from a collective trauma involves looking for the scars in "the tissues of [survivors'] social lives as well."[19]

Trauma theorists argue that individual trauma will be settled and put to rest through the process of "working through," which can restore memory and recover truth in order to eventually "[set] things right in the self."[20] With a collectivity, however, a discourse of cultural trauma needs to be created by those individuals and groups damaged by the event. The activity of generating a trauma narrative begins when various agents, which Jeffrey C. Alexander dubs "carrier groups," make claims regarding the nature of the wound and construct a narrative "about a horribly destructive social process."[21] The "trauma claim" is then projected to a larger audience and played out in the public arena until a trauma discourse is generated that can capture and express the crisis. Only through the creation of a trauma narrative can the trauma become a part of collective identity,[22] and only then can communities begin the healing process and eventually be rebuilt. A cultural trauma, writes Alexander, "occurs when members of a collectivity feel they have been subjected to a horrendous event that leaves indelible marks upon their group consciousness, marking their memories forever and changing their future identity in fundamental and irrevocable ways." Such an experience connects a group and allows its members to confront and come to terms with that which they perceive as traumatic. In this way, a cultural trauma has a unitive capacity as individuals pinpoint the cause of grief and are then responsible to it and to one another.[23]

The process of creating a trauma narrative does not happen in a vacuum, as Alexander attests: "In order for traumas to emerge at the level of the collectivity, social crises must become cultural crises."[24] He means that trauma must play out in the cultural arena and secure a stronghold in the collective memory and imagination, and a language must be found that can encapsulate and communicate the crisis.[25] Ron Eyerman posits that, as a cultural process, "trauma is mediated through various forms of representation and linked to the reformation of collective identity and the reworking of collective memory,"[26] while Alexander positions trauma as a cultural construct of sorts that is enacted in several cultural spheres. The religious arena, aesthetic realm, legal system, scientific world, mass media, political sector, and the cinema all have a crucial role in how traumatic collective events are "remembered" and articulated.[27] This is how, to quote Saul Friedlander, "memory comes."[28]

Both individual and collective trauma occasion a deferral between the event and its resurfacing, in the first case in one's mind and in the latter in the cultural sphere. This, a typical psychic defence mechanism, works to safeguard the subject from the horrors of the past. E. Ann Kaplan insists that traumatic memory is transferred to another part of the brain, as remembering is "dangerous." "Individuals and cultures," she argues, "perform forgetting as a way of protecting themselves from the horrors of what one (or the culture) has done or what has been done to oneself or others in one's society."[29] Thus, a widespread historical amnesia follows trauma-inducing social crises until the collective is ready to begin coping with and taking responsibility for the past. Such a reconciliation begins with the "mediation" of the event in the forms mentioned above by Alexander. This process is fraught with conflicts, as it entails a struggle over signification that is marked by a "double tendency" of avoidance ("mass forgetting" and campaigns to downplay or "deny a cultural trauma") and the compulsion to repeat (group endeavours to keep its memory alive in collective consciousness).[30] During this period, "meaning work" takes place in order to "tell a new story"[31] about the traumatized culture and a trauma narrative is created by identifying the following: the nature of the pain and that of the victim,[32] the relation of the "victim to the wider audience," and, most crucially, a perpetrator.[33] Recall is dangerous, as Kaplan maintains, as it compels the subject to return to the scene of the crime. Moreover, cultural remembering and working through traumatic injury begin a process of inquiry that will ultimately lead to the alteration of the master narrative, as collective trauma will inevitably be connected with collective identity.[34]

Kaja Silverman points out that not all attempts at reconciliation and identity reformation are successful: "The notion of historical trauma formation represents ... an attempt to conceptualize how history sometimes manages to *interrupt* or even *deconstitute* what a society assumes to be its master narratives and immanent Necessity."[35] Why only sometimes? For one, the new story ultimately should be a better one. But also, and most significantly in the Italian case, various stakeholders occupy dominant power positions over those traumatized.[36] With its tentacular reach, the Mafia is entrenched in and influences the political, economic, and entertainment sectors. It undeniably holds sway over several of the four criteria necessary for the creation of trauma as a new "master narrative"[37] as outlined by Alexander – establishing the nature of the injury, assigning victim status, relating the victim to the larger collectivity, and pinpointing the offender(s).

With the case of the Mafia, at first glance, the nature of the pain and that of the victim seem clear-cut, especially considering the killings of all those who found themselves in the wrong place at the wrong time or several high-profile murders, including the assassinations of anti-Mafia judges Giovanni Falcone and Paolo Borsellino in 1992 or thirteen-year-old Giuseppe di Matteo, kidnapped in 1991 and executed two years later in retaliation for his father's betrayal of Cosa Nostra. Many of the potentially traumatized, however, are perpetrators. What's more, thousands hold a liminal status within the organization, including many women and children. These individuals are bound to their clan through the code of honour, family loyalty, and, frequently, fear. Yet, as they have never committed any illegal act, the line between victim and victimizer is nebulous. In these cases, the third category, "relation of the trauma victim to the wider audience," is problematic, as Italian society at large has yet to recognize, let alone engage in, a dialogue regarding such grey areas. Essentially, the suffering of those who fit this category is denied. Finally, echoing the voice-over finale of Alain Resnais's *Night and Fog* (1955), "Who, then, is responsible?" The all-too-straightforward response is to place blame solely with the Mafiosi, who appear in news headlines as clear-cut criminals: killers, drug runners, or long-time fugitives of justice. But what of the many perpetrators who have posts in public office and big business? These people have never fired a gun or been directly involved in extortion, the eco-Mafia, prostitution, money laundering, drug running, or illegal trade, for example. Even the country's most recent prime minister is not above suspicion and has been accused of Mafia collusion. Given the ambiguous status of the Mafia, its affiliates, and those affected by it in the Italian cultural scene, it is unsurprising that national "forgetting" is not always innocent, for, as Kaplan maintains, "political interests generally enter into processes of national memory or non-memory."[38]

I now return to my earlier question: Can the Mafia be considered a cultural or a collective trauma, comparable, say, to that of the years of terrorism? On the surface, it appears that Mafia power and abuse have a stronghold in the Italian imaginary: Italy has witnessed periods of intense but brief anti-Mafia activity, as in the aftermath of the slayings of Falcone and Borsellino, for example; grassroots organizations in the form of collectives, small museums, archives, and anti-bribe campaigns have a presence in southern Italy; memorials to anti-Mafia martyrs can be found in cities throughout the country; the Mafia is a regular topic of conversation in the news and on talk shows; hundreds of films, documentaries, television series, and made-for-television movies have been produced on the subject over the last one hundred years. But, it is significant that Mafia-related socio-cultural movements and personal initiatives are either short-lived or exist in a vacuum. Most important, however, with the Mafia, Italy is lacking in hindsight. Italy's several Mafias are by no means things of the past, and continue to grow stronger and adapt to the times.

In sum, and of pivotal import for my study, Italy has yet to experience a period of post-Mafia dormancy necessary for the generation of a trauma narrative regarding the Mafia. As Bernhard Giesen argues, collective traumas "require a time of latency before they can be acted out, spoken about, and worked through."[39] Such a historical lacuna disavows the construction of a trauma discourse and of subsequent national mourning at large and makes it near impossible to acknowledge, and let alone attempt to alter, the Mafia's social, political, and economic causes so as to "prevent its recurrence as well as enable forms of renewal."[40] Fundamentally, although the Italian Mafia has most certainly traumatized (and continues to traumatize) numerous individuals and exerts a traumatizing potential over whole communities, it cannot yet be considered a source of cultural trauma due to its unremitting, and seemingly unending, nature. In essence, Italy does not inhabit a post-traumatic state during which time traumatic injury is understood and articulated as cultural trauma.

Film and Trauma Studies

My project attempts to overcome the dilemma of periodization and historicization as it relates to a national trauma discourse with regards to the Mafia by reflecting on it as it is now, and not after the fact. I am indebted to Shoshana Felman and Dori Laub's work on the traumatic aftermath of the Second World War, an event they consider not to be "encapsulated in the past, but as a history which is essentially *not over*, a history whose repercussions are not simply omnipresent (whether consciously or not) in all our cultural activities, but whose traumatic consequences are still actually *evolving*."[41] Specifically, I consider the particularities of filmic representations when a traumatic event persists indefinitely and occupies such a peculiar place in the public discourse that it might disappear for periods of time, only to resurface in all of its bloody horror. Recalling Eric Santner, I ask, Will the mourning process always be incomplete, displaced, or denied?[42] Will the past, in Henry Rousso's words "never pass" because *Trauerarbeit* is unfinished?[43] Ultimately, looking at the Mafia in relationship to national mourning takes our understanding of the Mafia and of trauma and mourning in new directions.

Several scholars have pointed out film's crucial role in shaping cultural identity in the wake of national traumas and consider how national cinemas might serve as vehicles for working through traumatic injury. The new millennium has witnessed a proliferation of film studies with a trauma focus. In the Italian scene, particular attention has been paid to representations of the Holocaust and Italian terrorism. In her discussion of the phenomenon of the fairly recent outpouring of Holocaust films in Italy, Millicent Marcus assesses the level at which Italians at large are ready to engage in the work of mourning so that they may overcome Holocaust trauma.[44] In several works on the *anni di piombo*, authors look at how films on Italian terrorism from the last forty years or so reflect the national grieving process or participate in the construction of a new master narrative that reveals the fragility of patriarchy, for example.[45] Outside of Italian studies, those writing on the Holocaust, nuclear war, horror and zombie films, the First World War I, the Second World War, or 9/11 suggest that films on the topic allow groups to address the anxieties of the psychological and political unconscious that are shocked by national trauma.[46]

In the summer of 2001, *Screen* published a "trauma dossier" in the hopes of opening a debate regarding trauma and screen studies at large.[47] Many of the questions raised in the contributions of the collection from a decade prior inform my study. In his discussion of the latency period as it relates to films that grapple with traumatic events, Thomas Elsaesser asks the poignant question "Why this or that film *now?*"⁴⁸ – a critical query for Mafia movies that might take as their subject matter a past event, but reference a chronic social ill. Trauma theory, he says, is "not so much a theory of recovered memory as it is one of recovered referentiality," which "can only be recovered through interpretation."⁴⁹ In turn, I explore what recent Mafia cinema says about the state of affairs in the present.

For her part, Kaplan's essay "Melodrama, Cinema and Trauma" looks at how the repetition of familial traumas (of class and gender) in the popular film form known as the melodrama serves a double purpose: the genre reveals "a traumatic cultural symptom" only to "seal over" such traumatic ruptures through routinely and neatly wrapping up all story lines so as to assure narrative closure. She argues:

> In repeating the traumas of both class and gender struggle, melodrama would, in its very generic formation, constitute a traumatic cultural symptom … The repetition of certain stories may betray a traumatic cultural symptom, while the mode's adherence to realism, and thus to closure, seals over the traumatic ruptures and breaks that the culture endured. The style reassures the viewer, who leaves the cinema believing she is safe and that all is well in her world.⁵⁰

Kaplan returned to these observations in *Trauma Culture*, where she wonders if and how collective traumas might be "translated" for a group by classical and dominant film forms.⁵¹

Contemporary Italian cinema is increasingly indebted to traditional film models such as melodrama, the film noir, the biopic, the political thriller, and the woman's film, and by and large follows the Oedipal logic familiar to such genres. The classical nature of such films might hinder the extent to which they are capable of capturing a "post-traumatic consciousness," which comes not with, as Joshua Hirsch explains, the representation of horror and atrocity, but with "the attempt to formally reproduce for the spectator an experience of suddenly seeing the unthinkable."⁵² A principal objective of *Unfinished Business* is to gauge the extent to which Mafia-related trauma might be successfully rendered in conventional film forms.

In the penultimate piece of the "trauma dossier," Maureen Turim turns towards films in which the staging of individual traumas invites the viewer to contemplate the larger cultural implications of psychic distress. One effect of such an undertaking, Turim argues, is the creation of empathy, which might result in "a comprehension of the historicity of trauma as a collective phenomenon."[53] Turim insists upon the frequent embroilment of individual and collective components of trauma and examines how the trope of the modernist flashback might aid in the creation of a trauma discourse. Films that employ such disruptive and fragmentary intrusions have the capacity to eclipse the distance between then and now and therefore might provoke the viewer into embracing the suffering of others. Such films embody "a meaningful return to historical memory,"[54] because, as Herman argues, "an understanding of psychological trauma begins with rediscovering history."[55]

The breadth of recent Italian feature films, documentaries, and made-for-television movies and mini-series on the Mafia might suggest that Italy has begun the process of working through that is essential for coming to terms with trauma and is now "living in an age of [Mafia] memory."[56] However, and with a few exceptions, newer Italian Mafia movies are made in the realist mode and conform to the traditional logic of desire that dominates the classical cinema. These films smooth over Mafia-related trauma in order to focus on stories that are both pleasurable and familiar. Many biopics conclude with the celebration of the life and death of an anti-Mafia crusader and suggest that the country is populated with heroes ready to combat evil at all costs, while films that focus on women in or around the organization sublimate their subversive potential into sentimental love stories. Ultimately, much recent Mafia cinema puts forth a fantasy of a nation united against Mafia villainy.

Such absolute and unambiguous depictions of the Mafia and of those in and around it are problematic to the construction of a traumatic (and eventually a post-traumatic) consciousness in that, as Janet Walker foregrounds in the final instalment in *Screen* that focuses on misremembering, the most successful examples of trauma cinema are non-realist, and approach the past in a way that speaks to the inherent unrepresentability of the trauma-inducing event. In its adherence to narrative closure and the consolidation of visual pleasure, contemporary Italian Mafia cinema is by and large realist and succeeds, to quote Hirsch, in making "the past masterable by making it visible."[57] Ultimately, the films of my study conform to classical models and do not have a specifically designed political agenda. As such, they are not revolutionary in their probing of a national crisis and therefore do not tend to lead to greater historical understanding. This is because, I would like to suggest, such a comprehension, as Michael Frisch maintains, "has come to seem a threat, even *the* threat to the authority of traditional political culture."[58] Historical understanding has the potential to alter Italy's dominant fiction, which consists of, as Silverman claims, the "images and stories through which a society configures consensus."[59] The dominant fiction allows subjects to assert a "normative identity"[60] and is the pith "around which a nation's and period's 'reality' coheres."[61] I argue that new millennium Mafia movies propagate the ideological fantasy of a nation united against Mafia malfeasance and thus disavow the recognition of the Italian Mafia as a national trauma and subsequently postpone national mourning at large.

In sum, film has a crucial role in shaping cultural identity in the wake of national traumas, and national cinema can help work through trauma and reflect the mourning process. I consider film to be the vehicle par excellence to gauge the level at which Italy has yet to engage in the work of mourning necessary to come to terms with Mafia-related trauma. Instead of participating in the trauma process, an undertaking that, as Alexander explains, will eventually alter collective identity, Italy inhabits a state of perpetual melancholia.[62] Both mourning and melancholy, as Freud points out, are responses to loss. The main difference between the two, however, is that the melancholic refuses to acknowledge and accept the lost object and instead internalizes it within the ego. Mourning entails grief work, or working through loss until the mourner is freed from the lost object. Whereas the mourner, after a painful process of letting go, is finally able to declare the object dead and begin to live again, with the melancholic, the loss itself is literally lost within the self and therefore cannot be worked through. The mourner understands that something is lost, but the melancholic "cannot see clearly what it is that has been lost" and subsequently experiences the loss of the ego itself.[63] Freud argues that the melancholic responds through a process of destructive internalization; for the melancholic, the only way to keep hold of the object is to obliterate it within the ego. On the one hand, to identify with the lost object allows the relationship to endure, but on the other, the ego will never successfully live up to what was originally lost and the now internalized object is debased and degraded; it takes on the qualities of the undead, as it floats between life and death.[64]

I situate my study of gender identity in the Mafia onscreen within this grey zone. In *Precarious Life: The Power of Mourning and Violence*, Judith Butler explains that while certain forms of grief are socially acceptable, and are "nationally recognized and amplified"[65] (for the victims of the World Trade Center or soldiers who die in combat), others, such grief for the thousands killed in Palestine by the Israeli military with US support and Arab peoples who are practitioners of Islam, are not.[66] This "disavowed mourning" produces a form of cultural melancholia that I suggest is akin to the situation in Italy with regards to the Mafia. Indeed, the process of working through traumatic Mafia memory is repressed and the process of mourning cannot be completed. Aside from a few high-profile funerals of anti-Mafia activists during the early 1990s, Mafia-related protests and social movements receive comparatively minor media attention. And this is especially the case for women involved in a variety of ways within the organization, who represent open wounds never allowed to heal.

My project places a particular emphasis on women with ties to the Mafia. I discuss a number of films in which vestiges of Mafia-related trauma emerge in the various forms of degradation and abuse that victims, perpetrators, collaborators of justice, or bystanders undergo, whether through murder, suicide, rape, abandonment, marginalization, or occlusion from the narrative. I also look at films where male characters based upon historical figures with non-normative sexual identities are recast as martyr figures and their non-conforming sexualities (according to Mafia norms) are erased from history. Similarly to the way that Julia Kristeva diagnoses France's *dépression nationale*,[67] I look at the mechanics of film identification and spectatorship and propose that trauma that has yet to be worked through on the national level is displaced onto these characters, who embody the country's unresolved grief. These characters are a visual reminder of the wound that will not heal; within them is discernible the site of unfinished mourning that reveals as much as it conceals. In several chapters, I read Mafia women as akin to the lost object for Freud's melancholic, in that as they are never properly mourned, they become internalized in the national ego ideal. As a result, we see that they are repeatedly debased on screen in a variety of forms. They are the misplaced target of Mafia villainy, and therefore confuse the national mourning process.

Victims, Perpetrators, Bystanders, *Pentite*: Mafia Women in Recent Italian Cinema

Numerous publications in the area of Mafia studies from the last twenty years or so have focused on the emergent role of women in the Mafia, as both perpetrators and victims.[68] Partially as a result of the phenomenon of pentitismo – that is, the trend over the past twenty years or so for Mafia men and women alike to turn state's evidence and to become collaborators of justice – it is now clear that women do occupy several roles within the organization, although they are far from emancipated. These women's "submerged centrality" is at odds with the more recent visibility of female anti-Mafia activists and protestors.[69] The Mafia is an esoteric "men only society" that, paradoxically, is surrounded by and aided by women. Quite ironically, according to Renate Siebert, Mafiosi work in service of safeguarding the mother, who is "the object of love and of hatred for whose defence and for whose possession the brotherhood was born, in conflict with the law of the father, [and who] symbolically represents possession of the earth." Thus, the maternal imago binds the group together. Siebert continues: "The secret which unites the fraternal members of the association, the *omertà* in effect, is the weapon turned against the father, the law, the state, the outside world, in defense of the world inside, in defense of a mother fantasized as uniquely good." The Mafia is dubbed the "mammasantissima," the most holy of mothers,[70] and, writes Adriana Cavarero, "horror has the face of a woman."[71] The face of the Mafia is feminine, yet its membership is exclusively masculine and heteronormative.[72] In such a hierarchy, women lead a precarious existence and are particularly powerless and vulnerable, "exposed at any instant to *vulnus* [wound]."[73] Indeed, as I argue in many of the following chapters, women are of utmost importance to the Mafia in their roles as wife and mother. They are the custodians of family honour and are responsible for instilling Mafia values, such as the cult of vendetta, in their children. Hence, as symbol they are central to the organization, yet they are excluded from membership therein. To recall Nira Yuval-Davis's work on gender and nation, women with ties to the Mafia "often symbolize the collectivity unity, honour, and the *raison d'être* of specific national and ethnic projects ... However, they are often excluded from the collective 'we' of the body politic, and retain an object rather than a subject position."[74] Fundamentally, the Mafia is a homosocial organization that denies access to women, demands normative behaviour, and repudiates same-sex desire.

There exist hundreds of Italian films on the Mafia. Yet, there is something striking with regard to how women in, against, or around the Mafia are envisioned in film, in particular in those films from the new millennium. In what I call the "first wave" of Mafia films, which range from 1949 to 1999, women were generally cast as types. To cite a few examples, Angela from Luchino Visconti's seminal Mafia movie *Il gattopardo* (*The Leopard*, 1963) can be seen as symbol of political transformism and *mafiosità*. Stereotypical images of the worried or grieving wife and mother are found in Francesco Rosi's *Salvatore Giuliano* (1961), Michele Placido's *Un eroe borghese* (*A Bourgeois Hero*, 1995) and Ricky Tognazzi's *La scorta* (1993) and *Excellent Cadavers* (1999). Films such as *Lucky Luciano* (Francesco Rosi, 1973) portray the simplistic Mafia mistress and Alberto Lattuada's dark comedy *Il Mafioso* (1962) depicts a blonde, naive northern wife who feels out of place in what she considers to be primitive Sicily. Several films represent clichéd femme fatale characters eager to lure the male lead to his doom. This is the case with Francesco Rosi's *Dimenticare Palermo* (*The Palermo Connection*, 1990) and Elio Petri's *A ciascuno il suo* (*To Each His Own*, 1967). Instead, Pietro Germi's *In nome della legge* (*In the Name of the Law*, 1949) and Damiano Damiani's *Il giorno della civetta* (*The Day of the Owl*) represent damsels in distress who are caught between men on opposite sides of the law.[75] In Giuseppe Tornatore's *Il camorrista* (1986), the protagonist's sister is a bitter spinster who works to ensure her sibling's success, and in Lina Wertmuller's *Mimi metallurgico, ferito nell'onore* (*The Seduction of Mimi*, 1972) women come off as the comical embodiment of wounded honour, which is also the case in Roberto Benigni's *Johnny Stecchino* (1991). Finally, in several political or engaged film noirs of the 1960s and 1970s, such as Francesco Rosi's *La mani sulla città* (*Hands over the City*, 1963) and *Cadaveri eccellenti* (*Illustrious Corpses*, 1976), women are nearly absent as, according to Mary Wood, the "narrative worlds of political *film noir* are highly masculinist, representing the past and public life in patriarchal terms, and marginalizing women."[76]

In more recent films, however, women at large have not necessarily come to occupy centre stage, but they have been cast in much more interesting, ambivalent, and complex roles, and it is to these films that I turn in my analysis. Indeed, this study offers, as Danielle Hipkins's important article urges, a "second take" on how gender is represented in recent Mafia cinema. Some of the women in films under consideration step out of the private sphere and are actively involved in mob business. Other interesting representations of women or the feminine demonstrate how directors are reluctant to continue to "suture Italian history and the male gaze," while in some films, sexual identity crises are downplayed and homosexuality is elided.[77]

Marco Amenta's film *La siciliana ribelle* (*The Sicilian Girl*, 2009) retells the story of the anti-Mafia martyr Rita Atria. The role of the Mafia mother, wife, or girlfriend has been expanded upon and problematized in Pasquale Scimeca's *Placido Rizzotto* (2000), Paolo Sorrentino's *Le conseguenze dell'amore* (*The Consequences of Love*, 2004) and Davide Barletti and Lorenzo Conte's *Fine pena mai: Paradiso perduto* (*Life Sentence: Paradise Lost*, 2007). And we have been granted a view into the inner sanctum of Mafia life through the eyes of the eponymous protagonist of Roberta Torre's *Angela* (2002), Lucia in Edoardo Winspeare's *Galantuomini* (2008), or Maria in Matteo Garrone's *Gomorra* (*Gomorrah*, 2008), while Oedipal crises dominate the narrative of Marco Tullio Giordana's *I cento passi* (*The Hundred Steps*, 2000), Stefano Incerti's *L'uomo di vetro* (*The Man of Glass*, 2007), and Claudio Cupellini's *Una vita tranquilla* (*A Quiet Life*, 2010).

In these films, several characters undergo profound personal traumas (such as rape or the murder of a son, father, fiancé, or husband) or die violent deaths by murder or suicide. It would seem that the enactment of such traumas on the screen might have the potential to directly involve the viewer in the national trauma of the Mafia. For example, in several recent Mafia movies, audiences engage in the collective mourning of male characters. This is the case of *I cento passi*, *Placido Rizzotto*, *Le conseguenze dell'amore*, and *L'uomo di vetro*, although in both *I cento passi* and *L'uomo di vetro*, the memorializing finale is only possible with the repression of the main protagonist's homosexuality. Complex visual and verbal coding in the films of my study, however, disavow such a commemorative gesture for many of the women in Italian cinema of the new millennium, as violence is staged in such a way to be quickly forgotten and displaced onto other narrative threads. In *Placido Rizzotto*, *Galantuomini*, *L'uomo di vetro*, and *Gomorra*, women are raped, sacrificed, or killed off out of the blue in order to further the narrative or to allow for narrative closure. In *Angela*, the title character is cast off in a perpetual state of exile and *Le conseguenze dell'amore* and *Fine pena mai* construct female protagonists as projections of male fantasy. In *La siciliana ribelle*, Rita is recast as a simplistic martyr figure so as to reinforce the film's Manichean message, while in *I cento passi* and *Una vita tranquilla*, women embody Oedipal conflicts. Ultimately, their status as martyr is made complicated and undermined as these women are silenced both literally and figuratively or stereotyped.

I am suggesting that a close examination of the apparent liminal presence of women and non-conforming identities in these films exposes the limitations of what counts as human in a Mafia context both onscreen and for the nation at large. Silverman states that there are three fundamental components to the dominant fiction: the binary opposition between male and female, the foundational identification of penis and phallus, and the primacy of the patriarchal family.[78] These three aspects, blatant in Italian life at large, are hyperbolized in Mafia culture. More to the point, Silverman argues that only a "historical trauma" with a direct effect on primarily male subjects is capable of disrupting the dominant fiction.[79] Until the Mafia is recognized as such, and a discourse begins in Italy that positions the Mafia as a national trauma on a par with that of the years of terrorism, women will continue to be scapegoated in Italian Mafia movies so that the national ego ideal can remain undamaged.

1 Oedipal Conflicts in Marco Tullio Giordana's *I cento passi*[1]

I joined the PSIUP with the anger and desperation of someone who wants to simultaneously break with everything and look for protection. Soon after, I fell madly in love with one of my young [male] comrades; I never expressed my desires, but I constructed a large part of my political life upon this schizoid condition, tumultuously.

Peppino Impastato, *Lunga è la notte*, 115–16

I've an infinite / hunger for love, for the love of bodies without souls. / Because the soul is inside you, it is you, but you / are my mother and your love's my bondage: / I spent my childhood a slave to this lofty, / incurable sense of immense commitment. / It was the only way to feel life, / its only colour, its only form: now it's over.

Pier Paolo Pasolini, "Supplica a mia madre"

I cento passi: An Anti-Mafia Martyr Film?

Marco Tullio Giordana's *I cento passi* (*The Hundred Steps*, 2000) is often discussed as the anti-Mafia martyr movie par excellence. The film, based on a true story, chronicles the life and death of passionate activist Giuseppe (Peppino) Impastato, born in Cinisi in 1948 into a family with ties to Cosa Nostra. His father Luigi Impastato was a small business owner indebted to Cinisi capomafia Gaetano Badalamenti and his uncle Cesare Manzella was a Mafia boss, murdered in a clan war in 1963. On 9 May 1978, Impastato was assassinated by Badalamenti's men, beaten to death and then blown up on the railroad tracks.[2] Millicent Marcus explores the various functions of commemoration at play in both Giordana's film and Pasquale Scimeca's *Placido Rizzotto* from the same year. In particular, she points out the memorialist impulse at work in both films and concludes that each represents "cinematic tomb inscriptions" that memorialize two forgotten martyrs to the anti-Mafia struggle.[3] And the same is said on a large scale in the majority of scholarship and reviews devoted to the film.[4] What's more, the film has been shown in schools and civic organizations throughout Italy, and used as a pedagogical tool to raise consciousness with regard to the anti-Mafia movement. Hence, it could be argued that the biopic introduces younger generations to Mafia-related trauma and inaugurates a new millennium of awareness of and protest against the Mafia in Italy.

At first glance, this appears to be the case: The viewer embarks on a journey of discovery with the protagonist, and is meant to identify with Peppino from the outset, to feel his anger and frustration as the Mafia relentlessly exploits his native town, to share in his tenacity during his heroic, local, and fruitless battle against the organization, to express shock and horror at his gruesome execution, and to finally shed a collective tear during the popular protest that acted as his memorial. In many ways, Peppino embodies the active male protagonist so typical of Hollywood cinema that Laura Mulvey takes to task in "Visual Pleasure and Narrative Cinema." Throughout the film, Peppino "demands a three-dimensional space corresponding to that of the mirror-recognition" – and we will return to the mirror later. Frequently, Giordana weds Peppino's image with the earth, and he thus becomes "a figure of the landscape," while, as an activist, he "command[s] the stage" and "creates the action" over and over again. The employment of techniques such as deep focus, on-location shooting, unobtrusive editing, and a predominately linear and uncomplicated narrative structure suture the viewer into the film while minimizing extra-diegetic intrusions so as to achieve a "realistic" portrayal of events.[5] Indeed, the film concludes with a montage of photographs showing the "real" Giuseppe Impastato, who looks uncannily similar to the actor, Luigi Lo Cascio, who interpreted him.[6] Thus, in the viewer's imagination, the actor has become the historical figure and representation is effaced by reality.[7] Moreover, the appealing and popular musical score represents, as Emanuele D'Onofrio argues, "that particular period as a mirror for contemporary society,"[8] and Catherine O'Rawe points out how the "soundtrack forms part of the middlebrow address" of the film.[9] Thus, on the surface, the anti-Mafia message of *I cento passi* is overt and uncomplicated.

Upon closer examination of the gender dynamics at play in the film, however, such an unequivocal reading falls apart. To cite the most glaring example, the staging of Peppino's homosexuality in the film is ambivalent and evasive. Alan O'Leary argues that the unitive ethos of *I cento passi* is helped in no small part by both the elimination of Peppino's homosexuality and the downplaying of his active militancy with the Democrazia Proletaria (Proletariat Democracy).[10] As such, it could be argued that *I cento passi* allows Peppino's martyrdom at the expense of both his sexual and political identity. Read further, Peppino's violent murder puts an end to not only to his anti-Mafia protests, but also to the feminine and non-violent ethos that he represents. As Mary Wood argues, the "defeat" of a new model of masculinity embodied by Peppino "signals the difficulty of adopting a 'new man's' role."[11] Although she is discussing new male roles in Italian films from the last twenty years at large, I would add that Peppino's unconventional masculinity is even more at odds in a Mafia milieu. In short, the overt reliance on conventional techniques and themes in the film only tells one side of the story and Peppino's death effaces his difference.

In the Name of Whose Father? Gender Identity in a Mafia Context

Borrowing from Herbert Marcuse's thesis regarding "Repressive Tolerance," Giovanni Dall'Orto argues that in Italy, homosexuality was repressed for so long that, until recently, it simply did not exist on the national level.[12] The Mafia, however, has not evolved at all. Male bonding defines the group, which Siebert designates as "esoteric," through such rituals as hunting, communal banquets, initiation rites, and blood brotherhoods, which are all meant, ironically, to enforce bonds with mother earth.[13] Homosocial desire, as Eve Kosofsky Sedgewick tells us, designates "social bonds of persons of the same sex." However, her use of the term presumes a "potential unbrokenness of a continuum between homosocial and homosexual," a continuum that the Mafia dictates must remain unambiguous.[14] "A man's first duty is to not be a woman," writes Siebert, and the goal of the Mafioso is to exorcise all feminine qualities from himself.[15] This form of homophobia, or the "hatred of feminine qualities in men,"[16] defines male homosocial relations in the Mafia, where masculinity is never a given, and must be constantly proven through generally violent measures.[17] Indeed, in a Mafia context, homophobia enforces heteronormativity. Hence, it is the very identification with the "abjection" of homosexuality, to borrow Judith Butler's terminology, that enables and produces heterosexuality. She poses the question: "If heterosexual identification takes place *not* through the refusal to identify as homosexual but *through* an identification with an abject homosexuality that must, as it were, never show, then can we extrapolate that normative subject positions more generally depend on and are articulated through a region of abjected identifications?"[18] The Mafia defines as abject all qualities that can be considered feminine – they must be disavowed or expelled in order for masculinity (the cult of death, of power) to remain intact. The fear of the abject is a fear of the feminine, or an anxiety about returning to the pre-symbolic stage before language and differentiation.

Mafiosi, Siebert argues, have a deeply ambivalent relationship with the feminine that results from the cultural tendency to "double the figure of the female as a woman on the one hand and, on the other, as a mother who can in some way suitably placate men's fear of women."[19] Paradoxically, they are acutely attached to the maternal yet repudiate the feminine in order to exalt the "Mediterranean Mother," "she who poisons her children's minds, she who underlies Mafia psychology and the presumed maternal culture of Mafia society; the woman who transmits the culture of vendetta, the woman who educates her children to Mafia 'values,' the wicked, revengeful woman who embodies the substratum of *Mafiosità*."[20]

In her discussion of the abject in horror cinema, Barbara Creed argues that "the mother is gradually rejected because she comes to represent, to signify, the period of the semiotic which the paternal symbolic constructs as 'abject.'"[21] Unlike the properly socialized Mafioso, in the film Peppino over-identifies with his mother Felicia and overtly repudiates his father Luigi. Indeed, he seems to never successfully overcome the "Mirror Stage," which, as Lacan explains, "is a drama whose internal thrust is precipitated from insufficiency to anticipation – and which manufactures for the subject, caught up in the lure of spatial identification, the succession of phantasies that extends from a fragmented body-image to a form of its totality."[22] The mirror constructs a previously fragmented self. Hence, the journey from semiotic to symbolic that takes place with the acquisition of language concludes with the subject's recognition and acceptance of a symbolic father, the Lacanian "Name of the Father," who embodies the law, who takes on the superego and who prohibits incest. Kaja Silverman explains that "the signifier 'father' has no relation whatever to the physical fact of any individual father. Instead, that signifier finds its support in a network of other signifiers, including 'phallus,' 'law,' 'adequacy', and 'mother.'"[23] In the film, Peppino is aware of these differences, but also recognizes that his father embodies the Law of father, that is, Mafia law. He tells his younger brother Giovanni when walking the "hundred steps" that separate the Impastato house from that of Tano Badalamenti that their father is not "old fashioned" but just "another Mafioso" like all the inhabitants of Cinisi. Peppino seamlessly equates his biological father with the superego: "my father, my family, my country ... I want to F*** it all." Furthermore, he emphatically tells Giovanni that they must rebel before they grow used to Mafia corruption and become exactly like everyone else. Hence, as is hinted at early on in the film, Peppino does not partake in the false recognition of wholeness and mastery that comes with the successful dissolution of the Oedipus complex. Moreover, Oedipal configurations onscreen shed significant light onto how gender identities are constructed and maintained in the Mafia. In particular, the film highlights the primacy of parental authority (or lack thereof) in the inculcation of Mafia values in children. In foregrounding the Oedipal narrative, Giordana lays bare the symbolic identity crisis that all inducted Mafiosi must undergo, a process that Peppino rejects. Ultimately, in *I cento passi*, Peppino's battle against the Mafia is really against his own father.

I cento passi is, to borrow from Teresa de Lauretis, "narrative and Oedipal with a vengeance," but with one exception.[24] Peppino predominantly conforms to the active "figure of narrative movement"[25] whose childhood questioning about the death of his uncle "generates a narrative, turns it into a quest."[26] He asks his mother the fateful question "What does is it feel like to die this way" (his uncle was blown to pieces by a car bomb in 1963), and her blunt yet revealing response, "You feel nothing, it's so brief," inaugurates Peppino's desire to know while portending his future death and martyrdom. Thus, narrative is based on a question of desire posed to the mother, the "mythical obstacle."[27] Conspicuous, however, is the absence of a female love interest in a film that works to support the active and masculine status of the "mythical subject."[28] Felicia stands in for this lack and demands a rereading of the Oedipus myth as it is played out in *I cento passi*. Ultimately, the collective gaze does not converge on a passive object of desire and this absence confounds traditional connections of visual and narrative pleasure.

Indeed, the primacy and complexity of the gaze is conspicuous in *I cento passi*. The film opens with the mirror reflection of a frustrated young Giovanni as he struggles with his bowtie while Peppino and Felicia are reflected in shallow focus as she brushes his hair in spite of her son's protests. From the outset of the film, it is implied that, unlike with Peppino, brother Giovanni's passing through the mirror stage was uncomplicated: his reflection is unfragmented and he acts the deferential son who obeys his father Luigi and accepts his power position. For example, when Luigi enters the room, Giovanni immediately asks him for help and his affect is cheerful and then obedient when Luigi reproaches Felicia for putting a bobby pin in his hair, which is a clear marker of femininity. Peppino, however, is much more reserved around his father, and seems to doubt his authority when Luigi grabs his chin and questions him on whether he memorized a poem and then warns him to not make a fool of the family. Throughout the film, Peppino's relationship with Luigi grows ever more contentious, while Felicia remains protective of her son and somewhat encourages his difference, in particular his anti-Mafia activity.

To some extent, *I cento passi* rewrites and sentimentalizes the father–son relationship, and downplays Luigi Impastato's Mafia involvement and paints him, especially towards the end of his life, as a misunderstood and lonely father who will protect his son at all costs. In the film he tells cousin Anthony during his visit to America that if "they" want to kill his son, they will have to kill him first, and, moments before Luigi's own death, he nostalgically recalls verses of the Leopardi poem "L'infinito," which Peppino recited as a child. The historical Luigi Impastato, however, was a Mafioso sent to *confino*, or internal exile for Mafia-related activity, in Ustica for three years under fascism and later was a tyrant in the home. In her memoir, Felicia Impastato explains that her husband had an open affair, her life with him "was hell," and his temper flared regularly.[29] The recasting of a kinder Luigi in the film privileges the family drama and foregrounds the Oedipal scenario, which broadens the film's reach, especially in the Italian filmic tradition, where Oedipal narratives have become a typical modus of understanding national history.[30] Of course, *I cento passi* is about the Mafia of Cinisi, but it is *also* about the anxieties and tribulations of a refractory young man who is at odds with local power systems.

Contrary to Peppino, who is a modern-day rebel with a cause, Giovanni is the dutiful son who implores his brother to stop making trouble and attempts to keep the peace in the family. For one, Giovanni becomes upset with Peppino after his brother turned their father's funeral into a protest against the Mafia. After this, and as they sort through Luigi's papers, an argument ensues and the pair struggles, arms locked, on the floor as Giovanni insists that he too is capable of heroism, that is, of standing up to Tano. Thus, in the aftermath of the father's death, Peppino's Oedipal struggle is momentarily displaced onto the fraternal relationship. Giovanni's normativity is also underlined when he finds a suitable partner named "Felicia" whose name, Peppino points out just after meeting her, is "come la mamma [like mom's]." For Peppino, Giovanni's path is all too easy, as he clarifies for his friend Salvo while they are photographing the Cinisi airport from a nearby hillside. In a discourse evocative of Giacomo Leopardi's poem "L'infinito," which young Peppino reads at a family gathering at the film's beginning, Peppino questions whether beauty should be privileged over political activism. But, as Laura Wittman argues, the "political experience of beauty is anything but objective," and such gestures (exchanging the ideology of politics for that of the pursuit of beauty) do not come easily for Peppino.[31] Giovanni, Peppino points out, chose the conventional path, one to be filled with simple houses, accompanying television sets, and window boxes full of geraniums. Peppino underlines that he envies his brother's normality, yet he could never live that sort of normative lifestyle. Thus, his reification of heteronormativity accentuates his difference. Indeed, while Giovanni chooses a suitable partner who is "like" his mother, Peppino is incapable of making any such life choice at all. Instead, he remains, to reference Pier Paolo Pasolini's poem "Supplica a mia madre" ("Prayer to My Mother"), a slave to his mother's love. To be sure, Luigi reminds Felicia that since divorce is now legal in Italy, she can leave him to marry her son, her "fiancé."

For several reasons, in *I cento passi* Peppino is not a normal man in the Mafia milieu, which is governed by the code of *omertà*, whose etymology, according to Giuseppe Pitrè, "non significa *umilità* ... ma *omineità*, qualità di essere *omu*, cioè serio, sodo, forte [does not signify humility, but 'manliness,' or being a man, someone who is serious, tough, and strong]."[32] To follow *omertà* means to act like a man, and sublimate and repress any effeminate qualities to enter into, in Renate Siebert's words, an uber-hetero-normative and homophobic "men-only society."[33] Mob thinking, in particular the thirst for revenge, de rigueur subservience of women, and hyperbolic emphasis on personal honour, finds its roots in the traditional family unit, whose structure is the blueprint for the Mafia hierarchy. And the agnatic or affinal "family" that one is born or marries into must always be subordinated to the ritualized "Family" into which the Mafioso enters through a symbolic ritual. In consequence, perhaps, "family" loyalties only go so far, as they are by demand subsumed to the larger interests of "Family."[34]

Oedipal Conflicts

Generational and kinship struggles are foregrounded in *I cento passi*, foremost in the mirrored "umbilical scenes" that take place roughly halfway through the film and make conspicuous Peppino's seditious relations with his father and inextricable bond to his mother. Millicent

Marcus employs the term "umbilical" to designate moments when "the film reveals the traces of its derivation from the parent text and discloses its interpretive strategy."[35] Indeed, these scenes, read in light of Pasolini's poem "Supplica a mia madre," lay bare both Peppino's umbilical attachment to the maternal and visceral sense of loss associated with the realization of the fragmented Oedipal self.

Tired of the constant roadblocks created by local authorities in their attempt to stage anti-Mafia rallies, Peppino and his comrades establish "Radio Aut," a self-financed radio station used to denounce the rampant corruption and Mafia activity of "Mafiopoli" (Cinisi). When Peppino's broadcasts air Tano's dirty laundry (his involvement in the drug and prostitution trade and his misappropriation of government funds meant to stimulate economic development in Southern Italy), Tano calls upon Luigi to silence his son. In a final attempt to curb Peppino's public and vocal anti-Mafia activities, Luigi interrupts Peppino while he is reciting the "windwill scene" from Miguel de Cervantes's *Don Quixote*, and beats his son to the ground. He dominates him and pleads with him to respect both church and family and to remember the commandment that he was taught as a young boy in church. Luigi implores Peppino to "honour thy father," a phrase that he repeats seven times, as he gently clutches and caresses his son's head. The camera is positioned on the floor and captures the pair in close-up, and the scene is framed to approximate a violent sexual attack, particularly as Luigi's violence is tinged with excessive intimacy. Peppino, however, refuses to sit by and to allow cycles of Mafia violence to continue, and he rebels against the metaphorical rape. Thus, his attempted parricide makes clear his refusal to "honour his father" as signifier of law and bearer of the phallus.

Luigi's plea to his son entangles the sacred with the profane and underscores connections between religion, power, violence, and honour in a Mafia context. John Dickie explains:

> Like mafia honour, mafia religion helps mafiosi justify their actions … Mafiosi often like to think that they are killing in the name of something higher than money and power, and the two names they usually come up with are "honour" and "God." Indeed, the religion professed by mafiosi and their families is like so much else in the moral universe of mafia honour, in that it is difficult to tell where genuine – if misguided – belief ends, and cynical deceit begins.[36]

Hence, it can be argued that Luigi's violent outburst helps "to obtain satisfaction for stained honour and to restore [his] reputation for manliness."[37] But Luigi's authoritarianism is coloured by compassion, which aids in the taming function of patriarchal authority in the Impastato household and spotlights the film's Oedipal narrative.

After standing up to his father, Peppino is exiled from the family home and retreats to a marginal space where he engages in a deeply eroticized encounter with his mother. Felicia directly opposes her husband's authority to visit Peppino in the garage-cum-bedroom that he now calls home to bring him his books. She walks in on him when he is sleeping, and he immediately asks after the work of Pier Paolo Pasolini and begins reading the politically engaged poem "Le ceneri di Gramsci" (Gramsci's Ashes) in the "voce grossa" that he adopts when attacking the Mafia. When Felicia protests, he chooses to read another poem, "Supplica a mia madre," in a softer and more intimate tone. The poem's subject matter, together with Peppino's gaunt and nearly naked body, deep intra-diegetic gazes, and the pair's reflection in the mirror reinforce the scene's erotic and voyeuristic nature. To be sure, notes in the screenplay indicate that "c'è qualcosa di strano in questa scena: Il giovane ragazzo seminudo e la donna nell'oscurità di un garage trasformato in alcova. Sembra più l'incontro clandestino di due amanti che quello di una madre che porta rifornimenti al figlio [there is something strange about this scene: the young half-naked boy and the woman in the darkness of a garage turned into an alcove. It seems more like a clandestine encounter between two lovers than that of a mother bringing supplies to her son]."[38]

References to Pasolini's film *Oedipus Rex* (1967, based in part, as Pasolini has said, on his own life) abound here and throughout the film, in particular in the way both films comment on the abuses of power. Allusions to Pasolini in *I cento passi* remind us that, as with the character of Matteo in Giordana's *La meglio gioventù* (*The Best of Youth*, 2003), Peppino's violent struggle against the Mafia is also one against his own father. Pasolini's most well-known political poem is literally pushed aside in favour of an encounter with highly Oedipal overtones. The camera slowly zooms in on Peppino as he recites the first two couplets of the poem, "È difficile dire con parole di figlio / ciò a cui nel cuore ben poco assomiglio. / Tu sei la sola al mondo che sa, del mio cuore, / ciò che è stato sempre, prima d'ogni altro amore [It's hard to say in a son's voice / what at heart I so little resemble. / You're the only one in the world who knows / what my heart always held, before all other love"], and then captures Felicia's rapt and attentive gaze as he concludes on the primacy of the mother's love. Peppino then coaxes her into reading the subsequent eight verses:

> Per questo devo dirti ciò ch'è orrendo conoscere:
> è dentro la tua grazia che nasce la mia angoscia.
> Sei insostituibile. Per questo è dannata
> alla solitudine la vita che mi hai data.
> E non voglio esser solo. Ho un'infinita fame
> D'amore, dell'amore di corpi senza anima.
> Perché l'anima è in te, sei tu, ma tu
> sei mia madre e il tuo amore è la mia schiavitù:
> For this, I must tell you what is terrible to know:
> in your grace was born my anguish
> You're irreplaceable. And for this
> the life you gave me is condemned to solitude.
> And I don't want to be alone. I've an infinite
> hunger for love, for the love of bodies without souls.
> Because the soul is inside you, it is you, but you
> are my mother and your love's my bondage.

As she recites in medium shot, Peppino is shown reflected in the mirror in shallow focus, looking downward, and his gaze is without address. Their eyes do not meet and he is immobile, and it is suggested that he remains trapped in the mirror phase, which, as an adult, condemns him to a solitary, anguished, and melancholic existence. When Felicia looks up from the poem, the camera briefly catches Peppino in medium shot as he closes his eyes seemingly out of despair and then switches back to a two-shot of the pair with Felicia in the foreground. As she continues reading, the camera slowly zooms in to a close-up of Peppino's downcast gaze, which reveals the pain of his otherness before cutting back to a medium close-up of Felicia shot from behind as she concludes her reading. After pronouncing the verse "your love is my bondage," she turns back to gaze fixedly at Peppino, and the screen fades to black.

This sequence, which is composed predominantly of a series of shot/reverse shots, confounds instead of solidifies the gaze in its reluctance to suture the viewer into the narrative framework. In classical cinema, the shot/reverse-shot formation consolidates meaning and effaces narrative intrusions. Here, however, Giordana foregrounds lack and absence and purposefully disorients the viewer by avoiding eyeline matches, violating the 180-degree rule and ending the scene without the expected reverse shot (the viewer is left literally in the dark at the scene's close). In her discussion of suture in narrative film, Kaja Silverman maintains that when the viewing subject becomes aware of the limitations of vision, feelings of imaginary plenitude sacrificed after passing out of the mirror stage give way to unpleasure. *Jouissance* disappears with the recognition of an absent field occupied by the "Absent One," who is the speaking subject of the cinematic text and who controls the gaze of the viewing subject and "has all the attributes of the mythically potent symbolic father: potency, knowledge, transcendental vision, self sufficiency and discursive power."[39] The speaking subject, however, must remain hidden so that viewing pleasure remains intact. The garage scene reveals the passivity of the viewing subject and discloses "the reality outside of that fiction,"[40] which is, precisely, Peppino's lack of mastery and wholeness in the face of the "coercive and castrating other"[41] that is the Mafia. This scene in *I cento passi* "ruptures the Oedipal formation which provides the basis of the present symbolic order"[42] through flagrantly foregrounding "the voyeuristic dimensions of the cinematic experience" and making manifest the absent field of vision.[43] Peppino is prisoner to his mother's love; he is unable to live outside of it. Yet, his enslavement, it is indicated, precludes him from entering another structure, the "most holy of mothers."

Innocenzo Fiore writes that "la donna è il potere mentre il maschio ha (dalla donna) il potere [women are power but men have power from women]." He means that women are the custodians of family honour (the key tenet of *mafiosità*) and that masculine authority is a direct consequence of whether women honour or dishonour the men in their lives.[44] In *I cento passi*, Felicia stands in direct opposition to the traditional Mafia mother in that she does not partake in any of the "active" functions generally demanded of women in the organization.[45] As discussed earlier, after her husband banishes Peppino from the house, she blatantly dismisses his power position by bringing her son books and supplies, and then, when Luigi is away in America, she welcomes Peppino back home. More to the point, she refuses to instil "cultural Mafia codes" in her children, and outright demands that her son's death not be avenged (after Peppino's murder she tells cousin Anthony that her son is not "one of you," and she does not want a vendetta carried out on the family's behalf.) As Ombretta Ingrascì tells us, "nella divisione di genere, la donna si occupa della cosiddetta 'pedagogia della vendetta.' Trasmette questa pratica incitando gli uomini, in particolare i figli, a riparare il torto subito, spingendoli a operare nel giorno dell'anniversario della perdita dell'onore [in the gender divide, women are concerned with the so-called 'pedagogy of vendetta.' They transmit this practice and incite men, in particular their sons, to right the wrong immediately, and push them to act on the day of the anniversary commemorating lost honour]."[46] Hence, Felicia subverts the concept of honour that is key to Mafia culture.[47]

I cento passi suggests that the motivations behind Peppino's crusade against both his real father Luigi and metaphorical father Tano stem not from resistance ideology but from a place of dependence upon his mother's love. The lack of a coherent anti-Mafia message with relation to Peppino is further thematized in the structure of "Supplica," as the concluding, yet unpronounced, couplets of the poem resonate with a sense of political engagement:

> ho passato l'infanzia schiavo di questo senso
> alto, irrimediabile, di un impegno immenso.
> Era l'unico modo per sentire la vita
> L'unica tinta, l'unica forma: ora è finita.
> Sopravviviamo: ed è la confusione
> di una vita rinata fuori dalla ragione.
> Ti supplico, ah, ti supplico: non voler morire.
> Sono qui, solo, con te, in un futuro aprile ...
> I spent my childhood a slave to this lofty,
> incurable sense of immense commitment.
> It was the only way to feel life,
> its only colour, its only form: now it's over.
> We survive, in the confusion
> of a life reborn beyond reason.
> I beg you, ah, I beg you: don't desire death!
> I'm here, alone, with you, in a future April ...[48]

Peppino's own death and subsequent martyrdom are foreshadowed here (in that the poet states that he does not want to die, that his life is over, and so on). Pasolini's reference to a "futuro aprile" recalls the failed resistance movement. The concluding lines of the poem are laden with a sense of defeat; now that the struggle is over, life has no meaning, and survival takes precedence over "impegno," or political commitment. The regressive, maternal, and semiotic state common to verses one through twelve is countered with a concluding voice that is historically aware and retrospective. The poem as it is represented in

I cento passi suggests that Peppino's identity is divided and that his political activism is the result of an unresolved Oedipus complex.

The Reconstituted Mirror

The historical Impastato admits that his political and sexual identities are interdependent. In a diary entry from 1965, Impastato writes: "Approdai al PSIUP con la rabbia e la disperazione di chi, al tempo stesso, vuol rompere tutto e cerca protezione. Mi innamorai subito dopo e fino alle follie di un mio giovane compagno di partito: non espressi mai i miei desideri, ma su questa mia condizione schizoide ho costruito larga parte della mia dimensione politica, tumultuosamente [I joined the PSIUP with the anger and desperation of someone who wants to simultaneously break with everything and look for protection. Soon after, I fell madly in love with one of my young [male] comrades; I never expressed my desires, but I constructed a large part of my political life upon my schizoid condition, tumultuously.]"[49] Here, Impastato implies that his political engagement is directly connected to his non-verbalized and repressed homosexual desire.

Considering Impastato's own musing on both his sexual leanings and his political activism, is the mise-en-abyme to Pasolini in *I cento passi* meant to suggest that Peppino's political anti-Mafia involvement is the result of his repressed homosexuality? As I have suggested elsewhere, I believe that references to Pasolini are meant to evoke the era to which his most well-known work can be dated, a period fraught with political and social unrest and economic uncertainty; that is, Pasolini becomes shorthand for a politically engaged moment in Italian history.[50] At the same time, the film constructs affinities between Peppino and Pasolini in life and in death. Such similarities are particularly apparent in the mother–son relationship, and Giordana has acknowledged that he modelled Peppino and Felicia's relationship on that of Pasolini and his mother Susanna Pasolini.[51] The protagonist's identification with Pasolini certainly suggests the *possibility* of a gay Peppino, as does the construction of Peppino's queerness out of difference from his brother's heterosexism, the inclusion of a male friend with whom Peppino seems to share an intimate bond, and allusions to an Oedipal relationship between mother and son (although, as George de Stefano points out, homosexuality as an "'unsuccessful' resolution of the Oedipal conflict [is a] discredited Freudian clich[é])."[52] Nevertheless, these all could be categorized as red herrings, mise-en-abymes to highlight Peppino's individualism, intellect, and rebellion. Ultimately, however, the privileging of the hegemonic masculine martyr narrative subordinates difference and as a result homosexuality is equated with psychopathology and nonconformity. Indeed, the metaphor of "illness as difference" perpetuated in the film mirrors the real-life Impastato's musings on his condition (not to mention Pasolini's own writings regarding his homosexuality).

Although many (such as his brother Giovanni Impastato) have debated and even denied outright that Impastato was homosexual, his sexual preference is no longer in question.[53] Impastato himself admits as much in the diary entry cited above. In subsequent entries, we learn that the relationship lasted for two years, and in 1968 he became involved with another young "compagno." This period, Impastato explains, was the most "heartrending" and "exciting" of his personal and political life. He oscillated between experiencing "bare desperation" and "moments of authentic exaltation and creative ability."[54] The diary, however, was only published in its entirety in 2006 after having been made public in 2003,[55] which begs the question as to whether Giordana was aware of Impastato's homosexuality before making *I cento passi*. Pioneering research by Dominic Holdaway tells us, however, that Giordana was privy to this information through his contact with and interest in a screenplay from 1998 that was never made: Antonio Carella's *Nel cuore della luna* treats Impastato's life and the aftermath of his death and includes a scene in which the protagonist's coming out to his close friend Enrico ends with the two men kissing.[56] In this scene, Peppino admits to having had a homosexual encounter while showering with a friend at the seaside. When his friend begins to soap his back, he remembers his mother bathing him as a child: "Mi è ritornata in mente mia madre quando mi faceva il bagno ... e mi accarezzava con le sue mani delicate ... lungo tutto il corpo ... quel ragazzo ... mi sorrideva ... [I remembered my mother when she bathed me ... and she caressed me with her delicate hands ... all over my body ... that boy ... he smiled at me]."[57] Of particular interest here is the collusion of this memory: the earlier recollection of his mother seamlessly transitions to the description of his friend. Peppino then cries out for help, exclaiming that he is "sick" – "aiutami! Io sto male!" which precipitates the erotic encounter between the two friends in the present day.

No such episode takes place in *I cento passi*, nor could it, although it is clear that Peppino's masculinity does not conform to gender norms in the Mafia (or to those demanded by patriarchal culture in general) and that the film does, borrowing from Silverman, "eschew oedipal normalization" through Peppino's relationship with his mother and the lack of a female love interest.[58] Ultimately, however, for Peppino's status as martyr to stay intact, his identificatory projection must remain normative and unthreatening. Thus, although *I cento passi* represents the Mafia as violent and capable of exerting a negative impact on a community, the organization's traumatic potential is tempered through Peppino's martyrdom, as his death has a unifying, redemptive, and curative capacity.

As de Lauretis argues, the classical narrative comes to a close when the modern-day Oedipus finds the heroine waiting for *him*,[59] when "narrative, meaning and pleasure" converge to "support the male status of the mythical subject."[60] And this is true with *I cento passi*. The anti-Mafia protest to which Felicia contributes her son's casket concludes the film and inaugurates Peppino's martyr status, which irrevocably answers the question "What does it feel like to die this way?" Indeed, as Marcus argues, "the victim's mother endows Tullio Giordana's entire film with the double function of epitaph and call to arms."[61] It is telling that brother Giovanni, whose gender politics are unproblematic, leads the mourners at the funeral march and thus ultimately acts as surrogate for Peppino's lacking masculinity. In the end, individual trauma is transformed into political and social action that has the potential, it is suggested, to actively combat the Mafia.

Yet, the unitive tenor of the film's conclusion is ironically realized through the disunion of Peppino's body, which was completely destroyed. The casket, however, stands in to reconstitue Peppino's fractured self, both his literal remains, which are scattered across the countryside, and his previously unconstituted ego. Indeed, the whole town, including the police chief, participates in the wake, which puts forward a social fantasy of justice that appears uncomplicated. In this way, the film suggests that the Mafia is potentially defeatable and the traumatic wounds inflicted by the organization will heal as long as one has a community with which to mourn those fallen in the anti-Mafia struggle. Cinisi represented in *I cento passi* mirrors, in one reviewer's words, all of Sicily, and Peppino's reconstituted identity is part of that reflection.[62] As such, his difference is sacrificed so as to solidify viewer identification, assure narrative closure, and reinstil *jouissance* in the realm of the Law. Ultimately, *I cento passi* suggests the impossibility of desiring differently in a Mafia context, both on and offscreen, and Peppino's death resolves his nonconformity.

2 Honour, Shame, and Vendetta: Pasquale Scimeca's *Placido Rizzotto*

In Corleone women are as dangerous as the lupara.
The Godfather (Francis Ford Coppola)

In fiction and life, rape is a special kind of crime in relation to narrative.
Lynn Higgins, "Screen/Memory," 307

Woman as a "scapegoat of men's fears"

Just some years ago, the town of Corleone engaged in a process of reinvention focusing on Mafia tourism and a proposed name change to "Cuor di Leone." Pasquale Scimeca's film *Placido Rizzotto* (2000) marks an important turn in this process: the eponymous character's martyrdom opens the doors for new advertising opportunities. It is now possible to buy products such as pasta or wine from the anti-Mafia association Libera Terra that promise "the taste of legality." The Placido Rizzotto cooperative owns and operates the popular Agriturismo "Portella della Ginestra," which was the summer residence of notorious Don Giovanni Brusca (made famous for murdering anti-Mafia prosecutor Giovanni Falcone in 1992) and another residence opened in 2009: the former dwelling of "boss of bosses" Toto Riina, run by the Pio la Torre cooperative.[1] While on site, vacationers can sip a wine called "Placido Rizzotto linea I cento passi," a label that recalls Giordana's film *I cento passi* of the same year, and for only 60 euros a night, sightseers can participate in the myth of a Mafia vanquished. One guest claims that "drinking a wine confiscated from mafia land gives it a special flavour – the flavor of legality."[2] Just a few years ago, as witnessed by the lawsuit brought against Time Warner by the Italian American Defense Association, the

Italian-American community was up in arms about the prejudicial identification of the Italian-American with the Mafia on *The Sopranos* (David Chase, 1999–2007); now Italy uses the mob to market itself to Italians and Italian Americans. In sum, Corleone and its surroundings have become minor tourist attractions, and all the while Cosa Nostra continues to operate effectively.

Placido Rizzotto (filmed on location in Corleone) treats the story of the title character who was murdered in 1948 by the Corleonesi, the Mafia clan that shares the city's name, as a result of his anti-Mafia activity with the trade union. Michael Corleone's fictional stay in the town that bears his name in Francis Ford Coppola's *The Godfather* (1972) takes place contemporaneously with the narration of Placido's story. Coppola's film positioned the city of Corleone as the birth of mafiosità, even though filming took place in the nearby towns of Forza d'Agro and Savoca. As George De Stefano points out, mainly as a result of the *Godfather* trilogy, Americans tend to conflate "Mafia" with Sicilian culture in general.[3] Mafia ethos in the film equals honour, justified vendetta, and traditional gender roles – "In Corleone, le femmine sono come la lupara [In Corleone women are as dangerous as the lupara],"[4] Michael is told by his bodyguard Fabrizio, and from Michael's stay in Corleone during the late 1940s up until about 1994, nothing was farther from the case as the town and surrounding areas witnessed hundreds of Mafia-related murders of "excellent cadavers," Mafiosi and bystanders alike.

Fabrizio was of course warning his boss to steer clear of Apollonia whom Michael had just laid eyes on for the first time during a walk through the countryside. The implication, of course, is that his advancements would bring dishonour to her family and shame to the girl, and ultimately provoke her relatives into avenging lost honour. Michael, however, plays his cards well and wins over the family and gets the girl, whose wrongful death by explosion fuels Michael's quest for vendetta and puts an end to the Sicilian episode. Indeed, her death is followed by a cut to New York, where Don Vito negotiates the terms of his son's safe return home with Don Barzini and the Five Families so that Michael can step in and take Sonny's place as the new godfather in training. In *The Godfather*, then, Apollonia is Michael's Sicilian MacGuffin, whose sole role, as Žižek explains, "is to set the story in motion but which in itself is 'nothing at all.'" Akin to the Hitchcockian object, Michael must have Apollonia; she is "vitally important" to him, as she would consolidate his "Italianness" and formally wed him to his father's land and namesake. Similar to the MacGuffin, she "is the purest case of what

Lacan calls *objet petit a*: a pure void which functions as the object-cause of desire."[5] Michael's desire to avenge the attempt on his father's life and the murder of his brother and Apollonia is bound up with the loss of Apollonia and the ethnic identity and cult of honour that she engenders. His thirst for vendetta, which is culturally ingrained in him, will never be satisfied.

Placido Rizzotto, as Amy Boylan argues, offers "a different view of Corleone" from that presented in Coppola's trilogy.[6] Instead, we see Mafiosi who use excessive violence to achieve their goals, such as rape and murder in the form of the *lupara bianca*, or make the body of the victim disappear. Mafioso Luciano Leggio, one of the men principally involved in Rizzotto's murder, retains none of the glamourous and paternal properties associated with the Corleone clan in the Coppola trilogy or, for that matter, in some historical accounts. Leggio himself seemed to have co-opted Don Vito's look and demeanour for his first court appearances in 1975.[7] Scimeca's film works to debunk Mafia mystique through the creation of a new hero whose courageous and tireless campaign in favour of the peasant class ends with his death. Nevertheless, *Placido Rizzotto* is not dissimilar to *The Godfather* and other classic Hollywood films where women are sacrificed in order to ensure that the Oedipal logic of the narrative remains intact. Two women in *Placido Rizzotto* are either brutally murdered or raped and the violence done to them is then sublimated into other storylines that propel the narrative forward and ultimately consolidate the martyr status of the film's hero. While the deaths of Placido and the shepherd boy in the film are based on historical accounts (with some deviation), the execution by hanging of a female partisan at the beginning of the film and rape of Placido's girlfriend Lia later on are completely invented. Anton Blok writes that "it is the task of the anthropologist or historian to find out what violence 'says' about honour, reputation, status, identity and group solidarity."[8] In this chapter, I argue that the representation of Lia's rape and the critical reception of it should be read as a synecdoche for the status of women at large in a Mafia context: they are routinely scapegoated and silenced onscreen and their stories channelled into culturally acceptable narratives. As such, *Placido Rizzotto* conforms to Molly Haskell's reading of gender as it is played out in mainstream cinema: "Women, by the logistics of film production and the laws of Western society, generally emerge as the projections of male values … Women are the vehicle of men's fantasies, the 'anima' of the collective male unconscious, and the scapegoat of men's fears."[9]

Public Rape

Critics tend to group Scimeca's film with Giordana's *I cento passi* and discuss how both are indebted to the neorealist tradition and foreground a pedagogical and ethical thrust which imparts a sense of "personal responsibility in the fight against organized crime"[10] or "transmit[s] the legacy of moral engagement and social justice for which their protagonists died."[11] Other than the common year of release, the two films share several concerns, most germanely the way little-known anti-Mafia activists are represented as martyrs and endowed with Christ-like qualities. As with Peppino in *I cento passi,* Placido is constructed from the outset as the spectator's ego ideal. The film opens with a double abandonment: first, when Placido's father Carmelo departs to perform his duties as campiere (field guard for the Mafia), the young Placido is left on his own amid the harsh and sundrenched landscape to tend the family's cattle. Once alone, the boy immediately bursts into tears, a gesture that reveals his vulnerability and positions him as an outsider to the patriarchal normative Mafia system. Moments later, we are shown Carmelo's arrest by Cesare Mori's men for "associazione a delinquere" (belonging to a criminal organization)[12] and, yet again, Placido's emotional response. Although the film omits Carmelo's jail time (he spent just over four years in the Ucciardone prison in Palermo), it implies that the father's absence and ill deeds compelled the son into action and initiated his quest for social justice. A held-held camera positioned from Placido's perspective captures Carmelo as he is taken away and his son runs after him. The subsequent reverse shot from Carmelo's point of view is an eyeline match of Placido running towards him, yet never catching up. Instead, a graphic match follows of an older Placido running through a contrasting geography of a dense and overcast forest in Brescia in an attempt to arrive in time, as we find out moments later, to stop a group of Nazis and Fascists from hanging five partisans.

Tension is created through cross-cutting: while Placido races through the forest, the soldiers prepare both the gallows and a picnic complete with wine, cigarettes, and music. As a Nazi officer sadistically kicks out the stands from under the feet of the first four victims, Placido arrives, screaming that the war is over while shooting and killing the picnicking officers. He then engages in a drawn-out battle with the remaining man, who is intent on finishing the task at hand of hanging the last person standing, the only girl among the group. During the mass hanging, the faces of the first four men are barely visible, and the camera captures only their legs in the throes of death. The girl, however, is repeatedly shot in medium close-up, she makes eye contact with Placido, and her gaze beseeches him to save her. Although he eventually kills the officer, he is unable to save the girl, who dies in his arms. Placido, bereft, returns to his native Corleone and immediately takes on the local Mafia.

Boylan argues that the inclusion of the war prologue creates a collective memorial to the victims of both Fascism and Nazism and to those like Rizzotto and Impastato who fought against the Mafia and as a result were murdered.[13] Thus, in suggesting that anti-fascist equals anti-Mafia, the film establishes an unambiguous hierarchy between good and evil that recalls Roberto Rossellini's treatment of Nazism and the partisan Resistance in the seminal neorealist film *Roma città aperta* (*Rome Open City*, 1945). The parallel could not be more apparent: Nazis are sadists, intent on killing at all costs.[14] In addition, the mise en scène of the public execution / alfresco meal recalls the perverse proximity of the torture chamber and decadent parlour in Rossellini's film. By the same token, Placido's martyrdom can easily be compared with that of partisan Manfredi: both are clearly cast as Christ figures (Placido's death is foreshadowed in the Passion play), and both are shown with arms outstretched in a manner suggestive of the crucifixion (Placido even has a literal cross behind him while doing so). In Rossellini's film, partisan Pina's death halfway through the film marks the inauguration of Italy's historical awareness (recall Marcus's assertion that "Neorealism may be said to begin with the death of Pina, which forces her story to open to history)."[15] In Rossellini's film, Pina is sacrificed to the real and her martyrdom is necessary so that Resistance heroes such as Manfredi and Don Pietro might eventually take a stand against the Nazis.

As is the case with *Placido Rizzotto*. The visceral grief expressed in Placido's reaction to the murder of the nameless and silent female partisan gives voice to his pathos and inaugurates the hero narrative. Her assassination creates the story and sets Placido's quest in motion. Yet, paradoxically, she has no place within it. Thus, she is not unlike the nameless and silent woman in Italo Calvino's short story "Zobeide" (from *Invisible Cities*) who runs naked in the dreams of the many men who pursue her without success. In an attempt to entrap her, these men arrive from all over the globe to construct a city that must, as Teresa de Lauretis comments, "be constantly rebuilt to keep woman captive." Zobeide is a cogent metaphor for how gender is represented onscreen. As both "source of the drive to represent and its ultimate, unattainable goal," woman is the wellspring of narrative and creates discourse; she is "the very ground for representation, both object and support of a desire which, intimately bound up with power and creativity, is the moving force of culture and history."[16] But she is absent from the narrative, from culture and from history.

Voyeurism, according to Christian Metz, implies distance: "If it is true of all desire that it depends on the infinite pursuit of its absent object, voyeuristic desire, along with certain forms of sadism, is the only desire whose principle of distance symbolically and spatially evokes the fundamental rent."[17] Placido violently pursues the memory of the young partisan and her lifeless gaze inscribes lack; it is the lost object that creates desire and propels the protagonist, and the narrative, forward. She is absent, and she is not alone. On the night of Placido's murder, his girlfriend Lia (based on Rizzotto's purported real-life fiancé Leoluchina Sorisi) is brutally raped by Luciano Leggio, the future head of the Corleonesi who then worked under mob boss Michele Navarra. The attack, which takes place roughly halfway through the film, is invented. Critics who write of the rape tend to either mention it briefly and move on (David Rooney feels that it is "unduly hammered")[18] or zero in on an ambiguous expression that passes over Lia's face for just a second just when Luciano is completing the act that implies, in their words, pleasure on the part of the victim. Luana Babini writes that Lia "closes her eyes in an expression that betrays pleasure,"[19] while the reviewer from *La Repubblica* says that she "prova piacere allo stupro [takes delight in her rape]," but adds that this seconds "un vecchio pregiudizio che speravamo morto [an old prejudice that we hoped was long dead]."[20]

As Lynn Higgins argues in her piece on *Last Year at Marienbad*, "in fiction and life, rape is a special kind of crime in relation to narrative." She means that rape is frequently rewritten and "discursively transformed into another story."[21] Although in this instance she is talking about how rape defences frequently gravitate around not *who* committed the crime but instead whether a crime was even committed at all, her argument is appropriate to the representation and interpretation of Lia's rape. First off, the film (and its critical reception) leads us to believe that Lia takes some sort of pleasure in the sexual violence done to her. Furthermore, Luciano rapes Lia in part to carry out a vendetta against Placido, as Luciano's sadism is initiated when Placido publicly provokes him in the piazza just after Placido and Lia are passionately kissing. Read this way, the rape furthers Placido's martyrdom while effectively silencing Lia, as it puts a definitive end to her local rebellion against her family (her mother, a relative of Luciano, prohibited her from seeing Placido).

What's more, in the case of the actual Leoluchina Sorisi, her post-filmic life is rewritten in historical accounts and she is overtly vilified. Rape, as Tania Horeck argues, is frequently "structured as a scene through which a multitude of conflicts are staged."[22] In particular, Horeck puts forth the term "public rape" as a way to get us thinking about "the collective investment in narratives of rape."[23] She is especially interested in how rape as it is represented in the public domain functions "as the site of collective identification"[24] to reveal cultural fantasies about sexual difference. The representation and critical interpretation of rape in Scimeca's film raise important questions about anxieties around spectatorship. As well, the staging of Lia's rape reveals a "naturalization of patriarchal thinking" that serves a double purpose: Leoluchina Sorrisi is violently punished retroactively onscreen for purportedly cavorting with the enemy years after Rizzotto's death, while it is insinuated that, at some level, the fictional Lia finds physical gratification in her rape. This, along with the reaction of critics to Lia's purported pleasure, shows, in the words of Lynn Higgins and Brenda Silver, how easy it is to "ventriloquize definitions of rape that obliterate what might have been radically different perceptions."[25]

Vilifying Leoluchina Sorisi

Historical accounts of Leggio's arrest on 14 May 1964 point out that he was taken into custody while hiding in Leoluchina Sorisi's home. Dickie writes that, until then, Sorisi was "above suspicion" due to her earlier involvement with Rizzotto.[26] Other commentators are much less generous. Anti-Mafia activist and martyr Giuseppe Fava is perhaps the most vocal detractor of Sorisi. He claims that Leggio was not found in her house, but in her bed, and that he was "accudito e curato da questa donna. Non che ci fosse un rapporto umano. Però era nella sua casa. Io ho cercato questa donna, l'ho cercata a Corleone, l'ho cercata dovunque, da tutte le parti, non l'ho trovata più [nursed and cared for by this woman. Not that there was a human relationship between them. But he was in her house. I looked for this woman, I looked for her in Corleone, I looked for her everywhere, all over the place, but I never found her]." We wonder what might be the desired outcome of Fava's woman hunt. Fava then expresses the ineffability of the situation and wonders, "Ecco qui la realtà va oltre qualsiasi immaginazione. Perché una donna che è innamorata di un uomo, che assiste alla sua fine e ama anche la sua maniera di morire, poi può far tenere dentro la propria casa e curarlo, accudirlo e nasconderlo l'uomo che si presume lo abbia ucciso [This is where reality surpasses imagination. Why would a woman who is in love with a man, who stands by him until the end and even loves how he dies, can nurse, care for and hide the man who supposedly killed her love?]"[27] Merlo Francesco claims that she "finì nel letto di Liggio [ended up in Leggio's bed,][28] while journalist Enzo Biagi details Sorisi's emotional and tender reaction to Leggio's arrest: "Raccontano che quando i poliziotti catturano Luciano e lo portano via in autolettiga, Leoluchina Sorisi, amorevole e premurosa, gli aggiusta i capelli, lo bacia, e scoppia in un pianto irrefrenabile [They say that when the police captured Luciano and took him away in an ambulance, Leoluchina Sorisi lovingly and tenderly stroked his hair, kissed him and then burst into uncontrollable tears.]"[29] This, from the woman who reportedly cried "a chi me l'ha ucciso mangerò il cuore [I'll eat the heart of whoever killed him]" when Rizzotto's remains were identified at the foiba, or grotto, at Rocca Busambra just over twenty-one months after his murder on 10 March 1948.[30]

Sorisi's account of Leggio's presence in her house raises more questions than answers. She claims that she only protected him out of fear, as Leggio had threatened to kill her relatives if she did not comply with his demands. She maintains: "Fui costretta perché altrimenti avrebbero ucciso mio fratello e mio cugino, non potevo rifiutare perché conoscevo la ferocia di Liggio [I had to because otherwise they would have killed my brother and my cousin, I couldn't refuse because I knew what Leggio was capable of]."[31] Furthermore, later in life, she denied both ever being romantically involved with Rizzotto and declaring that she ever would eat the heart of those responsible for his death. She also stated that she was actually secretly engaged to Pasquale Criscione, the man who is said to have delivered Rizzotto to his murderers or was one of them.[32]

Renate Siebert interprets the chain of events, in particular Leggio's arrest in Sorisi's home, in terms of what she dubs "the discreet charm of violence." She originally questions whether Leggio was arrested before Sorisi could complete a long-awaited act of revenge: "There are known stories of women who became the lovers of a murderer with a vendetta in mind." But Siebert moves on to propose Sorisi's story as emblematic of "the attraction of evil" and the dialectics of passion between victim and victimizer that so define gender relations in the Mafia.[33] She wonders what happens when fantasized violence is not sublimated into "love, tenderness and companionship," but becomes routine.[34] She also proposes that women who fall in love with Mafiosi most likely have not developed an ego "strong and mature enough to be able to reconcile intimacy with the social world, inner worlds with the world outside."[35] These women, it is suggested, need the men in their lives for ego validation, regardless of how their partners make a living. Siebert's interpretation regarding the sadomasochistic attraction to power in a Mafia context presupposes Leggio and Sorisi's romantic involvement, which is not surprising given the widespread commentary in the media that assumes a relationship between the two. What is unsettling, however, is how this backstory plays out on the big screen. It is striking that in a film like *I cento passi*, the main protagonist's homosexuality is elided in order to ensure the continuation of narrative pleasure, while in *Placido Rizzotto*, a violent, traumatic, and fictional rape is included in the film with a similar result.

The "practical" reasons for which the rape is visualized are several. For one, vendetta for Lia's allegiance to a man who opposed the Mafia, a gesture that her mother clearly endorses, albeit uncomfortably, as she sits by downstairs while the rape occurs, and does nothing. In short, Lia brought shame upon her family by rejecting the sovereignty of family honour through her association with Placido. Her act was extremely brave and dangerous as she refused to remain, borrowing from Siebert, "complicit in the perpetuation of abusive and domineering relationships." Ultimately, Lia's insubordination provoked vendetta as a means to punish and silence her in perpetuity.[36] But also, the act works to further vilify the Mafia through aligning extreme violence with the character of Luciano Leggio, the worst of all bad guys. Indeed, Leggio was twenty-five when Rizzotto was assassinated, while in the film he appears a decrepit and ill-kempt man in his mid- to late forties, a casting choice that furthers Scimeca's malignant vision of Luciano and the organization that he embodies. In addition, the rape symbolically furthers Placido's punishment post-mortem, much like his death by *lupara bianca* deprives his family of burial rites and intensifies their grief.

The one critic's discussion of the brief "pleasurable" expression that passes over Lia's face recalls Siebert's discussion regarding the allure of violence and begs the question as to whether Scimeca was familiar with Siebert's analysis of the Leggio/Sorisi case. A similar dynamic is brought up in an interview between Scimeca and Vito Zagarrio, when the director is asked to comment upon the problematics tied to "sadomasochismo, all'umilizione [sadomasochism, to humiliation]" especially apparent in the rape scene. He dodges the question, and instead discusses violence as present in another film, *Il giorno di San Sebastiano* (*Saint Sebastian's Day*, 1993), and insists that this film is historically accurate. This is the second time that Scimeca refuses to engage the interviewer on the question of the rape. Earlier, Zagarrio asked Scimeca to consider themes relating to sadomasochism, sexuality, and psychoanalytic conflicts between men and women as apparent in *Placido Rizzotto* and *Il giorno di San Sebastiano*.[37] Again, the director sidesteps the question and instead discusses the social, civil, and ethical impetus to his filmmaking and expresses his desire to tell the stories of a peasant world that is on the verge of disappearing. His silence on the matter underlines my contention that the rape in *Placido Rizzotto* is abruptly channelled into other stories focusing on the heroes and villains of Mafia folklore. Tania Modleski positions Hitchcock's *Blackmail* (1929) as a film that "poses the issues of rape and the silencing of women with almost exemplary clarity" and discusses how films that brutally assault women appeal mainly to men. Rape and violence, Modleski maintains, "effectively silence and subdue not only the woman *in* the films – the one who threatens patriarchal law and order through the force of her anarchic desires – but also the women watching these films." Thus, women are doubly silenced and "can enjoy them only by assuming the position of 'masochists.'"[38]

Luciano is an aging, balding, crass, and overtly violent and impish man with whom the spectator is not positioned to identify. Yet the film suggests that sadistic violence might be sexually gratifying for Lia, which is in line with popular pornography storylines and the outdated musings of Freud's disciple Hélène Deutsch. In her two-volume *The Psychology of Women*, Deutsch categorized female sexuality as intrinsically masochistic, and affirms that the female psyche is "connected with masochistic ideas."[39] Rape fantasies are a normal part of female sexual development, she argues, so much so that they "often have such irresistible verisimilitude that even the most experienced judges are misled in trials of innocent men accused of rape by hysterical women."[40] The film leaves no doubt in the viewer's mind regarding the truth-value of Lia's rape. But the scene is structured in such a way as to instil a seed of doubt in the spectator, one that several critics pick up on.

Filming the Primal Scene

The rape and its aftermath, which occurs roughly halfway through the film, is cross-cut with two other storylines: first, that of Lia's mother's betrayal and then of Placido's looming abduction. When Luciano enters Lia's room while she is sewing and forces her onto her bed, she immediately and repeatedly calls out for her mother. The rape is staged in a peculiar way, and is in line with other European films made in the new millennium that include, in Horeck's words "ever more graphic and 'authentic' rape scenes."[41] In Scimeca's film, realism is accomplished through use of a fixed camera that shows the pair originally framed from the side as Luciano forces himself onto Lia and removes some of her clothing and then from above as he rapes her. During the struggle, cross-cutting first shows Lia's mother on the stairs; she is clearly aware of what is happening, but chooses the Mafia over her daughter. During the rape, two cuts show Lia's mother in the kitchen as she covers her ears. Notable throughout the entire sequence is the lack of the shot–reverse shot formation and the fixed camera creates a claustrophobic atmosphere that is anything but pleasurable to watch. Although not as drawn out as the nine-minute rape scene shot in one unbroken take in Gaspar Noé's *Irréversible* (2002), the struggle and the rape in *Placido Rizzotto* are prolonged, and take up about two minutes of screen time.

In her discussion of the controversial documentary *Raw Deal: A Question of Consent* (Billy Corben, 2001), Horeck turns towards Christian Metz's reading of the fictive aspect of voyeurism to help contextualize the diverging reactions to an alleged rape caught on camera. Voyeurism, it is maintained, "rests on a kind of *fiction*, more or less justified in the order of the real ..., a fiction that stipulates that the object 'agrees,' that it is therefore exhibitionist."[42] It is presumed that the object consents, and this presumption has to do with, in Horeck's words, "how spectators see things they already believe."[43] Although others have maintained that Lia experiences fleeting sexual pleasure, I argue that her expression can be read in various ways. The brief look that passes over Lia's face is ambiguous, and is not clearly suggestive of pleasure. After a prolonged struggle against her attacker during which Lia repeatedly scratches him on his back with both hands, drawing blood, she finally gives up, and relaxes her hands in what could look like an embrace. At this moment, her head tilts back, her eyes close and her lips slightly part. It remains up for question, however, if Lia experiences sexual arousal in sexual violence. "The cinema," Christian Metz argues, "retains something of the prohibited character peculiar to the vision of the primal scene ... The cinema is based on the legislation and generalisation of a prohibited practice."[44] Metz associates cinematic scopophilia with the primal scene, which is an unauthorized act of looking that will have consequences for the voyeur. Kaja Silverman argues that in the Metzian reading of voyeurism, spectatorship does not facilitate "mastery and sadism" but instead "passivity and masochism."[45] Masculinity that is threatened in the fantasy of origin must be compensated, that is, the passive subject first needs to regain mastery so that the power relations of the primal scene can be reversed. In this way, voyeurism in this context is read "as a compensatory drama whereby passivity yields to activity through an instinctual 'turning around' and reversal."[46] Just as with the primal scene, we are not supposed to be there, yet, once there, cannot stop watching. And this is particularly true in the case of rape, which is a crime that typically takes place far from the human eye. The problematic representation of the rape scene in Scimeca's film, to quote Horeck's analysis, "draws arresting attention to the ambivalence of spectatorship, and the question of our complicity and participation in scenes of violence."[47] The rape places the spectator in an uneasy and passive position that must be upended, a position that is reinforced by Lia's mother, who could help her daughter, yet chooses not to. Ultimately, when Lia relaxes, we can as well, and the film moves on to a narrative that reinscribes the omnipotence of the masculine viewing subject.

The succeeding shot is of Placido and his comrades as they jovially walk through the streets of Corleone and bid each other good night following the successful meeting of the trade union. A cut back to Lia's bedroom depicts the aftermath of the rape and Lia's failed revenge: she is reflected in the mirror, naked and shaking, as she takes Luciano's gun and points it at him. Unfazed, he holds up his hand to take the gun from her. At this moment, Lia is naked, while during the rape she was still mainly clothed. Her nudity accentuates her vulnerability, and thus further victimizes her, while also positioning her as an erotic object of contemplation. The camera then returns to Placido as he says his goodbyes to his friends and is pursued by Pasquale, and then returns to Lia one last time, who covers herself and cries. Finally, a close-up reveals Luciano's watch: the time is 9:50 p.m., and he takes his leave and calls out to Pasquale once outside Lia's home. At this point, the film's narrative takes a decisive turn as the genre switches to that of a typical "whodunit." The final forty minutes of the film chronicle the deaths of both Placido and the shepherd boy and their fathers' quest for justice. The circumstances behind Placido's murder, which are, in Captain della Chiesa's words, "only true in parts," are recounted through diverging flashbacks by three different characters: Pasquale, Vincenzo Collura, and Giovanni Pasqua. Competing narratives, funereal marches through the centre of town, chases in the woods, interrogations, and accounts of assassinations in Australia characterize the film as a *giallo*, or Italian mystery. *Placido Rizzotto*, which began as an anti-Mafia martyr narrative, abruptly turns into a provocative mystery, and this generic tone continues until the film's close.

Upholding the Dominant Fiction

The first woman to appear in the film is violently murdered, while the first man that we see (the film opens with a slow pan that settles on Carmelo as he prepares his mule for the day's work in the field) will stand for witnessing and commemoration. Although first cast as a Mafioso, Carmelo is soon redeemed through his creative role as *cantastorie* ("story-singer"). Indeed, the frame tale of the wandering storyteller brackets the film and endows Placido's story with a mythic dimension. After Placido returns home, a cut to Carmelo introducing the key players of his son's story positions the father as custodian of his son's memory while simultaneously diminishing his earlier misdeeds. Although Carmelo and Placido, while working in the fields or at the dinner table, quibble over the latter's defiance of Mafia law, Carmelo ultimately breaks *omertà* after his son's murder and aggressively works with the police to pursue his executioners. During the final scene of film, we see Carmelo as *cantastorie* sitting on a bench despondent, his head buried in his hands without an audience to hear his story. Although he is alone, his son's story has been told, and his memory has been brought into the public domain. Carmelo's malfeasance is quickly elided, which furthers the construction of Placido as an unambiguous anti-Mafia activist. Placido's quest is based on straightforward concepts such as justice, equality, and liberty from oppression. For example, in an anti-Lampedusian gesture during a meeting of the labour union whose mise en scène recalls the realist painting "Il quarto stato [The Fourth Estate]" (Pellizza da Volpedo, 1901), Placido urges his fellow Sicilians to wake up and to look inwards to find the courage to stand up to the "honoured society." Scimeca's treatment of Placido's murder consolidates his martyr status and, as Boylan maintains, the film "bestows meaning upon his death."[48]

Placido's martyrdom is solidified at the end of the film through Pio La Torre's call for arms cum eulogy that follows fictionalized video footage of the arrest of Pasquale, Vincenzo, and Luciano. Of note is the choice to cast additional actors to play Pasquale Criscione and Vincenzo Collura in order to lend further veracity to the invented arrest footage. These men somewhat resemble the actors, but look different enough to suggest to the audience that we are watching actual arrest footage. No second actor interprets Leggio, however, as inconsistency in the depiction of the inveterate villain might detract from the film's unambiguous message regarding good and evil and the impossible place of women within such an unequivocal struggle. Looking amused and resistant, Luciano is forced out of what we learn a few moments later to be Lia's home. After he is led away, the camera lingers in the doorway and captures Lia as she rocks back and forth in a chair in the corner. A fade-out is followed by the opening words of la Torre's speech in which he implores the citizens of Corleone to fearlessly fight for justice in memory of Placido. While he speaks, cross-cutting shows Lia as she leaves her home, suitcase in hand, and then throws a rock at her mother who has followed her outside. La Torre's diegetic voice-over, "a single stick can be broken, but a hundred sticks, a thousand sticks, cannot be broken," reminds the viewer of Lia's violation and underlines her precarious status. Lia represents an open wound that cannot heal or be worked through, and her grief will remain unresolved; her personal trauma has no place in the dominant martyr narrative and her act of rebellion against her mother is an empty gesture. In the end, her story is subsumed into another narrative: that of Placido and other anti-Mafia martyrs such as Pio la Torre and Carlo Alberto della Chiesa that the film means to memorialize.

The film ends with a montage of images of Luciano, La Torre, della Chiesa, and Rizzotto accompanied by a script that recounts significant episodes in their lives and the circumstances behind their deaths. Once more, Luciano's image is that of the actor who interpreted him, while the latter three are depicted with historically accurate documentary photos. We learn that Leggio died in prison, la Torre was killed by the Corleonesi in 1982, and della Chiesa was assassinated on Leggio's orders. Rizzotto, we are told, has no tomb where he can be mourned and his "miseri resti" lay in a sack in the basement of the Court of Appeals in Palermo. However, on 10 March 2012, Rizzotto's remains were positively identified using DNA testing exactly sixty-four years after his death in 1948. This event attracted international news coverage and the trade union leader received a state funeral in Corleone on 24 May 2012.

In the year 2000, the film commemorates Leggio's victims and is a visual reconstitution of Placido's absent body. What, though, of Lia? Unlike Philomena, who was raped and mutilated by Tereus, Lia has no creative outlet for her trauma. And the film implies that she is not able to articulate her losses and make meaning of the violence done to her. While Philomena is able to convey her story through her weaving, the rape forever silences Lia; she is speechless until the film's close, and even remains true to *omertà* in her interrogation session with della Chiesa. Exiled from the narrative, Lia is the "absent Woman ... that serves as the guarantee of masculinity, anchoring male identity and supporting man's creativity and self-representation."[49] The film implies that Lia is not able to articulate her losses and make meaning of the traumatic experience of rape. The film's finale perpetuates the "dominant fiction," which Silverman describes as an "ideological belief that a society's 'reality' is constituted and sustained." In essence, Placido's "'exemplary' male subjectivity cannot be thought apart" from the ideology that the film promotes.[50] *Placido Rizzotto* suggests that Italian society is populated with male heroes ready to combat evil at all costs. Ultimately, a collective memorial to the men who perished at the hands of the Mafia supplants the memory of the violence done to Lia.

3 Mafia Woman in a Man's World: Roberta Torre's *Angela*

That's his wife, and he can do as he pleases.

Angela (Roberta Torre)

In patriarchal society, to desexualize the female body is ultimately to deny its very existence. The "woman's film" thus functions in a rather complex way to deny the woman the space of a reading.

Mary Ann Doane, "The Woman's Film," 80

Angela: A True Story?

Roberta Torre's film *Angela* from 2002 is unique in its focus on a *donna di mafia*. The title, appearing moments into the film and followed by the line "based on a true story," refers to the eponymous protagonist and sets the stage for an in-depth look inside the Mafia, supposedly from the point of view of one of its women. A subtitle conveys that the film is set in 1984 in Palermo, during a period of intense Mafia activity in the capital.[1] In its interest in truth value, Torre's film is in line with other Mafia movies from the new millennium, such as Marco Tullio Giordana's *I cento passi* or Pasquale Scimeca's *Placido Rizzotto*, both from 2000, that tell the "true stories" of the struggles of two anti-Mafia martyrs, Peppino Impastato and Placido Rizzotto. These films, which focus on two men who fought the Mafia from within, readily establish a good guy / bad guy dichotomy. That is, Peppino and Placido fight for freedom and justice while Mafia bad guys Gaetano Badalamenti, Michele Navarra, and Luciano Leggio come off as quintessential villains. Typically, as Laura Mulvey tells us, the hero is the "more perfect, more complete, more powerful ego ideal conceived in the original moment of recognition in front of the mirror," a definition that applies to Peppino, Placido, and several other onscreen anti-Mafia martyrs.[2] Torre's representation of Angela, however, is ambiguous, in terms of both the protagonist's ties Cosa Nostra and her desire to construct a life outside of it. *Angela* marks a departure from these and other recent Mafia biopics that clearly position the spectator on the side of the (eventually) fallen and memorialized hero. This list also includes Michele Placido's *Un eroe borghese* (*A Bourgeois Hero*, 1995), Alessandro di Robilant's *Il giudice ragazzino* (*The Boy Judge*, 1994), and Ricky Tognazzi's *La scorta* (1993) or *Excellent Cadavers* (1999). These films are all loosely based on the true stories of various anti-Mafia crusaders – judges, lawyers, labour union organizers, bodyguards, or socialists – who are murdered as a result of their stance against the Mafia.

In its focus on a woman in or against the Mafia, *Angela* has very few on screen predecessors; the only exceptions being Marco Amenta's documentary short *Diario di una siciliana ribelle* (*One Girl against the Mafia*, 1997) about the pentita and eventual suicide Rita Atria and Giuseppe Ferrara's made-for-television drama *Donne di mafia* (2001), which chronicles the daily ins and outs of a group of women "married to the mob." Torre has frequently claimed that *Angela* is not a film about the Mafia.[3] Perhaps. However, in her position of wife of a mobster from Palermo, Angela has control over daily Mafia business and is entrenched in the organization as a drug runner and accessory to murder. Much about Angela's depiction reveals some of the core tenets of Mafia code and culture, above all the essential and culturally ingrained commitment to *omertà*, and codes of conduct that demand compulsory fidelity for women and exaggerated virility for men.

Unlike other more recent Italian Mafia movies that depict heroic and fact-based male characters who most often perish in their morally grounded struggle against Mafia violence, Torre's representation of a desirous woman in a man's world is fraught with tensions that reflect a national sense of unease with the idea of Mafia women. In the pages that follow, I will look at what happens when Angela transgresses her gender constraints and makes choices that dramatically contradict her prescribed role as a Mafia wife and mother. As we will see, once exiled from her community, Angela has very few, if any, options, and it follows that she has no arena in which to vocalize and thereby work through her grief. Unlike her Mafia movie contemporaries, she is anything but commemorated. Fundamentally, *Angela* offers an innovative take on the mechanics of film identification and spectatorship and pushes the limits of the Mafia melodrama, while foregrounding the double bind of

Mafia women in the new millennium: on the one hand, they are ever more present in mob business, while on the other they are obliged to be invisible, and their autonomy is overshadowed. Indeed, Angela perfectly encapsulates this new woman in the Mafia: she is torn between her sense of loyalty to both her Mafia Family and nuclear family and her desire for independence and sexual satisfaction.[4]

Angela is the third film of what Áine O'Healy has dubbed Roberta Torre's "Sicilian cycle," which also includes two musicals, *Tano da morire* (*To Die for Tano*, 1997) and *Sud Side Story* (2000).[5] The former is a garish exposé into the life, death, and afterlife of low-ranking Mafioso Tano Guarrasi and the latter offers a cynical twist on Shakespeare's Romeo and Juliet who are recast as a Sicilian street singer and Nigerian sex worker. While in the musicals gender roles are set in stone, this is far from the case in *Angela*. The film is positioned from Angela's perspective, and the camera follows her throughout the streets of Palermo, where she delivers cocaine hidden in shoe boxes for her husband Rosario Parlagreco, a.k.a. Saro, a mid-level mobster and shoe store owner, and meets Masino Santalucia, Saro's godson and right-hand man with whom she engages in a passionate affair. When Saro's clan is arrested and Angela's indiscretion is revealed to her husband, she is shunned, and the film closes on an image of Angela as she perennially waits at the port for her lover's return. When under arrest, however, Angela refuses to break *omertà* to save herself, and possibly also Masino. In this way, paradoxically, she remains true to Mafia culture, yet no longer has any place within it. Ultimately, in the last third of the film, Angela is reduced to a liminal figure, and is deprived of voice and agency. Catherine O'Rawe argues that *Angela* demonstrates "the impossibility of the 'woman's film' in the mafia context," as it is not possible for the viewer to "know" Angela and identify with her at all.[6] As we will see, Angela stands apart from the classical heroine of the woman's film who suffers the age-old conflict between romantic longing and familial duty precisely because of her position as a Mafia woman. The woman's film frequently concludes when the excessively desirous female lead either dies or is reabsorbed into a bourgeois romance. Instead, Angela becomes an exile, and is left adrift in a no (wo)man's land. Hence, although Torre initially announces her intent to tell the "true story" of a generally unscreened facet of Mafia culture, in the end the viewer is left at an impasse: Angela's "unknowability" further confirms the ambiguous place of women in the Mafia context and the unease with which contemporary directors represent them.

The Double Bind of Mafia Women

As neither victim nor complete perpetrator, Angela is hard to categorize. Through her active involvement in her husband's illegal activities and transgression with Masino, Angela Spina is not the typical Mafia wife. To be sure, much of her behaviour is troubling, in particular her general lack of shame or guilt coupled with the resignation with which she either stuffs bags of cocaine into shoe boxes, which she delivers because "since she's a woman, she can do deliveries without being stopped," or cleans up the blood of Signor Santangelo, who was murdered in Saro's office. This final example is telling: she is not disgusted in the least, and completes her task with banal indifference. Furthermore, when arrested, she demonstrates a complete lack of remorse for her crimes. As a deviant woman, Angela is not exceptional, just fairly mundane. O'Rawe points out that generally the criminality of deviant women has to be "overdetermined."[7] Angela, by contrast, lives a fairly routine, systematic life. She runs the shoe shop, makes deliveries, goes out with her husband, and attempts to keep her daughter Minica's behaviour in check. Unlike many women with ties to the Mafia, Angela's characterization is much less ambiguous, as her active and willing participation in the drug trade most surely categorizes her as a perpetrator. For example, Angela has a better handle on drug trafficking then some of Saro's associates, makes drugs deals in front of a young girl, deceives the police while they follow her, and volunteers to do drug runs when it is not necessary. At the same time, however, she is far from emancipated.

In "Becoming Visible: Did the Emancipation of Women Reach the Sicilian Mafia?," Valeria Pizzini Gambetta argues that women's heightened visibility within organized crime (in arrests and trials, for example) does not necessarily imply that women have obtained power status within the organization. It is true that many women are actively involved in several aspects of mob business and have historically stepped in to fill significant roles left empty as a result of the death or incarceration of a male family member.[8] However, in that these women, like Angela, were never inducted into Cosa Nostra, they hold no influence within it. This is alluded to early on in the film when Santangelo, the man eventually murdered in Saro's office, is uncomfortable accepting the drug drop from Angela, telling her that "this is not a job for a woman." Akin to the experiences of many real-life women connected to the Mafia, Angela's arrest is only a ploy to obtain insider information regarding her husband's activities and therefore to catch a much bigger fish.[9] In addition, the police wrongly believe that having Angela listen to recordings of her intimate phone calls with Masino will prompt her to talk. Instead, her retort – "If you think I would get others arrested to save myself, you do not know me well. You're wasting your time." – demonstrates her loyalty to Mafia values.

Angela's double bind is made most obvious in a scene that echoes the famous finale of Coppola's *The Godfather* (1972). The door shut on Kay during Michael's induction as new godfather to the Corleone clan bars her from this key ritual and excludes her from the inner workings of the Mafia. Yet, the following take frames her solidly within the doorway, which alludes to the paradox of Mafia women: they are central to the family as wife and mother but, at least traditionally, must remain silent, subservient, and invisible. In Torre's film, Masino shuts the door on Angela after she asks Mimmo about the availability of a 50,000 lira bag of cocaine. His gruff "We're talking about important things" excludes her from "men only" Mafia business, but only up to a point, as Angela continues to spy on Saro and his clan throughout the film. Moreover, Masino's incendiary rebuttal has nothing to do with his take on Angela's involvement in mob business. Instead, he is only sublimating his jealousy after he spied on Angela and Saro while they were playfully kissing. He explains to his companions that Angela bothers him as she always gets in the way. Neither support Masino's position, and Mimmo responds: "That's [Saro's] wife, and he can do as he pleases," and then points out her utility to the business. In this way, Torre ambiguates Coppola's straightforward take on space, place, and gender roles in a Mafia context.

Throughout the first two-thirds of the film, Angela repeatedly attempts to frustrate her proscribed gender parameters: She works the streets as a drug runner, relentlessly spies on her husband and his cronies, negotiates profitable deals for the family, and allows her desire for Masino to grow. Up until the group arrest, the spectator follows Angela on her journey of self-discovery and is positioned to identify with her, to feel her frustration as a woman in a man's world, her gentle, almost motherly love for her husband and passion for Masino. Torre frequently shoots Angela with a handheld camera in the shadows as she darts through the streets of her neighbourhood near the Ballarò market, or in the dark, where she is framed so that her face is obscured when, for example, she attempts to eavesdrop on her husband and his associates. However, frequent shots of her dark and emotive eyes demonstrate her frustration, alienation, and ultimately her desire for something prohibited. At the same time, she is regularly sexualized through following shots that languidly track her through the streets of Palermo and close-ups of her red nail polish and brooding eyes.

Let us not forget, however, that, like Kay Corleone before her, Angela's supposed autonomy never existed. She is followed, watched, photographed, and bugged even in what she thought were her most private moments. For example, when Masino drives Angela home after their first sexual encounter, the non-diegetic sound of Pino Daniele's "Appocundria" imbues the scene with nostalgia and malaise, sentiments furthered by the mise en scène: the pair is filmed in a two-shot as the car appears to be floating through the sky. As they drive, a recording of their earlier conversation setting up their encounter is interspersed with the music. The camera then tilts skyward and cuts to a shot of an official who is reading the transcript of the same conversation from the beginning while the melody and original exchange between the two can still be heard. Thus, Torre underlines Angela's lack of emancipation, which is furthered after her arrest when she is watched not by the authorities, but by Saro's men, who hope to catch her with Masino. Also, towards the end of the film, when Angela is in full breakdown, Torre includes a heavily pixilated shot of her in close-up that resembles footage from a surveillance camera and recalls earlier scenes when Angela and Masino were followed, and their conversations taped. Hence, Torre suggests that Angela's desire at the end of the film to begin anew is futile, as her autonomy was regularly limited as Saro's wife and drug runner; in essence, her independence was a fiction, as was Michael's confession to Kay.

Is Angela then a victim? A perpetrator? Does she represent the enslaved condition of Mafia women at large? Does her desire to "leave" because she "wants a change," as she tells Saro during a car ride just after her flirtation with Masino begins, suggest a subtle rebellion against the daily ins and outs of mob life, or only imply that she knows that, if she stays, her affair, and the accompanying fallout, is imminent? Torre does not suggest clear answers to any of these questions. Instead, the director, like the viewer, does not know what to do with Angela, a woman clearly "inside" the system and true to Mafia ethos yet in possession of her own desires. Torre's ambivalent representation of Angela echoes a general sense of unease around the notion of Mafia women in Italy. Mafia women, at least in Cosa Nostra, present a legal and cultural conundrum: increasingly, some can hold key roles in the organization, yet, in that they are not officially inducted as members of the Mafia, convicting them of Mafia-related crime is quite a challenge. As Teresa Principato maintains, their role is central, but distinct, from that of their male counterparts:

> Cosa Nostra tends not to admit women to its own inner circles, not so much because of archaic male chauvinistic concepts ... but because it assigns them a precise role, irrelevant for the penal code (as well as law enforcement), but still crucial: the role of caretaker and communicator of the cultural codes at the basis of the organization, such as: the division of others into categories of friend-enemy; a certain sense of honor; the duty toward the vendetta, omertà, etc.[10]

On top of this, of course, is obligatory fidelity, the violation of which is punishable by death for all parties involved. Most germane is a comment by Joe Bonanno: "If a family member discovered that his wife had gone to bed with another Family member, he was justified in killing him."[11] Although several antiquated legal loopholes, such as penal code 587, the "crime of honour" that provides the comedic pith to Pietro Germi's film *Divorzio all'italiana* (*Divorce Italian Style*, 1961), have been done away with in the legislature, they are part and parcel of Cosa Nostra. As Siebert argues: "A woman is basically considered to be a man's property, and the bond that ties the man to the women is that of possession. This ancestral, almost meta-historical bond is the background that men share."[12] In the film, as so frequently in the real world, Mafia law wins out. Although Angela is found not guilty of her crimes by a court of law, she is punished twofold for her amorous transgression. At first, when her husband exiles her from her family, and presumably from any contact with her daughter Minica; but more saliently at the film's close, when she is banished from everyone and everything and is likened to the undead while she despondently awaits her lover.

The Mafia Melodrama

Although *Angela* unveils the inner workings of a small-time mob family and sheds light on the emerging role of women therein, it is difficult to categorize *Angela* as simply a Mafia movie, which, in both the Italian and the American context, is generally situated from the male point of view and focuses more or less exclusively on "male" issues and problems such as tracking down bad guys or the legal system, honour, *omertà*, and virility in a "men only society." Yet, as O'Rawe has convincingly argued, *Angela* is far from being a "woman's film," a genre that sheds light on the female condition and is dependent upon the knowability of the female protagonist in the domestic sphere.[13] However, in its focus on private conflicts, the clichéd and failed love story, a bereft protagonist, and appeal to a female viewer,[14] *Angela* follows the genre rules for a melodrama; in particular, the "fallen woman" melodrama made popular in the 1920s and early 1930s that finds its antecedents, as Lea Jacobs argues, in nineteenth-century popular culture.[15] Jacobs describes one of the first visual representations of the fallen woman, which shares thematic and visual similarities with Torre's film: a series of three paintings by Augustus Egg (1858) depicts a woman's fall from grace from upper-class wife and mother to bereft and suicidal outcast. The series, according to Jacobs, "implies a loss of both class and familial status."[16]

Unlike Egg's fallen heroine, Angela is punished twofold: once for excessive desire, which led to her dalliance, and also for her earlier transvestitism while masquerading as a made man, a plot twist in line with Mulvey's reading of castration anxiety and film spectatorship. Mulvey argues that film is a medium that creates and reinforces desire through objectifying the threatening female characters.[17] Indeed, Mulvey discusses scopophilia in cinema as a system of repression and projection on the part of the audience that allows for a redirection of our "voyeuristic fantasies" onto the actors while simultaneously identifying with the "male" image and fetishizing or punishing the female protagonist.[18] In *Angela*, however, a woman, and not a man, is on centre stage. This focus on a female protagonist troubles traditional notions of film spectatorship and identification and problematizes the logic of Mulvey's theory of castration anxiety.

The treatment of female spectatorship offered by Mulvey in her follow-up article, "Afterthoughts on 'Visual Pleasure and Narrative Cinema' Inspired by King Vidor's *Duel in the Sun* (1946)" is helpful to understand this quandary. Here, Mulvey looks at "films in which a woman central protagonist is shown to be unable to achieve a stable identity, torn between the deep blue sea of passive femininity and the devil of regressive masculinity."[19] As a Mafia woman in a man's world, Angela lives this dichotomy. While active in the organization and venturing outside of the household, she is under surveillance, and is the persistent object of the male gaze. Interestingly, she is also an active agent in her own self-presentation and sexualization. However, when we are positioned to identify with her towards the end of the film, she is in a state of unending breakdown and is excluded from the symbolic.

Mulvey argues that in the western or the melodrama, the mechanics of Oedipal nostalgia are laid bare. Women protagonists accept masculinization at a very high price (punishment or death, for example) and "masculine identification" is unworkable and ultimately fails. While the male spectator sees his ego ideal in the active male hero, the female viewer's experience of identification is masochistic. For the female protagonist and spectator, the very possibility and then impossibility of identification leads to nostalgia for that which never could be, that is, the enactment of the heretofore repressed active phase of development. Mulvey asserts that "the female spectator's fantasy of masculinisation is at cross-purposes with itself, restless in transvestite clothes." This nostalgia or "sadness" then reaffirms the pitfalls in representing "the feminine in patriarchal society."[20] In the end, we are duped, temporarily persuaded by a fantasy that can never be.

As is Angela: her arrest evinces her various trespasses and marks a dramatic restyling of her representation. Her vibrancy and activity are tied to her sexuality, and at the moment of her arrest, her masquerade is swiftly undone. Her eroticism, constructed through her active and willing involvement in mob business, was underscored through costume and performance, such as red silk blouses, scarlet nail polish, repeated shots of her intense stare accented by heavily made-up eyes and the nuanced portrayal by Donatella Finocchiaro.[21] Mulvey observes that the "female presence as centre allows the story to be actually, *overtly*, about sexuality: it becomes a melodrama."[22] However, after Angela is arrested, her allure is quickly dismantled: at the station, a series of mug shots are taken of her against a white background while she is wearing a white blouse. After the final photograph is snapped, the screen fills with white light and Angela slowly vaporizes as if she were a spectre. Then, her nails are cut, her jewellery is taken from her, and she is dressed in prison garb and locked in a cell; the two doors and one window that close on her reiterate her abrupt transformation. From this point on, Angela is for the most part desexualized and frequently resembles the walking dead. Rather than engaging with the object of her desire or participating in her milieu, she withdraws into memory, her gaze is without address, and we see her physically divided from both her husband and Masino via glass barriers.

Mary Ann Doane reads the aforementioned double bind of the female protagonist in the melodrama and woman's film, and bemoans the consequences of the de-eroticized female gaze: once the female gaze is "de-eroticized,"

> the female spectator has two options for modes of entry [into the film]: a narcissistic identification with the female figure as spectacle, and a "transvestite" identification with the active male hero in his mastery ... In patriarchal society, to desexualize the female body is ultimately to deny its very existence. The "woman's film" thus functions in a rather complex way to deny the woman the space of a reading.[23]

The de-eroticizing of the female protagonist is hyperbolized in uber-patriarchal Mafia culture, where the denial of female sexuality is de rigueur, and is also blatant in Torre's film. Angela, a once desiring subject, is transformed into a passive object of discourse, who is talked about and looked upon as if she were an accessory to a film that purportedly focuses on her condition. To be sure, Saro orders her to "disappear" from his life and her litigator informs the court that "her psychophysical conditions have notably worsened," and that she "cannot be held accountable for her actions, being completely incapable of intent or will." Angela is also described of being "of unsound mind." During the trial, where she appears in a state of breakdown, Angela's psychological condition is the focus of dialogue, while after its conclusion, she becomes despondent and slips into a depression. Thus, the development of her character is analogous with that of the female protagonist of melodramas that, according to Doane, "mobilize a medical discourse." In these films, the newly disenfranchised female lead "can only passively give witness as the signs of her own body are transformed by the purportedly desexualized medical gaze, the 'speaking eye,' into elements of discourse."[24]

Angela's marginalized condition is underscored in her final meeting with Masino, which takes place after Saro is sentenced to eleven years in prison. The couple role plays an escape that will never take place. No longer custodian of her own desires, Angela can only play-act and follow Masino's lead. In this way, her wordlessness and passive simulation demonstrate her complete lack of control over her own life and offer a bitter commentary on how much has changed in terms of the mechanics of identification in the film. In essence, Angela's role playing hints at an Oedipal nostalgia, or an impossible desire to return to a world governed by clearly coded gender rules which finds its archetype in mafiosità.

The Abject Melancholic

During the film's finale, Angela swiftly comes undone. She goes to the bar by the port to await Masino as directed so that the pair might flee Palermo to begin life anew, but he never arrives. Was he murdered by Saro's henchmen, which is suggested when Saro refers to him as a "dead man walking"? Or did he simply abandon Angela to save himself? Torre never tells us. Masino's plea to Angela to not give up on him, and to return to the bar by the port every day until she sees him as he promises to "show up eventually" accompanies repeated tracking shots of Angela at a table, waiting, as the rain pours down outside the window. She is shot both from within and from outside the restaurant, where she is obscured by the rain, and is barely recognizable. These shots are interspersed with dissolves to other patrons in the bar, a technique that creates a dizzying and unreal affect, while simultaneously conveying a sense that days, if not weeks, have passed in a sequence lasting about ninety seconds. In fact, a repeated shot of a clock over Angela's shoulder confirms that she has only been waiting several hours. Until Saro learns of Angela's affair, time was clearly demarcated in the film by frequent cuts to a calendar that displayed the dates when events transpired. During the last twenty minutes of the film this episodic device is absent, a gesture that foregrounds Angela's loss of a social identity and expulsion from her sodality.

During the last moments of *Angela*, the theme music predominant throughout the film transitions into a dissonant jazz piece by The Cool Elements that slowly escalates to a crescendo while Angela appears ghostlike in her near-empty home. She is without make-up, her nails bare and ragged, and she sobs, grieving the loss of Masino and with him her only chance of escape. A pan to a close-up of a stuccoed wall upon which is reflected the shadow of the falling rain cuts to a medium long shot and then an extreme long shot of Angela's back in black silhouette at the port, where she stares out to sea. Captions inform the viewer that Masino has still not returned, that Saro was released from prison in 1995 and never saw his wife again, and that Angela now works in a tailor's shop and that she can often be found at the bar by the port. The screen slowly fades to black to leave Angela immobile, perennially trapped in a time loop, between the "now" of that rainy day during the

1980s and the forever after as implied in caption. This closing image is at odds with the opening scene of the film, when Angela is presented for the first time: a roving camera tracks a blurry shot of the storeroom of the shoe store, where Angela is barely visible in the corner. Moments later, Angela is shot in close-up with the room in shallow focus while she sings, smokes a cigarette, and checks her hair, jewellery, and make-up in a mirror, all of which demonstrate, as O'Healy notes, an "anxiety regarding her visibility" that is present throughout the film.[25] Unlike in the finale, at the beginning of the film Angela stands out among her dreary and blurred environs.

I would like to recall my earlier discussion of the melodrama and masculine identification, by which the failure on the part of the female protagonist to live out the dream of successful masculinization is generally imbued with melancholy. Freud's categories of mourning and melancholia are appropriate to Angela's state. Mourning, as Freud argues, involves working through loss. "When the work of mourning is completed," Freud tells us, "the ego becomes free and uninhibited again" and at that point can reattach itself to a new object that serves as a substitute for the original loss, a process that helps to restore the psychic economy of the subject.[26] It is not clear, however, if Angela comprehends exactly what has been lost. Furthermore, as an exile, she is incapable of mourning her losses, both that of her lover and the much larger loss of her community. In that she does not understand the reasons for her grief, she cannot work through it. Instead, she lives in a state of melancholy, characterized by "a profoundly painful dejection, cessation of interest in the outside world, loss of the capacity to love, inhibition of all activity, and a lowering of ... self regarding feelings ... [Melancholy] culminates in a delusional expectation of punishment."[27] Angela experiences, as Freud explains, a narcissistic "*identification* of the ego with an abandoned object," made clear in her obsessive returning to the scene of the crime, which, as the narrator implies, goes on in perpetuity.[28] Identification allows Angela's relationship with both Masino and the world to which he belonged to continue, at least in her mind. However, in that the Masino that Angela imagines will never successfully live up to the original man with whom she fell in love, Angela's melancholy will no doubt continue and play itself out as an unabated cycle of self-punishment.

Angela's melancholy demonstrates her unworkable position: no longer inside the system, her only options are to completely betray her past by becoming a *pentita* or to escape with Masino. Angela is unwilling to commit the former and barred from the latter, and as I argued earlier, she inhabits a liminal state between a community that no longer recognizes her and a country that has yet to come to terms with and recognize what she represents. The film might suggest that, after her exile, Angela will achieve a certain level of autonomy through finding respectable employment as a seamstress. However, her compulsion to return to the port and to not move on and fully integrate into the symbolic implies that she is incapable of working through Mafia-related trauma.

Angela's condition can be expanded with Julia Kristeva's notion of the abject. Above all, Kristeva argues, the abject is what must be repressed so that the symbolic order may remain intact. Tangible examples are hinged on the body: the ultimate abject object is the corpse: once alive, now dead, part of us, drastically different from us. But also blood, pus, faeces, sweat, and urine, that which the subject must "thrust aside in order to live."[29] When Kristeva writes that the abject is a "precondition of narcissism," she means that the subject, in the process of identity formation, must jettison the maternal in order to enter language.[30] As such, the abject is never fully other, and can be likened to a siren that beckons the subject back to the chora, the space of the pre-symbolic. The abject, the signifier of trauma, evidences the space where "meaning collapses,"[31] draws "attention to the fragility of the law," marks a threshold, and delineates difference.[32]

Angela, who "does not respect boundaries, positions, rules," and who is "in-between, ambiguous," experiences abjection throughout the film, in particular during the finale. She clearly "disturbs identity, systems, order" in both her Mafia kinship group and with the judicial system.[33] In that we are not clearly positioned to identify with her, Angela's motives are unclear throughout the film and she is, according to O'Rawe, "totally devoid of affect."[34] Her lack of shame, guilt, and remorse baffle the prosecutor, whose moral code is completely discordant with honour politics. He asks her, "What's this foolish honour that's keeping you quiet? What are you trying to do? Who are you trying to save? They wouldn't do the same for you. I don't know anything about this so-called honour. Explain it to me once and for all." Angela is disinterested in answering; here and elsewhere she sleepwalks through the film.

Abjection can be likened to melancholy, as both are boundary or limit states. Also, melancholics, like the abject object, "which modernity has learned to repress, dodge or fake," do not properly suture environments.[35] Past and present, inside and outside, and life and death intermingle and threaten the symbolic order, which in the economy of the film is grounded in rigid gender conventions and the honour code. Angela must be scapegoated, cast out in order for Mafia values to remain intact. Fundamentally, no redemptive act closes the narrative and Angela never aggregates her surroundings, which raises compelling questions regarding identification and spectatorship. In order to abrogate the abject, the viewer will often identify with or forgive the female victim in some way, which helps close the narrative and leaves viewing pleasure intact. While Angela's punishment should end the film and restore some sort of order, in that she is neither fetishized nor reabsorbed into the dominant narrative, she disturbs rather than consolidates meaning.

In traditional melodrama, the female protagonist tends to bring the narrative to a close through some sort of social ritual: generally through the marriage act, but also, as in the case of *Duel in the Sun*, through her demise. With the fallen woman film, the woman frequently repents for her wrongdoings, yet remains an outcast and lives the rest of her wretched days on the streets as a prostitute or mendicant.[36] The woman's transgression and punishment inscribe a moral code within the film, thereby reinforcing the dominant social order and making sense of the whole story. In Torre's film, Angela neither literally repents – "pentirsi" – as she chooses to stay true to the Mafia code, nor does she repent for her affair with Masino. Thus, Angela's lack of atonement suggests a national inability to see women in their position as desiring subjects. As such, she is doubly punished: she is exiled from both her blood family and mafia Family, but more to the point, she is literally cast off in a state of exile at the film's close. On a deeper level, however, Angela as abject connotes a problem: that is, the trauma of the Mafia that hangs over Italy, yet is frequently disregarded so that the image of the nation is left unblemished. Indeed, neither killed off nor redeemed, and certainly unmourned, Angela is left ghost-like and clanless; she is an open wound not worked through, much like that of the community that shunned her.

4 The Mafia Noir: Paolo Sorrentino's *Le conseguenze dell'amore*

> But let's get back to our Sophie! Her mere presence seemed a feat of daring in our sulking, fearful, unsavory household.
>
> After she had been with us for some time ... we could not help fearing that she might one day disturb the fabric of our intimate precautions or suddenly, one fine morning, wake up to our sleazy reality ...
>
> We made strides in poetry, so to speak, just marveling at her being so beautiful and so much more obviously free than we were. The rhythm of her life sprang from other wellsprings than ours ... Our wellsprings were forever slow and slimy.
>
> The joyful strength, precise yet gentle, which animated her from her hair to her ankles troubled us, alarmed us in a charming sort of way, but definitely alarmed us, yes, that's the word.
>
> Louis-Ferdinand Céline, *Journey to the End of the Night*, 407–8

> What will concern me here [are] the alterations ... implied by the *confrontation with the feminine* and the way in which societies code themselves in order to accompany as far as possible the speaking subject on that journey. Abjection, or the journey to the end of the night.
>
> Julia Kristeva, *Powers of Horror*, 58

The Mafia Noir

The vast majority of reviews and scholarship devoted to Paolo Sorrentino's *Le conseguenze dell'amore* (*The Consequences of Love*) from 2004 discuss the film's noirish and neo-noirish elements.[1] The film, which takes place primarily in the contained world of a nondescript hotel in Lugano, Switzerland, follows the daily routine of Titta Di Girolamo, a former investment banker who lost 220 billion euros of Cosa Nostra's monies in a venture gone awry. As punishment, he is exiled from Italy and forced to live a solitary existence as an errand boy delivering several million dollars of Mafia money to a Swiss bank once or twice a week. Like most protagonists of film noir, Titta chain-smokes incessantly, is reserved, depressed, disillusioned, and cynical, and carries inside of himself a deep secret, which he refers to as his "segreto inconfessabile [unconfessable secret]." In keeping with the genre, Titta is also the film's voice-over narrator through whose perspective we are presented with a visually complex milieu characterized by elliptical editing, jarring jumpcuts, shallow focus, dramatic angles, and an amber pallet. All of these techniques imbue the film with a sense of anxiety while unsettling us and keeping us on our toes as we are introduced to a series of characters and a set of clues that, it is suggested, if properly followed, will unveil the pith of the "consequences" announced in the film's title. In typical noir fashion, the hermetically sealed world of the anti-hero begins to unravel once he falls for the beautiful and alluring Sofia, who works as a bartender at the hotel. The discovery of emotion leads Titta to break all his routines and to commit a series of acts that directly challenge the Mafia and lead to his demise. As he is slowly lowered into a vat of wet concrete at the film's close, his memory returns and he dies a redeemed man, having discovered the value of friendship, love, compassion, and atonement, all vital qualities that stand in stark opposition to the Mafia and its cult of death, forgetting, and self-interest.

His murder is "extraordinary" or "daring," "rocambolesco," a word mentioned frequently in the film that is meant to contrast with a normal or boring death along the lines of old age or illness in the aforementioned prison-hotel. In short, Titta's death, and therefore his life, have meaning, a narrative twist in line with the "noir redemption film" in which, as Palmer argues, the intrusion of the past can offer a "revival of faith, both secular and religious, in the difficult yet ultimately achievable perfectability of human nature."[2] None of this, it is suggested, would have happened had Sofia not implored Titta to interact with and recognize her. Mary Wood calls Sofia a "catalyst" who represents a challenge to power and whose presence in the protagonist's life ultimately creates chaos and exposes "the face of the contemporary Mafia."[3] However, just before Titta departs for Sicily to attempt to explain the theft of nine million dollars of Mafia money, Sofia is abruptly effaced from the narrative through her supposed death. If Titta's death is extraordinary, hers is mundane: while apparently on her way to pick up Titta at the hotel to celebrate his fiftieth birthday in the countryside, she distractedly answers her cell phone, which causes her car to veer off the road and crash into a tractor in the middle of an empty field.

This arbitrary accident lacks narrative motivation and at first glance appears completely discordant with the typical culmination of the femme fatale's storyline, whose collapse is generally intimately bound up with that of the protagonist. Although such an expungement from the narrative comes across as inconsistent with the plot, I argue here that Sofia's seemingly irrational death is necessary for Titta to transcend his depression and the confines of his Mafia-made prison so as to eventually reach a state of enlightenment. Sofia provokes Titta's rebellion, but, in doing so, she threatens the traditional logic of desire prevalent in Italian Mafia movies from the new millennium and must be eliminated. In the pages that follow, I will read Sofia as a symptom of Titta's repression. In particular, I will look at the figure of the femme fatale as informed by Julia Kristeva's discussion of the abject feminine and demonstrate the impossible place of female desire and autonomy in Italian Mafia cinema. To be sure, Sofia's erasure from the narrative is without consequence, while Titta is redeemed through death.

"To each ego its object, to each superego its abject"

The contrast between the Mafia and Sofia could not be more apparent: Mafiosi in the film are hard-core thugs or sophisticated businessmen who privilege money and power above all else. They commit murder without remorse, killing targets and bystanders alike, and readily double-cross one another. In the film, the organization is humorously likened to an enlarged prostate when the commission interrogates Titta at the "Hotel New Europe." The panel of Mafiosi sits at a conference table that is backed by a large sign reading "Hypertrophy of the Prostate: Refresher Course." But the comic allusion is overshadowed by the pragmatic depiction of Cosa Nostra as an international, deadly, and uber-affluent organization with a strict hierarchy whose members are professionals, "calculating and ruthlessly efficient, but never flamboyant or 'colorful.'"[4]

Conversely, Sofia, who is played by Anna Magnani's granddaughter Olivia Magnani, is depicted as otherworldly. She is remarkably beautiful, dresses elegantly yet simply, and moves with catlike grace.[5] She is mysterious; we only know that she has worked at the hotel for two years, is taking driving lessons in order to get her licence, and is mildly interested in Titta. We understand little of her attraction for the protagonist, and remain ignorant of her motives, although one reviewer comments, and I assume ironically, that "she does get a sports car out of the deal."[6] Men are drawn to her, and early in the film, one man is so mystified by her presence that he walks directly into a streetlamp, as Titta observes from his hotel room. Thus, the film suggests that Sofia is a distraction, but one who carries repercussions for those who fall victim to her allure. Moreover, from the film's outset, she is positioned as a mystery that is both unattainable and elusive, and she is akin to a siren who threatens but also beckons to the subject, much like the site of abjection.

Sofia's affinity with the abject object is announced early in the film when Titta listens to a woman reading the following passage from Louis-Ferdinand Céline's *Journey to the End of the Night* in the bar in the hotel:

> Then anything can happen! A bargain! Think of the saving, getting all your thrills from reminiscences ... Reminiscences are something we've got plenty of, one can buy beauties, enough to last us a lifetime ... Life is more complicated, especially the life of human forms ... A hard adventure. None more desperate. Compared with the addiction to perfect forms, cocaine is a pastime for stationmasters. But let's get back to our Sophie! ... We made strides in poetry, so to speak, just marveling at her being so beautiful and so much more obviously free than we were. The rhythm of her life sprang from other wellsprings that ours ... our wellsprings were forever slow and slimy. The joyful strength, precise yet gentle, which animated her from her hair to her ankles troubled us, alarmed us in a charming sort of way, but definitely alarmed us, yes, that's the word.[7]

Sorrentino makes no secret of how his film is inspired by the writings of the controversial nihilist. Affinities in the connection of Titta and Sofia and that of Ferdinand Bardamu, Celine's cynical anti-hero, with his Sophie are conspicuous in the film.[8] The protagonist has to make a choice: to go on with his uncourageous, restrained, and backward-looking existence or begin to live through the body of a perfect and vital other. Just before this passage, Bardamu meets Sophie for the first time, and after detailing her exquisite body and "miraculous skin," he immediately equates eros with death, bodily decay, and a crisis of language. Before Sophie's "godhead" could be "mauled by [his] shameful hands ... Death and Words must give their permission first." Also, he declares that a "cultivated man needs to be rolled in a dense layer of symbols, caked to the asshole with artistic excrement, before he can tear off a piece."[9] Sophie/Sofia represents a border state, the unsymbolizable and uncontrollable site of abjection that must be cast out so that identity can remain intact.

In *Powers of Horror: An Essay on Abjection*, Kristeva focuses heavily on the trope of abjection in Céline's work, in particular his preoccupation with "those females who can wreck the infinite." Women in Celine are "Janus-faced," they give life only to snatch it away.[10] "To each ego its object, to each superego its abject," writes Kristeva. While the object is "definable" and settles the ego, the abject does quite the opposite. It unsettles precisely because it comes from within, and evokes the pre-symbolic space of the maternal body and the loss of differentiation that this body represents. Yet, the abject is violently excluded by the superego so that identity, borders, and sanity can be maintained. With the construction of Sofia as abject, *Le conseguenze dell'amore* implies that Titta has internalized the superego, read here as the Mafia. Hence, Sofia will be "jettisoned" by Titta "into an abominable real, inaccessible except through jouissance." Kristeva equates the abject with jouissance, as both are "parachuted by the other" and embody a site before the acquisition of language that can drive the subject to the point of extinction, which, as I will demonstrate, is the outcome of Titta's encounter with Sofia.[11]

In the first few minutes of the film, Sofia is constructed as an unobtainable and impossible "ob-ject, a boundary and a limit."[12] *Le conseguenze dell'amore* opens on a static extreme long shot of man standing still on a moving walkway. The long take lasts two full minutes and the various elements of the mise en scène – cavernous cold space, neon lighting reflected on tile walls and the fixed posture of the subject – together with the melancholic cadence of Lali Puna's aptly named "Scary World Theory" "disturb" the viewer and imbue the film with a sense of apprehension and mystery.[13] As the man, who we later learn is a porter working for the bank where Titta deposits the Mafia money, gradually approaches the right side of the frame, we see that he is holding onto a chain that is attached to a black suitcase that will reappear time and again throughout the film. When he reaches the end of the walkway, the non-diegetic music is abruptly taken over by the sound of the suitcase's wheels as they briskly roll against the grated metal floor. The camera pans right to follow the porter on his delivery, but this movement is interrupted by a disorienting cut to Sofia, who unhurriedly joggles a cocktail shaker in the belle époque–styled bar. An escalating sound bridge of the wheels of the suitcase connects the two divergent narrative spaces. Then, the camera quickly zooms in to capture Sofia in medium close-up while she turns her head to look over her shoulder to the extreme left of the frame as if she were watching the porter walk into the bar. Thus, desire is quickly transferred from the suitcase, a standard prop in the mystery genre, to Sofia, both of whom work together to launch the narrative. Both the suitcase and Sofia are sources of fascination and are presented as mysteries to be solved. The suitcase is regularly delivered to Titta's hotel room by a tall, beautiful, and enigmatic woman who wears sunglasses and is dressed in black. She waits for visual confirmation from Titta and then departs without ever uttering a sound, thus augmenting the sense of intrigue regarding an inanimate object. The suitcase and Sofia are akin to the "object-cause of desire," which is "not what we desire, what we are after, but, rather, that which sets our desire in motion." As "objet petit a," Sofia is positioned as unattainable, because, according to Slavoj Žižek, desire is "metonymical; it shifts from one object to another," which is clear in the opening moments of the film.[14] It follows that desire can never be satisfied, which presents a challenge to narrative cinema in its demand for formal resolution. However, the journey continues nonetheless.

The Femme Fatale: A "symptom of man"

In many ways, Sofia is a typical fetish object of the male gaze who creates desire and sets the narrative investigation in motion, but in essence is without a substantive identity, as Danielle Hipkins has pointed out.[15] Fetishism, writes Mary Ann Doane, "is a phallic defense which allows the subject to distance himself from the object of desire (or, more accurately, from its implications in relation to castration) through the overvaluation of a mediating substitute object."[16] Sofia is frequently shown in close-up and medium shot as she glides through the space of the hotel, and three times she is the object of Titta's gaze as he watches (or recalls watching) her naked torso that is reflected in the mirror while she changes for work. Also, men attempt to look down her blouse or, in the case of Titta's half-brother, make advances towards her that she rebuffs. As the object of the spectator's gaze, she is, in Laura Mulvey's words, "the perfect [stylized] product" who reassures rather than threatens.[17] And this is the case with the entire film, whose mise-en-scène is stylized, editing rhythmical, and tone sedate.

Sofia as fetish obviates Titta's fear of castration, which is equated with his sense of dread regarding loss of phallic mastery. Fetishism, according to Kristeva, is a defence mechanism against depression, and fantasy can "replace the denial of psychic pain ... due to object loss."[18] While in Lugano, Titta is disempowered by the Mafia, and he reacts by carefully controlling all aspects of his life: from his dress and composure to whom he talks to, where he sits, with whom he dines or plays cards, the precise hour and day that he injects heroine (Wednesdays at 10:00 a.m.) and the annual routine of having his blood cleaned. Sofia breaks these regimens, which, as I have said, eventually leads to greater insight on the part of the protagonist.

However, their relationship (or, more accurately, Titta's relationship with Sofia) is slightly different from that of the typical femme fatale with her doomed male victim. In her study on the femme fatale, Doane insists on the figure's traumatic potential. In that she "never really is what she seems to be,"[19] she is threatening, unpredictable, ambivalent, and therefore apparently unmasterable. She is a "figure of fascination"[20] because she blurs boundaries between subject and object, passivity and activity, pain and pleasure, ego and superego. As a projection of male desire, she is a construct; an "articulation of fears surrounding the loss of stability and centrality of the self, the 'I,' the ego."[21] In that she is a "symptom" of male anxiety, she is not an empowering symbol. She has no autonomy in herself and is only a "carrier" of power.[22] She is a "secret"[23] that must be revealed, which makes her an ideal character for the film noir, whose plot is centred around a mystery. Moreover, the classic femme fatale manipulates men through her sexuality, frequently taking advantage of intimate knowledge of the protagonist's secret past and causing his downfall. As such, she embodies evil and must be effaced from the narrative through punishment or death.[24]

Sofia complies with these qualifiers, but only up to a point. Most aptly, she does nothing to actively and consciously motivate Titta's undoing. Instead, it is her mere presence that unsettles him. This way, she is in line with the moniker of "donna intrigante" that director Kurt Bernhardt bestowed on Marlene Dietrich in a 1929 interview: she was "an intrigante, pure and simple."[25] Contrary to the femme fatale, who "consciously uses her sexual allure to destroy others," the "intrigante" only "fosters intrigue," and "just can't help being an object of so much passion and desire," and is ultimately "most desperately trapped by fate and circumstance."[26] Unlike the femme fatale, then, the intrigante is a victim. And one crucial difference between Sofia's character and that of the femme fatale of the film noir is the lack of a physically present third player who has a direct relationship with the woman, whom Žižek calls the "obscene-knowing father." This father is not the absent, yet omnipotent, "Name of the Father" but his "obscene, uncanny, shadowy double." He is violent and cruel, an "absolute Master for whom there are no limits," who is frequently embodied by the all-powerful gangster who actively exploits the femme fatale. He is also omniscient, and is aware of the threat of parricide that hangs over the noir universe.

Although no "obscene father" is physically manifest in *Le conseguenze dell'amore*, the Mafia hangs over the entire film and acts as his stand-in. Recalling Doane, in this relationship, Žižek claims, woman "finds herself occupying the impossible place of the traumatic Thing."[27] What he means is that woman covers up the real crisis in the noir: the aforementioned "relationship to the obscene father,"[28] read here as Titta's association with Cosa Nostra. It is only natural that the male protagonist will clash with the obscene father, the deviant stand-in for "the guarantor of the rule of Law,"[29] in order to test his own power while attempting to prove the other's impotence. In this discordant relationship, woman is an exchange commodity between father and son, a "figure of masculine fantasy" who helps to maintain the fiction of Oedipal mastery. "The function she performs," writes Žižek, "is exactly homologous to that of the Name of the Father, i.e., she renders it possible for the subject to locate himself again within the texture of symbolic fate."[30] However, in the film noir, the relationship between the protagonist and the femme fatale is invariably untenable and its failure exposes the unfeasibility of heteronormative sexuality and happy endings. In this unhappy triad, woman is nothing in herself, just "the symptom of man" who is eventually pushed to nonexistence. "A Symptom," Freud tells us, "is a sign of, and a substitute for, an instinctual satisfaction which has remained in abeyance; it is a consequence of the process of repression."[31]

A Desire for Death

In acknowledging the pull that Sofia has over him, Titta foresees his own death, as Sorrentino points out: Titta is "un hombre que vive como si estuviera muerto y que, cuando decide vivir, descubre que tiene que morirse [a man who lives as if he were dead and when he decides to live he discovers that he must die]."[32] In his customary position in the bar, Titta writes in his journal, but then stops to watch Sofia as she changes her top behind a semi-closed door behind the bar at the end of her shift. He surveys her naked back from behind, and a slow zoom-in reveals her face partially reflected in a mirror. A cut to the page of the diary discloses his entry: "Progetti per il futuro [Future projects]," which he follows up with writing, "non sottovalutare le conseguenze dell'amore [never underestimate the consequences of love]" while he watches Sofia leave on what he believes to be a date. The realization of desire triggers a flashback to his wife in her wedding dress who beams at the camera as she pulls her veil away from her face. We then return to the present, where Titta lethargically masturbates under the covers in his hotel room. However, eros is immediately saturated with melancholy as we are privy to an array of Titta's fantasies. His first memory is that of his wife in the hospital holding their child and then happily saying "ciao" to Titta directly to the camera. After we return briefly to a nearly immobile Titta, another cut to his wife on their apparent wedding day shows her veiled and despondent, completely lacking any of the joy apparent in the earlier memories. A montage then follows, consisting of brief images of several beautiful women whom Titta has encountered in the mall or in the hotel, and concludes on the memory of Sofia changing in the bar; however, in Titta's fantasy world, this time her breasts are visible. A cut follows to Titta in profile as he smokes and looks out the window, and an eyeline match reveals the subject of his vision: two shots of massive slewing cranes that hang over the city during the first light of day. This perspective is disorienting, as it does not match at all the view from Titta's room of rooftops and city monuments shown earlier in the film. However, these projections specifically recall the mise-en-scène of the film's finale when Titta is lowered into a container of wet concrete by a large crane in an abandoned quarry. Hence, his demise is apparently the consequence of his obsession with Sofia.

On the journey towards abjection and the encounter with the feminine, Kristeva writes: "What will concern me here [are] the alterations ... implied by the *confrontation with the feminine* and the way in which societies code themselves in order to accompany as far as possible the speaking subject on that journey. Abjection, or the journey to the end of the night." Sofia, like her Célinian predecessor, denotes knowledge, is "bound for the infinite," and entices Titta to join her.[33] In Titta's fantasies and memories, women are positioned as overdetermined castrating figures who lead the protagonist to the end of his night. What they embody – jouissance, the chora, the maternal, the semiotic – threatens the symbolic and points towards its vulnerabilities, in particular the weak or lacking paternal figure. Men in the film are dying, mentally imbalanced, cruel, and lecherous. Titta's father is "already dead" and their relationship is non-existent, while his brother is a womanizing globe-trotter. We learn that Titta let his half-brother, who is twenty some years his junior and clearly looks up to Titta, go hungry as a baby when Titta gluttonously ate his dinner in front of him. The elderly and childless Carlo, a down-and-out gambling addict who lives in the hotel that he used to own with his wife Isabella, takes lithium, a drug used to treat bipolar disorder. The film depicts masculinity in a state of crisis and represents men who are on the verge of collapsing back into the "pre-objectal relationship"[34] of the maternal body. "One of the sources of Célinian abjection," writes Kristeva, "no doubt lies in the bankruptcy of the fathers," because they are impotent and incapable of supporting their progeny.[35]

However, this fragile patriarchy is set up against the all-powerful Mafia that exerts absolute control over Titta's life, even though he believes he has outsmarted the organization. Prompted by his half-brother, who visits Titta and implores him to move beyond his narcissism and be nicer to Sofia, Titta breaks with his regimen and sits at the bar. When he tells Sofia "maybe sitting at this bar is the most dangerous thing I've done in my life," he is far from exaggerating. However, the romantic narrative is interrupted by the violent intrusion of the Mafia in Titta's life: they have been sent to Lugano to commit a murder and use his room as a base camp. Titta's demeanour immediately morphs; when he is with the two hit men, he is nervous and fearful, and demonstrates vulnerability. After their departure, he learns that Sofia has been taking driving lessons, a fact that prompts Titta to steal 100,000 dollars from the Mafia so as to give her a BMW convertible. At the bank, he pulls off a major bluff that concludes with a bank employee "finding" the exact sum of the missing amount of money in the suitcase so as to not risk losing Titta's (but really the Mafia's) lucrative account. After Titta leaves, the bank manager calls for the porter to take the money to the vault, and what follows is a long shot positioned from a fixed location behind the porter, who stands on the moving walkway with the suitcase attached to his hand on the way to the vault. At this point, we have come full circle and now understand the opening sequence of the film as the dénouement of Titta's deception, and are advised to be on the lookout for other clues to help decipher Titta's relationship with the all-powerful father.

The theft allows Titta to buy Sofia an elaborate gift, but, more to the point, it is a means to rebel against the Mafia, and to regain the illusion of autonomy and potency. Once again, the suitcase is representative of elusive desire, an engine that creates suspense and propels the narrative. It is interesting that the film's original title was *L'uomo della valigia* (*The Man with the Suitcase*). When Titta reveals his extravagant gesture to Sofia, she is uncomfortable accepting until later that night when Titta, high on heroine and wholly vulnerable, reveals all of his secrets to her, thereby earning her trust. The two then make a date to celebrate Titta's fiftieth birthday the following afternoon: "I'll come pick you with my car," she tells him, and Titta falls into a deep sleep that lasts the night, most likely for the first time in years, as he is a relentless insomniac. He is awakened in the morning by the routine delivery from the nameless Mafia intermediary, and as he prepares for the trip to the bank, it is clear that he is not alone, as the two gangsters have returned to steal the suitcase. Titta complies with all of their orders and then informs Cosa Nostra of the theft, and the Mafia immediately summons him to Sicily to explain himself to boss Nitto lo Riccio, who has been on the run for a quarter of a century. He then waits for Sofia, but owing to the car crash she never arrives, and Titta is oblivious as to the reason why.

As I mentioned earlier, in that Sofia's death is not tied to or motivated by elements of the film's diegesis, it takes the viewer by surprise. The scene begins with a shot of Sofia's eyes reflected in the rear-view mirror as she races along a country road distractedly listening to techno. A series of cuts to a sprinkler evokes the finale of Michelangelo Antonioni's *L'eclisse* (1962), which also chronicles a failed meeting. The accident occurs suddenly and is preceded by a series of rapid and confusing takes that include point-of-view shots of the road ahead, images of a dummy flagman dressed in orange and holding a signal light while mechanically waving a bright banner, and close-ups of the roadblock and of Sofia's purse as her phone rings. Sofia ignores all the warning signs (the roadblock, the flagman, the signal light) and seems intent on driving into the barricade at breakneck speed until she reaches for her phone, swerves off the road, and crashes head-on into a stationary tractor. We do not see the crash, as, instead, the camera pans to the left to rest on the face of the mannequin, who stares out to the distance with lifeless bright blue eyes. We then return to Sofia, who is inert in her car, which is now drenched by the water from the sprinklers.

The film suggests that Sofia desires death, and runs into it head-on. Cautionary signs abound – the roadblock covered in yellow tape, several pylons, the large pseudo-workman – and remain unobstructed in her line of sight. Here, Sofia conforms with the essence of the femme fatale: she is nothing but a projection, a lure who unconsciously mediates Titta's relationship with the obscene father. Her role completed, she is no longer necessary to the narrative and is thus expunged, appropriately in a vehicle procured with Mafia money. We see her only one more time, in an ambulance, where it is unclear if she is dead or alive. Her glazed-over eyes and slack jaw imply that she is lifeless, but a paramedic is taking her pulse, which confers an aura of ambiguity to her condition. In that she is a source of abjection, it follows that she is left in a border state, and her story terminates without proper narrative closure. Furthermore, we have no sense as to whether Sofia has a community of people who might grieve her possible death, which, as we will see, is not the case for Titta.

The mannequin can be read as an uncanny doubling for the symbolic father, who supports the symbolic order and thereby radically opposes the death drive. In his discussion of the three stages of Lacanian doctrine as they relate to the end of the analytic process, Žižek argues that the death drive implies "the annihilation of the signifying network, of the text in which the subject is inscribed, through which reality is historicized – the name of that which, in psychotic experience, appears as the 'end of the world,' the twilight, the collapse of the symbolic universe."[36] The death drive then reveals the null that the symbolic order strives to conceal. In that she is representative of jouissance and of excess, Sofia radically breaks with the pleasure principle in her desire for death. Sofia, as I pointed out earlier, is a symptom of man, which means that she is a "signifying formation which confers on the subject its very ontological consistency, enabling it to structure its basic, constitutive relationship to *enjoyment (jouissance)*."[37] With Sofia's disappearance, Titta's symbolic universe unravels while he journeys to its epicentre.

An Ethical Suicide?

As a figure who fosters mystique and intrigue, the femme fatale is unthreatening. However, when she invariably breaks down towards the noir's close, she "fully [assumes] her own fate," and her identity is unmasked as pure death drive. As such, she resists control and embodies a disintegration of masculine sovereignty. The noir protagonist can react in one of two ways: by rejecting her and the drive that she assumes in order to regain phallic mastery and reassert symbolic law or by identifying with her "as symptom" and running head-on into his suicidal destiny.[38] Titta does the latter. When he returns to Italy to face the commission, he admits that he knows the whereabouts of the suitcase containing nine million dollars, but that he will not divulge its location. "You stole my life, so I am stealing your suitcase," he tells Lo Riccio, even though he knows that this gesture will bring about his death. Thus, Titta's deliberately willed suicide is the ultimate act of protest against the big Other.[39] At the same time, however, this type of transgression in the noir reveals how "intersubjective, 'public' symbolic space has lost its innocence: narrativization, integration into the symbolic order, into the big Other, opens up a mortal threat, far from leading to any kind of reconciliation."[40] Death is the only outcome for the protagonist in the noir universe who wants to know more, who questions and disturbs the "neutrality" of the symbolic order, as does Titta when he steals twice from the Mafia.

During the journey to the site of his execution, Titta finds himself at the point where "the game is already over." When the noir protagonist is between two deaths, one symbolic and the other real, Žižek maintains that he desperately desires to tell his story, but "every attempt at narrativization ... is by definition lethal." The noir is unlike the classic detective novel at whose end the investigator makes sense of the mystery and events are "integrated into the symbolic universe," which allows for the restoration of law and order. The noir, however, precludes happy endings in which the hero defeats the villain, finds love, and reinstates symbolic law. Hence, the genre is characterized by a "structural imbalance," as its protagonist cannot be inscribed through narrative into the big Other.[41] As such, the noir threatens the *"sense of reality"* that is obligatory to maintain the dominant fiction. It follows that the life story of the noir protagonist can only be told during the moments when he inhabits the precarious in-between state in which Titta finds himself during the last ten minutes of the film.[42]

Indeed, it is here that we are granted total insight into Titta's character, but also understand that the Mafia, Titta's symbolic community, will remain intact, will go on without him, and will be unaffected by his death. An elaborate flashback sequence begins that reveals the intricacies of Titta's major deception as the song "Lipstick and Chocolate" plays in the car, whose words express, according to Wood, a tension in Titta's character "between patience and ability, recklessness and sensuality."[43] We learn that he found the courage to break out of his passivity and that he killed the two Mafiosi and re-obtained the suitcase thanks to his in-depth familiarity with the hotel. However, one of his three travelling companions informs Titta that the Mafia knew all along about his "petty" theft of 100,000 dollars, and looked the other way. In this way, his act of rebellion is trivialized and he is reminded of his lack of agency. Once Titta is tethered to the crane, the men continue to coerce him into divulging his secret by reminding him of the power of the organization and its honour code while promising him that he can start a new life. Rather than comply with their demands, he remains speechless, and as he gradually approaches the concrete, a distinct melancholy tone pervades the film. From this moment on, the Mafiosi are silent and, when Titta gazes down at his imminent tomb, we are privy to three projections from his mind that imply generosity, love, and friendship.

We first learn what has become of the suitcase: Titta left it anonymously for Carlo and Isabella as a gesture of atonement for earlier humiliating Carlo in front of his wife and friend when Titta publicized Carlo's habitual deceptions during their card games. Thus, through his death, Titta has purchased life for the aging couple who believed that they would monotonously meet their end in their metaphysical prison. As Titta's legs become enveloped by the sludge, the escalating din of the machinery abruptly transitions to the sound of Sofia zipping up her coat as the camera tilts to follow the movement of the zipper and then rests on a close-up of her face as she gazes off-screen somewhat Delphically before walking out of the frame. The source of this distorted memory is the first time that Sofia addressed Titta early on in the film, saying "arrivederci" to him right after she zipped up the same coat after curiously studying him for a short while. Titta, however, never meets her gaze. Also, this is the first time we hear her name, as a colleague says, "Ciao, Sofia" as she leaves the bar.

When Titta's head is close to being submerged, we see a point-of-view shot of the quarry that resembles an apocalyptic landscape, but is soon transformed in Titta's mind into a dense snow bank. A sound bridge of the shrill wind connects the two disparate geographies, and, as the concrete swallows him up, Titta recalls his best friend Dino Giuffrè who works for the electric company ENEL in the northern region of Alto Adige repairing power lines. Titta imagines his friend perched high up in the air amidst the snowy backdrop. Even though they have not spoken for twenty years, Titta is convinced of his friend's loyalty, as we learn through a voice-over: "Only one thing is certain. I know it. Every now and then, at the top of an electricity pylon, in the midst of a snowy landscape, against a cold, biting wind, Dino Giuffrè stops, melancholy assails him, and he then starts to think. And thinks that I, Titta Di Girolamo, am his best friend." The declaration of undying amity is accompanied by a point-of-view shot of a nearby pylon whose cables stretch out towards the infinite, and the film comes to a close on Dino's perspective of a dense dark forest that turns to complete black before the film's title appears one final time on the screen. With this finale, Titta has created an illusory audience to mourn him, and his anonymous death by "lupara bianca" is transformed into a gesture of commemoration. Dino, and with him Carlo, Isabella, and Sofia, thus become the custodians of Titta's memory, and the latter's previously fractured symbolic identity is restored in the mind of a phantasmatic other who, the film implies, will mourn him in perpetuity. The finale of *Le conseguenze dell'amore* recalls the solemn funeral procession outside of the hotel at the film's beginning that seized the attention of Titta and Sofia. No such rituals are conducted in Sofia's honour. While Titta leaves behind an (albeit imagined) community to remember him, Sofia is abruptly effaced from the narrative and no commemorative gesture marks her apparent passing.

In his discussion of ethical suicide, Žižek asks, "Why is suicide the only successful act?" He means that the act (ethical suicide) designates a repudiation of the symbolic, a radical transformation of the agent. "In it," he argues, "the subject is annihilated and subsequently reborn (or not), i.e., the act involves a kind of temporary eclipse, *aphanisis*, of the subject ... By means of it, I put at stake everything, including myself, my symbolic identity; the act is therefor always a 'crime' a 'transgression' namely of the limit of the symbolic community to which I belong."[44] Which is what happens in *Le conseguenze dell'amore*. Titta is akin to Antigone, whose gesture of protest, as Žižek argues, excludes her from her community and represents a symbolic suicide. Both are self-destructive and "offer ... no positive program," and only insist on their "unconditional demand."[45] In the noir, such an ethical gesture of protest against the Mafia is only possible with the disintegration of Sofia, and while Titta will live on in the mind of his imagined community, mourning for Sofia is disavowed.[46] As a femme fatale, source of abjection, and "symptom of man," Sofia's presence is required in the film to the extent that she mollifies Titta's anxieties. Once his ego is fortified and his humanity is finally recovered, Titta is able to stand up to the governing Mafia father. And, while Titta dies redeemed, the Mafia is unaffected by his protest and remains a symbolic traumatizing community that repudiates the feminine. Indeed, Sofia is jettisoned from the narrative and from history, which makes perfect sense, as, following Lacan, she never existed in the first place.[47]

5 Men of Honour, Man of Glass: Stefano Incerti's *L'uomo di vetro*

Partial insanity = psychic disease; Mafia = social disease; political Mafia = social disease; corrupt power = social disease; prostitution = social disease; syphilis, genital warts, etc. = physical disease that reverberates in the sick psyche since childhood; religious crises = psychic disease caused by these diseases; These are the diseases that I, Leonardo Vitale, am victim to, and am now resurrected in the faith of the true God.

Leonardo Vitale, cited in Salvatore Parlagreco,
L'uomo di vetro: Il caso di Leonardo Vitale, 26

Mafia = autorità = male sociale [Mafia = power = social disease]

L'uomo di vetro (Stefano Incerti)

The Mafia is not a part of Leonardo's life ... His problems are caused by maternal anxieties. His search for atonement is caused by unconfessable sins. Oedipus is guilty, not Pippo Calò or his uncle, the Mafioso and assassin. They call it *the truth of the non truth*.

Parlagreco, *L'uomo di vetro*, 113

"The first mafia *pentito* who was never believed"

In 1984, Tommaso Buscetta broke *omertà* and began collaborating with the Italian justice system, divulging to the authorities the inner workings of the Mafia. He revealed to Giovanni Falcone Cosa Nostra's hierarchy, its methods of operation and codes of conduct, and identified numerous key players in the organization. As a result, hundreds of arrest warrants were issued which led to the conviction of 342 Mafiosi at the Maxi-trial of 1987.[1] Another consequence of the "Buscetta theorem" was the murder of Leonardo Vitale on 2 December 1984. Vitale was gunned down in broad daylight in the city of Palermo while returning from mass with his mother Rosalia Vitale and sister Maria Vitale. He was murdered as Buscetta's testimony confirmed Vitale's own declarations to the authorities some eleven years earlier in 1973. Up until Buscetta's revelations, Vitale was "safe" because his testimony was not taken seriously, as he was considered mad, of unsound mind, schizophrenic, and partially insane. Vitale was arrested in 1972 and was accused of being involved in the kidnapping of Luciano Cassina, son of Count Arturo Cassina. After spending forty-seven days in solitary confinement, Vitale was released for lack of sufficient evidence, but then, the following year, experienced a crisis of conscience and a religious reawakening which led to his confessions and a series of revelations about the Mafia. He then spent the next eleven years travelling between various Italian prisons and mental institutions where he was treated with analysis, heavy drugs, and regular rounds of shock therapy. He was finally released in 1984, and spent his last months at home in Palermo with his mother and sister. He understood how Buscetta's testimony put his life in jeopardy and revealed in an interview just a few days before his death, "Ormai mi ammazzeranno [now they will kill me]."[2]

Stefano Incerti's film *L'uomo di vetro* (*The Man of Glass*, 2007) tells the story of Leonardo Vitale, "the first mafia *pentito* who was never believed," to borrow from the subtitle of Salvatore Parlagreco's homonymous 1998 book *L'uomo di vetro: Il caso di Leonardo Vitale: il primo pentito di mafia che non fu creduto*, upon which the film is loosely based. Both Incerti's film and Parlagreco's exposé forward the thesis that Vitale's madness was in part constructed, and I will go into more detail on this later. It is posited that his prolonged internment in the asylum setting heightened his underlying anxieties and contributed to a series of breakdowns, outbursts, and an alleged suicide attempt. Indeed, Vitale *had* to be classified by the Mafia as "of unsound mind" so that his testimony would not be taken seriously. Various stakeholders, as Girolamo Lo Verso maintains, "lo volessero invece 'pazzo' [instead wanted him to be 'insane']"[3] because, in the words of Parlagreco, "solo un pazzo può tradire la mafia [only a crazy person can betray the Mafia]."[4]

In this way, the film is in line with Michel Foucault's theories regarding madness as a socially constructed and mediated phenomenon that morphs throughout the centuries. He writes: "Madness cannot be found in its raw state. Madness only exists in society, it does not exist outside of the forms of sensibility that isolate it and the forms of repulsion that exclude or capture it."[5] Whereas during the twentieth century madness is reduced to a "natural phenomenon, linked to the truth of the world," during the age of Shakespeare and Cervantes it had a revelatory function, "for example, Lady Macbeth begins to speak the truth when she becomes mad." Ultimately, confinement has suppressed the "depth and power of revelation to the experience of madness."[6]

Incerti's film constructs Leonardo as a martyr figure and a mystic who was manipulated by the system for much of his adult life before being assassinated by the Mafia. Although some complicated familial relationships from his past are hinted at in the film, *L'uomo di vetro* ultimately suggests that the Mafia is responsible for Leonardo's breakdowns. This is not the picture that emerges from various legal documents, testimonies, and memoirs on the Vitale case, however. Most commentators agree that Vitale was driven crazy after his initial arrest, which is a thesis that the film shares. What is missing from the film, however, is reference to a series of childhood traumas and personal recollections that reveal that Vitale experienced an ongoing crisis regarding his sexual identity and believed that he was homosexual.

The film works to further normalize Vitale by dramatizing and fictionalizing a relationship that Vitale had with a young woman named Pina. While Pina is only summarily discussed by Vitale's family in interviews and is briefly mentioned in Vitale's own letters and testimonies, she takes on a central role in the film, where she is recast as Anna Siringo. Leonardo and Anna's relationship is developed quite fully in *L'uomo di vetro*. What's more, the two have intercourse on the beach, and Anna's narrative comes to an abrupt close when she is raped by Mafia soldiers and then, a few sequences later, leaves town. Leonardo's relationship with Anna and her eventual rape are two key elements in *L'uomo di vetro* that aid in constructing the protagonist as an average heterosexual male who turned against the Mafia and as a result became its victim. Moreover, the film elides Vitale's sexual difference and downplays his Oedipal crises, while implying that his spiritual conversion is the result of vehement anti-Mafia sentiment. In this way, the normalizing operation that takes place in *L'uomo di vetro* is akin to what we see in Marco Tullio Giordana's *I cento passi*, as discussed in the first chapter: both Vitale and Impastato are ultimately remembered as fallen anti-Mafia martyrs whose ambivalent "inner enemy" is externalized and made incarnate in the Mafia, a much more straightforward adversary.[7]

The "Other" Mirror

The opening scene of *L'uomo di vetro* establishes Leonardo as the film's ego ideal. While the screen is still black, we hear someone entering and then starting a car. As the engine revs and the car is set in motion, Carlo Muratori's song "Mpare" begins. After the title "*L'uomo di vetro*" appears on the screen, the film cuts to a close-up of Leonardo as he drives through the streets of Palermo, and the city is presented to us through his perspective. A sound bridge of the engine establishes Leonardo as the driver of the car that we heard a moment earlier. Thus, the film implies that his perspective exceeds that of the traditional voice-over narrator. As he drives his red Fiat Spider through Palermo, shots of the city walls, the Teatro Massimo, and the Teatro Politeama alternate with images of Leonardo, who is wearing sunglasses and is smoking. He is on centre stage while his surroundings are out of focus, and he appears calm and in control of his environment. When he pulls up to an office building, a young woman runs out to meet him, and the two drive out of the city and into the woods, where they passionately kiss. During the film's incipit, Leonardo is presented as the active male hero common in the classical cinema as discussed by Teresa de Lauretis. He "crosses the boundary" of the city and "'penetrates' the other space" of the diegesis. In that we see the city through his eyes, he is constructed as "the active principle of culture, the establisher of distinction, the creator of differences."[8] While Anna is gazed upon by both the viewer and the protagonist and is "fixed in the position of icon, spectacle, or image to be looked at," Leonardo "commands at once the action and the landscape, and ... occupies the position of subject of vision, which he relays to the spectator."[9]

Thus, the film initially implies that Leonardo is well rounded and secure in his sexual identity, and has what his Mafia peer group would consider to be a normal relationship with a woman. The following scene, however, suggests that Leonardo is out of place with his fellow Mafiosi, who mock and belittle him. While the group is sunbathing, they poke fun at his manhood, tell him that his uncle will spank him and send him to bed and then attempt to chide him into taking violent action against Rappareddu, a man who has been stealing lemons from his uncle. Thus, a disconnect is established between how we are positioned to see Leonardo and how he is viewed by others.

We are quickly presented, however, with Uncle Titta, a more powerful male figure to whom Leonardo looks for guidance and reassurance.

Titta is kind and patient with his nephew, discourages violent measures, and instead reminds Leonardo that those who are respectful of others are treated with respect themselves. Titta is modelled on Vitale's real-life uncle, Giovanni Battista Vitale. The death of Vitale's father when he was eighteen profoundly affected him and prompted Vitale to find a substitute father figure in the guise of his uncle.[10] "Titta," as he was called, was a man of honour who had already begun inducting his nephew into Cosa Nostra by having him kill a dog, then a beloved horse, and then, when he was seventeen, a man. Vitale willingly did his uncle's bidding, as he wanted so desperately to please him, to fit in, and become like everyone else in his Mafia kinship group.

In *L'uomo di vetro*, Titta is presented as a benevolent symbolic authority figure whom Leonardo desires to emulate. Throughout the entire film, Leonardo never speaks unkindly of his uncle, which is not the case with the historical Vitale, who maintains that, after his confessions and conversion, he no longer feels affection for his uncle as Vitale is profoundly changed, feels an inner peace and understands right from wrong.[11] It is striking that Giovanni Battista Vitale's murderous past is elided in the film. During his confession, Vitale recalls that his uncle tells him, "Vedi le mie mani? Sono sporche di sangue e quelle di tuo padre anche di più [See my hands? They are dirty with blood and your father's were even more so]," which prompts Vitale to realize that his father killed more people than his uncle had.[12] In the film, however, the memory is rewritten so as to malign his father and humanize his uncle. After Leonardo is released from his first period of incarceration, he tells his family, "One night I dreamt of dad, his hands were covered in blood." His uncle quickly dismisses the potentially trauma-inducing memory by jokingly suggesting that they play the lotto for good luck. Later on, and just before his confession, Leonardo complains that he wants to go back to work at his uncle's building site as his current job delivering flowers is "woman's work" and that the thorns prick his delicate hands. Titta then asks to see Leonardo's hand, which he touches and tenderly affirms that it is just like his own. In *L'uomo di vetro*, the sins of the father are neutralized and minimized, and the blood is washed clean.

The historical Vitale, however, was preoccupied with blood and spoke of it regularly, describing it as "un'impurità [an impurity]." Blood represented "la morte, l'uccidere, sono le mani lorde sue, del padre, dello zio, della mafia, ma il sangue è anche il femminile, le mestruazioni, il parto, il sesso [death, killing, his filthy hands, his father's, his uncle's, the Mafia's, but blood is also the feminine, menstruation, birth, sex]."[13] "Per essere uomo [to be a man]," maintained Vitale, "dovevo uccidere e fare l'amore con le prostitute [I had to kill and make love with prostitutes]."[14] A Mafia boy, writes Lo Verso and Lo Coco, "must be fearless, violent and interested in girls."[15] Murder was a way to consolidate Vitale's threatened masculinity. The Mafia then was Vitale's cover, and becoming a man of honour translated into proving his masculinity, which also entailed repressing any non-normative suspicions about his sexual identity. Thus, Vitale's relationship to the Mafia and to his uncle is much more complicated than it would appear in the film.

In *L'uomo di vetro*, Leonardo's attraction to and veneration of his uncle draws him towards the Mafia, into which he is inducted after he murders two men in order to please Titta. During his confessions, which in the film take place on the altar of a church at Leonardo's request, he calmly recounts how he murdered Luigi Mannino and Giuseppe Bologna as a means to obtain the friendship of his uncle. He killed as a favour to Titta and "followed him everywhere, and in everything that he did." While Leonardo explains that he was "very attracted to his [uncle's] personality," we see a reflection of Titta who is shaving in a mirror, and it is assumed that Leonardo is not present in the flashback. Two shots later, when Titta cuts himself on the cheek, we hear Leonardo admit that he never was concerned about his own life, and that he "only cared about being like others, being a man, like [his] uncle Titta." The blood on Titta's cheek is symbolically manifest in the following scene, during which Leonardo is inducted into Cosa Nostra. Leonardo's finger is pricked and he then holds a burning saint card, and takes his oath, "My flesh will burn like this holy picture (santina) if I do not maintain this oath," in front of his proud uncle. Leonardo then reminisces that he "had become a man, a man of honour, like Uncle Titta."

Leonardo strove to become the other more powerful and undisputedly virile man reflected in the mirror, who is performing the "manly" ritual of shaving. The mirror then becomes Leonardo's access point into the Mafia, which, as Alan O'Leary argues, can be considered "a heterotopic form of social organization."[16] Heterotopias, Foucault tells us, are "counter-sites" that one enters into via compulsion or ritual.[17] These "other spaces" are enclosed and have their own rules and regulations. The Mafia qualifies as a heterotopia of compensation, that is, a "space that is other, another real space, as perfect, as meticulous, as well arranged." In the Mafia, "existence is regulated at every turn," and "each person carrie[s] out his/her duty."[18]

Leonardo hopes to fashion a "perfect" self as imagined in his uncle's mirror image, and Foucault argues that the mirror functions as a heterotopia: "It makes this place I occupy at the moment when I look at myself in the glass at once absolutely real, connected with all the space that surrounds it, and absolutely unreal, since in order to be perceived it has to pass through this virtual point which is over there."[19] Foucault's discussion of the mirror in relation to heterotopic spaces recalls Lacan's "mirror stage," as, in both cases, the mirror functions to construct the subject by projecting "the formation of the individual into history" and linking "the *I* to socially elaborated situations."[20] Although the Lacanian mirror stage is structured around the concept of misrecognition (the subject imagines a more perfect and more complete self as projected in the mirror), both the mirror stage and heterotopias help situate the subject in the symbolic order, which, in the case of Leonardo, is the Mafia. "From the standpoint of the mirror," specifically his uncle's reflection in the mirror, Leonardo discovers his absence "from the place where [he is]."[21]

Thus, Vitale as rewritten in Incerti's film joined the Mafia, the dominant social group of his neighbourhood, to win the approval of a surrogate father figure and to fit in and become like everyone else. In his own reminiscences, Leonardo's weak imago is restored when he becomes a man of honour. Ironically, however, once he betrays his Mafia brotherhood, he is expelled from a heterotopia of compensation and is forced into a series of psychiatric hospitals and prisons, which Foucault considers "heterotopias of deviation," or "those in which individuals whose behavior is deviant in relation to the required norm or mean are placed."[22]

Social Disease and Psychic Disease

L'uomo di vetro proposes that Leonardo's religious awakening that led to his collaboration with the authorities is the result of his realization that Mafia ethics are fundamentally wrong and that the organization must be stopped at all costs, even at the price of his own safety and liberty. Thus, the reconstituted mirror image that he so desired is shattered by the acquisition of a moral code. Vitale's memoirs and testimonies tell another story, however, one that is much more complicated and messy. In the film, Leonardo burns his clothes while in prison because, as he subsequently explains to a panel of psychiatrists, "they were bought with money that wasn't earned with an honest job." At that point, the four men begin asking him a series of questions: Has he ever had fits ("delle crisi")? Has he ever heard voices? If so, what are they saying? As Leonardo explains that he has felt demoralized and that he sometimes talks to himself so as to cheer himself up, the suspenseful non-diegetic music escalates while the camera rapidly cuts from the faces of the psychiatrists to Leonardo, who becomes increasingly distressed and agitated. After Leonardo proclaims that he has found inner peace upon confessing his crimes, one man asks him to discuss the relationship between his parents, and Leonardo adamantly affirms that such a detail is inconsequential, and that what is important is fighting the Mafia. At this point, another man asks Leonardo if he read *The Godfather*, to which he responds that he had seen the film. When prompted as to whether he liked it, Leonardo looks incredulously at the panel. The following shot is a close-up of a bedpan filled with faeces that sits atop an issue of *Epoca* magazine from February of 1972. The camera then pans up to reveal that Leonardo is writing "Mafia = autorità = male sociale [Mafia = power = social disease]" in human excrement on the wall of his cell.

This sequence underlines the thesis that Leonardo's psychic malady was in part "created" by his institutionalization and psychoanalysis. The insinuation put forth by the panel of psychiatrists is that Leonardo invented his testimonies after having watched Coppola's film, and it is suggested that his subsequent act of rebellion is a reaction to not being believed. Here, Leonardo acts out angrily after he meets with doctors who clearly do not take his confessions seriously. At another point in the film, he has an outburst when learns of the "suicide" of his cousin, which was orchestrated by the Mafia in order to further agitate him.

And many close to Vitale share this opinion regarding the origins of the historical Vitale's insanity. His mother and sister believe, for example, that "le sue crisi non erano dovute alla follia, ma alle cure [his crises where not caused by madness, but by the treatments],"[23] while Vitale himself declares, "Non ero pazzo ... La pazzia è la conseguenza della psicoterapia. Tutto quello che è accaduto è stato voluto dalle autorità [I wasn't crazy ... Madness is the result of psychotherapy. Everything that happened was desired by the authorities]."[24] Also, Bruno Contrada, the ex-chief of police of Palermo's homicide division and the first man to hear Vitale's confessions and statements, affirms that he was not crazy, and that "il carcere, il manicomio giudiziario, le sofferenze gli hanno nuociuto [prison, the criminal asylum, and his suffering caused him harm]."[25] To be sure, his family and the Mafia favoured Vitale's confinement for different reasons (in the case of the former to keep him alive, while the latter meant to ensure that he was never taken seriously). Ultimately, Vitale's madness was "costruita, fabbricata [constructed, fabricated]," and he was allowed to "passare per pazzo [pass as crazy]," precisely because the words of a madman have no weight.[26]

And this is where we understand the title of Parlagreco's book, which references Miguel de Cervantes's short story "Man of Glass," one of the author's "exemplary novels." The narrative focuses on Tomás Rodaja, a brilliant man who, as a result of being poisoned, becomes convinced that his body is made of glass. He is taken for insane, and attracts large crowds, who enjoy listening to his satiric critique of contemporary Spanish society. However, once he is "cured" of his illness, his musings are no longer of interest to the population, and he is left alone to starve before setting off for Flanders, where he is killed in battle.[27] Like Tomás, Vitale "era pazzo nel suo comportamento pratico, ma i suoi discorsi erano savi e veri ... Ottenne la parola grazie alla sua follia. Poté parlare pochissimo da savio [was crazy in his practical behaviour, but his discourses were wise and true ... Thanks to his madness, he had the floor. Once he was sane, he could talk very little]."[28]

Thus, the sequence from the film when Leonardo writes on the wall of his cell suggests that his mental illness is a product of the asylum, a thesis, as we have seen, that is also advanced with regards to the historical Vitale. More to the point of my analysis, Leonardo's reaction to not being believed foregrounds the more straightforward anti-Mafia position that *L'uomo di vetro* promotes: the Mafia is a social ill that is situated with other hegemonies such as the judicial system, both of which repress Leonardo and censor his revelations. Vitale's own memoirs, however, betray a much more complicated relationship between Vitale and the Mafia. He writes:

> Seminfermità mentale = male psichico; mafia = male sociale; mafia politica = male sociale; autorità corrotte = male sociale; prostituzione = male sociale; sifilide, creste di gallo ecc. = male fisico che si ripercuote nella psiche ammalata sin da bambino; crisi religiose = male psichico derivato da questi mali; Questi sono i mali di cui sono rimasto vittima, io, Leonardo Vitale risorto nella fede nel vero Dio [Partial insanity = psychic disease; Mafia = social disease; political Mafia = social disease; corrupt power = social disease; prostitution = social disease; syphilis, genital warts, etc. = physical disease that reverberates in the sick psyche since

childhood; religious crises = psychic disease caused by these diseases; These are the diseases that I, Leonardo Vitale, am victim to, and am now resurrected in the faith of the true God].[29]

Here, we see that Vitale is discussing three types of disease: social, physical, and psychic. While the Mafia, the political Mafia, corrupt power, and prostitution are categorized as social diseases, syphilis and genital warts are classified as physical disease, and partial insanity and religious crises fall under the rubric of psychic diseases. What's more, he states that his religious crisis is caused not only by his sense of guilt owing to his involvement in the Mafia (a common thesis promoted in the film) but also by venereal disease, his relationship with prostitutes, and his underlying mental illness.

Unlike in the film, Vitale admitted at several occasions in interviews and in his writings that he felt that he was part male and part female, and that he believed that he was a "pederast." He also doubted his virility and recounted that he went to prostitutes so that he could feel normal, although he never enjoyed it. He also thought that his penis was too small, especially in comparison to his father's, and he was profoundly distressed after witnessing his mother and father lying naked together after they had intercourse. He also admitted to having been sexually intimate with his sister Maria Vitale and mused about the possibility that the two might marry after his mother passed away.[30] As Parlagreco argues, "La mafia non fa parte della vita di Leonardo ... I suoi guai sono dovuti alle ansie materne. E la ricerca di espiazione è causata da peccati inconfessabili. Il colpevole è Epido, non Pippo Calò o lo zio mafioso e assassino. La chiamano *verità della non verità* [The Mafia is not a part of Leonardo's life ... His problems are caused by maternal anxieties. His search for atonement is caused by unconfessable sins. Oedipus is guilty, not Pippo Calò or his uncle, the Mafioso and assassin. They call it *the truth of the non truth*]."[31] In essence, Vitale's relationship with his family unit is anything but inconsequential.

In his testimonies, Vitale experiences a profound coming to terms with God, whom he blamed for "i brutti pensieri che ... attraversavano la mente [the bad thoughts that crossed his mind]."[32] Vitale admits that these "idee fisse [obsessive ideas]" about sex began after he saw his parents lying in bed just after completing the sex act.[33] Following this moment, he felt different and he saw himself as impotent and sexually inadequate. Also, as mentioned earlier, he wondered if he were attracted to men. Vitale's reaction to having witnessed the primal scene can be informed by Freud's case history of the young Russian aristocrat Sergei Pankeieff, whom Freud referred to as the Wolf-Man. Indeed, the case histories of Vitale and Pankeieff share some shocking similarities.

Typically, as Freud argues, the revived memory of the primal scene leads to neurosis as the recollection establishes castration anxiety and creates confusion regarding sexual identity. After the Wolf-Man witnessed the sex act between his parents, he internalized the traumatic memory that only surfaced later when he dreamt that a pack of white wolves were sitting among the branches of a tree outside his bedroom window. "The wolf that he was afraid of was undoubtedly his father,"[34] writes Freud, "from whom in the end he feared castration."[35] This is because, during the sex act, the boy identifies with his mother whom he views as castrated while simultaneously desiring sexual satisfaction from his father. Freud explains the dream thusly: "Longing for sexual satisfaction from [the boy's] father – realization that castration is a necessary condition of it – fear of the father."[36] Subsequently, the Wolf-Man was fixated with defecation and he developed a "hostility towards women,"[37] although he maintained sexual relations with them, "but he did not enjoy this possession."[38] Freud also attests that the Wolf-Man was homosexual at the level of the unconscious.[39]

The Wolf-Man "remained fixated, as though by a spell, to the scene which had such a decisive effect on his sexual life."[40] In order to assuage his internal anxieties, the Wolf-Man became preoccupied with religion and identified with the figure of Christ[41] and experienced an "obsessional piety."[42] In essence, he sublimated his sexual urges into a culturally accepted form. Like the Wolf-Man, Vitale was consumed with the idea that he was sexually inadequate as a result of catching sight of his father's penis, which was "grosso e potente [large and powerful]," while his mother's sexual organs looked like the "genitali di un bambino o alle ali di un Uccello implume [a (male) child's genitals or the wings of a featherless bird.]"[43] Also akin to the Wolf-Man, Vitale did not find pleasure in sexual relationships with women, and he feared finding a wife, as he thought himself incapable of consummating the marriage. Also in both instances, a religious conversion appeared to resolve crises regarding sexual identity. Both the case of the Wolf-Man and Vitale point towards the key role of belatedness, or "Nachträglichkeit," in the construction of the traumatic narrative: in the case of the former, a dream triggered the trauma-inducing event, while Vitale's memories were jogged during psychoanalysis and when he gave his testimony.

L'uomo di vetro, however, omits Vitale's childhood trauma and its repercussions regarding his sexual identity. Instead, the film suggests that Leonardo primarily desires to reconcile himself with his murderous past, which he does when he is resurrected in God's faith. One scene, however, does allude to Leonardo's complicated Oedipal scenario. While taking the Rorschach test at a clinic, Leonardo interprets several plates (IX, III, II, X) in relatively benign terms and sees within them cheerful images: a bird skeleton, a butterfly, two snails reflected in a mirror, and a garden that is replete with an eagle, tulips, clouds, and "a dragonfly, a little one." Plate VIII, however, reminds him of "a woman's womb or the place where faeces are expelled." His reading of plate VIII in terms of feminine reproductive organs as abject suggests that Leonardo equates birth with defecation, which alludes to the "fantasy of rebirth" discussed by Freud in the case of the Wolf-Man. According to Freud, the Wolf-Man believed that his maladies would be cured once he was able to "let himself be sexually satisfied by his father and [bear] him a child … Here, therefore, the phantasy of re-birth was simply a mutilated and censored version of the homosexual wishful phantasy."[44] The child would come in the form of a stool, a "softened substitute"[45] for a fantasy of intercourse with the mother. In this way, "two incestuous fantasies are united."[46] In the film, however, the complex Oedipal scenario is neutralized through performance; Leonardo is smiling, he is serene and is enjoying the task at hand and he seems to have nothing but filial love and devotion for his mother. The historical Vitale, however, admitted that the act of covering himself with faeces helped him to distinguish right from wrong and recognize that his past actions were impure and unclean.[47] Vitale overcame abjection by controlling his body and purifying his mind. As with the Wolf-Man, human excrement can redeem and renew. In sum, the roots of Vitale's illness are much more ambiguous then they appear in the film.

The Ultimate MacGuffin

Vitale's mother Rosalia Vitale and his sister Maria Vitale were profoundly devoted to him. Rosalia Vitale followed him from asylum to asylum, and let rooms nearby so as to best tend to her son's needs. Also, mother and daughter were dedicated to maintaining that Vitale was sane: he was not crazy, they said, the judges only "lo dichiarano matto per aiutarlo [declared him mad in order to help him]."[48] *L'uomo di vetro* reflects this defensive relationship and portrays the family as an isolated unit intent on supporting and nurturing Leonardo, especially after the disappearance of Titta, who is murdered by the Mafia. Also in the film, mother and sister are adamantly opposed to Leonardo's relationship with Anna; she is an outsider whom they do not trust and also blame for his initial incarceration. Anna is educated, has a job, learns to drive, is frequently outside in the sun, laughs and enjoys her friends and work, and for most of the film wears bright colours. Instead, Rosalia and Maria are mostly shot inside their house or in prisons and asylums. They wear mostly darker colours, are frequently upset and brooding, and have no attachments or personal interests other than Leonardo's welfare and protecting the family name.

Moreover, Anna is cast as Leonardo's conscience; after his initial arrest, she asks him why he did not tell the police what he knew about the Mafia. Later, he writes a letter to her telling her that he wants to confess as a means to save his soul and also asks for her forgiveness before asking forgiveness from God. Leonardo implores his sister to deliver the letter to Anna, and when Maria responds that their mother would not approve, Leonardo queries whether she no longer loves him and then gently caresses and kisses her neck. She then wonders if he still loves Anna ("l'ami ancora?") to which he responds that he loves only her ("voglio bene solo a te.") Although this scene hints at the incestuous tie between the siblings, such a relationship is minimized, as it becomes clear that Leonardo is playing up their relationship so as to manipulate his sister into doing his bidding and delivering the letter, which she does.

Thus, Anna is positioned to contrast with Leonardo's mother and sister, who are tied to their Mafia kinship group. Anna is nothing like the traditional Mafia wife and mother, who has "un grande potere di vita e di morte [a great power of life and death]."[49] According to the logic of the classical cinema, her transgressive behaviour – Anna is independent, a freethinker, and does not follow *omertà* – cannot go unpunished. Like Lia from Pasquale Scimeca's *Placido Rizzotto*, Anna is raped in retaliation for her boyfriend's anti-Mafia activity. And, also like Lia, following the attack, Anna leaves town for an unknown destination, at which point she is summarily expelled from the film's diegesis.

I would like to recall my earlier discussion of the construction of Leonardo's heterosexuality in *L'uomo di vetro*, whereby the development of the relationship between Leonardo and Anna glosses over the fact that Vitale believed that he was homosexual. Hence, Anna provides Leonardo's lacking masculinity. As Kaja Silverman puts forward, "female subjectivity represents the site at which the male subject deposits his lack"[50] and "lack would appear to be inscribed into cinema through the female body."[51] This operation certainly takes place at the beginning of the film, where Leonardo is constructed, albeit briefly, as the active protagonist typical of the classical cinema. In fact, the opening sequence and the second time that Leonardo and Anna spend the afternoon together early on in the film mark the only two instances where Leonardo appears carefree and unencumbered by mental anguish. Thus, to borrow from Slavoj Žižek, Anna "is of vital importance" for Leonardo in that she consolidates his masculinity.[52] Anna can be likened to the MacGuffin so common to Hitchcock's cinema, which is something to be "explained, interpreted." According to Žižek, "the MacGuffin is clearly the *objet petit a*, a gap in the centre of the symbolic order – the lack, the void of the Real setting in motion the symbolic movement of interpretation ... a pure semblance which lures the hero into the Oedipal journey."[53] Like the MacGuffin, Anna is a "pretext" who generates the story, but in essence is "nothing at all."[54]

The final meeting between Anna and Leonardo takes place, the film tells us, in March of 1973, after he is released from his first extended stay in the mental hospital. Anna has changed: she has a modern haircut, wears glasses, and has obtained her driving licence. Leonardo has changed as well: he looks more childlike and is unsure of himself and can no longer drive, as he is considered "an idiot." The two quickly re-establish their connection and are subsequently shown on a beach, where they appear to be having sex in the middle of the day. While Leonardo gyrates atop Anna, he exposes her breast to the camera. Her passion is matched by Leonardo's growing frustration as he realizes that he is unable to perform. Anna is not discouraged and covers his face with kisses and caresses his head and back as she lovingly tells him that she realizes that she is not yet very good at intercourse, but promises to learn. Leonardo then rebuffs her, and tells her that he must get going as there is work to be done and that his cousin Salvatore has promised to take him to get a granita. When he walks hastily away, Anna attempts to cover herself while looking despondently in a pocket mirror, as she is on the verge of tears.

The normal viewing pleasure derived from watching the sex act is interrupted by Leonardo's performance anxiety. To cite Linda Williams, this scene marks a "cinematic coitus interruptus," that is, the build-up of anticipation around Leonardo and Anna's relationship comes to nothing. As such, the viewer is left frustrated and confused, which mirrors Anna's reaction and thus prompts us to both identify and sympathize with her.[55] In that Leonardo demonstrated much passion for Anna before his arrest, the film suggests that his inability to perform sexually is a result of feeling debilitated and disturbed because of his incarceration and medical treatments. This is not the case, however, with the historical Vitale, who regularly discussed his lifelong aversion to both intercourse and the female body.

The open-ended sexual plotline between Anna and Leonardo is unequivocally resolved with Anna's rape, which is staged in a peculiar and troubling way. After driving home at night, Anna locks her car and walks to her front door. As she enters the building, she turns towards the camera with a horrified look on her face. An unidentifiable man pushes her inside while she struggles and another follows who then shuts the door after checking to ensure that they are unobserved. The film then cuts to Leonardo in his cell, who is praying a rosary before repeatedly washing his hands and then burning his clothing. What happened, we ask, to Anna? Was she raped? Kidnapped? Beaten? Murdered? The answer comes a few minutes later, just after Leonardo writes "Mafia = autorità = male sociale" in human excrement on the wall of his cell. In the following scene, Anna's face is shot in close-up with her surroundings in shallow focus. She looks offscreen and appears traumatized, and she is visibly shaken and has difficulty breathing. Time has passed since we last saw her: her clothing is different and sunlight enters the room. She then stands up, grabs her suitcase and begins to pack. This scene, lasting fifteen seconds, ends briskly with a cut to Leonardo's cousin Salvatore moments before he is murdered by the Mafia. We are left to assume that what happened behind closed doors was an act of sexual violence and possibly a gang rape. We never see Anna again and we have no idea as to where she might be going.

The choice to only show the before and the after of the scene of the crime attests to, in Mieke Bal's view, "the difficulty in representing rape." Rape, she maintains,

> makes the victim invisible. It does this literally – the perpetrator first covers her – and then figuratively – the rape destroys her self-image, her subjectivity, which is temporarily narcotized, definitely changed, and often destroyed. Finally, rape cannot be visualized because the experience is, physically as well and psychologically, *inner*. Rape takes place inside. In this sense, rape is by definition "imagined"; it can only exist as

experience and as memory, as *image* translated into signs, never adequately objectifiable.⁵⁶

The staging of rape in *L'uomo di vetro* suggests that Anna's identity is completely obliterated. She lost her freedom, independence, and confidence and is effectively silenced. We never see her resist her attackers or say "no." Thus, the power of consent is taken from her and she is a victim of patriarchal Mafia law. Like the rape of Philomena before her, Anna's rape is unrepresentable precisely because her body becomes "a cipher for masculine values."⁵⁷ Early on in the film, Anna confirmed Leonardo's normative identity. Now, her body is used, presumably, to ensure his silence.

It is suggested that Anna is raped in the film in retaliation for Leonardo's ongoing confessions. However, there is no implication in the film that Leonardo is ever made aware of the attack, and therefore would react to it in any way. He does ask his mother about Anna later in the film, "and Anna?" but Rosalia does not answer his question. The sexual violence done to Anna is completely invented, which is not the case with the staged suicide of the historical Vitale's close friend and cousin Salvatore Vitale. Although Salvatore Vitale's death is "archivato come suicidio [classified as a suicide]," it is commonly assumed that the Mafia orchestrated his poisoning in order to send a message to Vitale regarding the potential repercussions of his continued betrayal.⁵⁸ The film suggests that Salvatore's death did just that as, after Leonardo sees a newspaper with the headlines regarding his cousin's suicide, he carves a cross on his stomach with a knife. This act of self-mutilation confirms his insanity and leads to the release of all those whom Leonardo had earlier implicated in his testimony.

Anna is crucial in the beginning of the film (she normalizes Leonardo's sexual identity and acts as his conscience), but then she is forgotten once the narrative becomes focused on the Oedipal battles between good and evil, Mafia and anti-Mafia. She is, in fact, the ultimate MacGuffin, as she is cast as a mere plot device who is disregarded and exorcised from the film once she is no longer necessary and serves no further purpose in terms of narrative development.⁵⁹ Anna's rape is then one of the "fictional elements" added to the film as a means to enhance the narrative, and the trauma of her rape is elided from the diegesis.⁶⁰ Anna's body is used to forward the narrative and her rape further vilifies the Mafia, which the film constructs as the "social disease" principally responsible for Leonardo's breakdowns.

Martyr, Mystic, Madman

In *L'uomo di vetro*, Leonardo is cast as a Christ figure who is martyred in his battle against the Mafia. Most reviews of the film foreground such a heroic representation. He is a "pentito e martire [collaborator of justice and martyr]" who endures a "martirio personale [personal martyrdom]."[61] His suffering positions him as a "novello Cristo chiamato a immolarsi per la salvezza dell'anima sua [second Christ ready to sacrifice himself to save his soul],"[62] and his rebellion is "heroic."[63] Leonardo's Christological qualities are foregrounded in the film. Notably, his confessions take place on an altar of a church, as if he were a priest saying mass. Hence, Leonardo is shown to feel genuine penitence for his sins, and is thus a *pentito* in the truest sense of the word. Also, one of the cover articles of the *Epoca* magazine present when Leonardo defiles his cell with excrement is entitled "Gli uomini del mistero: Paracelsus, medico, mago e profeta [Mystery Men: Paracelsus, Doctor, Magician and Prophet]," which is an overt reference to Leonardo's mystical conversion. Furthermore, after his first round of electroshock therapy, he lies nearly naked in bed where his mother bathes him. This scene is staged, in one reviewer's words, "come fosse una rappresentazione della pietà [as if it were a representation of the Pietà]."[64] Fundamentally, Leonardo's madness is heroic and revolutionary; the antimafia prosecutor tells him, "if everyone were mad like you, the world would be a better place."

Leonardo's narrative comes to a close after his memory regarding his past crimes has been wiped clean as a consequence of repeated electroshock and drug therapy, which is a thesis suggested in several studies on the historical Vitale.[65] He is a shell of his former self, his eyes are glazed over, and a guard watches over him at all times, even when he goes to the bathroom. A new prosecutor named Carlo Minniti arrives to question Leonardo so as to build the case against all those indicted. When he asks Leonardo to start from the beginning and to tell him everything, Leonardo's narrative is disjointed, incomplete, and vague; he remembers killing two men, but unlike in his earlier confessions, does not cite their names and does not recall how they were murdered. He concludes, "comunque, sono morti [anyway, they're dead]" before asking for a cigarette. As he smokes, a sound bridge of a gentle wave takes us to an image of a calm sea abutting an empty sandy beach. We come back for a moment to Leonardo, who is lost in thought, before returning to the seaside. This time, however, a younger, composed, and serene Leonardo stands in the centre of the frame, and the camera follows him as he walks to the left. As he exits the scene, the screen fades to black and the narrative concludes. Thus, Leonardo has conjured up an image of himself as healthy and unconfined that corresponds to earlier representations of him before his arrest and subsequent breakdown. He (and we) imagine him as purified and reborn; his guilt and crimes are washed away. This is not the case for Anna, who, like Lia in Scimeca's *Placido Rizzotto*, does not engage in the mourning process necessary to come to terms with the violence done to her.

It is significant that we are not witness to Leonardo's murder in the film. True to the biopic form, *L'uomo di vetro* includes an epilogue that conveys noteworthy details regarding the Vitale case: "The trial took place only six years later. Leonardo Vitale was condemned to twenty-seven years, which were converted in appeal to eleven years in a hospital for the criminally insane. Most of the people that he accused were acquitted." Ergo, Leonardo Vitale, both in real and filmic life, was scapegoated so that hundreds of other perpetrators could go free. A second citation appears on the screen and foregrounds Vitale's martyrdom:

> Released in June, 1984, he was killed a few months later on the 2nd of December, while coming home from Sunday Mass. Unlike State justice, the Mafia saw the importance of his revelations and inexorably punished him for having broken the code of silence. Let's hope, even after his death, that Vitale will gain the credit he deserved and deserves. – Giovanni Falcone

This proclamation tellingly comes from Falcone, who also lost his life at the hands of the Mafia eight years after Vitale and, together with Paolo Borsellino, is Italy's most commemorated anti-Mafia martyr. Falcone's words were pronounced during the maxi-trial in 1986 and elevate Vitale to the status of others fallen in the battle against the Mafia, such as Placido Rizzotto and Peppino Impastato. Leonardo is constructed as a scapegoat who takes on the weight of the world in his anti-Mafia struggle and his death, citing Girard, "brings about communal cohesion."[66] Thus, together with Falcone, Borsellino, Impastato, and Rizzotto, Vitale's murder is depicted as meaningful and capable of uniting a community against the Mafia.

One critic writes that the historical Vitale welcomed death, as "non è più un uomo diviso a metà, ha scelto da che parte stare e ha deciso di espiare così la propria colpa di aver ucciso [he is no longer a man divided in half, he chose which side he stands on and decided to thus expiate his guilt of having killed]."[67] Incerti's film supports this straightforward reading. Leonardo's attraction towards the Mafia and involvement in gang life are principally motivated by a desire to reconstruct a failed paternal figure. However, his incarceration leads to a spiritual crisis, which prompts Leonardo to develop a moral code. Ultimately, he chooses good (God) over evil (Mafia) and, although his extended confinement makes him anxious and paranoid, he is and will remain unencumbered by the inner demons that haunted and traumatized the historical Vitale since his youth. Such a cohesive finale that privileges the anti-Mafia martyr narrative while downplaying Mafia-related trauma, including the rape of Anna, echoes the conclusion of *I cento passi* and places both films squarely in the tradition of the biopic, a genre that has traditionally proved reluctant to represent anything but heteronormative sexual identities. "Homosexuality," writes George F. Custon, "was one of the most censored bits of behavior in the public narratives of the biopic."[68] The last image we see in *L'uomo di vetro* is a documentary photograph of Vitale, who is smiling broadly and looking into the camera while handcuffed, while the final images in *I cento passi* are photographs of Peppino Impastato talking with his colleagues, enthusiastically giving speeches, laughing, and, in the final image, tranquilly looking out a window. Thus, in both *I cento passi* and *L'uomo di vetro*, the documentary image is a final memorializing gesture that offers the final word on Impastato and Vitale as recast in Giordana and Incerti's films, and we remember them as unambiguous in their struggle. In the end, *L'uomo di vetro* finds a neat sense of closure: the audience celebrates Vitale's sacrifices as the film eclipses both Vitale's complicated Oedipal drama and his suggested homosexuality.

6 The Female Mob Boss: Edoardo Winspeare's *Galantuomini*

> The birth of the Sacra Corona Unita brought about the loss of our land's virginity. Until then, during the 1980s, Salento was uncorrupted by the cancer of criminality. Then, it exploded and I was there and I heard talk of killings, drugs, arms trafficking, and I asked myself "why?" The extraordinary thing is that the Sacra Corona Unita is the only Mafia as of yet to be defeated.
>
> Interview with Edoardo Winspeare

Key Facts
   Group name: Sacra Corona Unita
   Level of threat: Medium
   Status: Active
           "Serious and Organized Crime," *Jane's Intelligence Review*, 2009, 40

> It is as though the fact of having a female point of view dominating the narrative produces an excess which precludes satisfaction.
>
> Laura Mulvey, "Notes on Sirk and Melodrama," 43

Women of Honour?

The title of Edoardo Winspeare's film *Galantuomini* from 2008 translates most commonly as "gentlemen," but other acceptable renderings are "honest men," "men of their word," or "men of honour" – a translation with a specific Mafia referent – although the film's festival title in the United States and in Australia was *Brave Men*.[1] Thus, the title announces an interest in exploring the psychology of "men of character" within a Mafia context.[2] Instead, as becomes apparent moments into the film, the viewer is not positioned to identify with a male anti-Mafia prosecutor or a Mafioso, but with Lucia Rizzo, a woman who has acquired significant status as a female mob boss of a clan of the Sacra Corona Unita ["United Holy Crown"], Italy's "newest" Mafia, which is located in the southeast region of Puglia.[3] She is the first character who speaks in the film, and *Galantuomini* concludes on a medium shot of Lucia after she turns her back on the possibility of love and walks relentlessly in the direction of the camera and towards an unknown future. Throughout the film, we have access to Lucia's memories, witness tender moments between her and her son, her friends, and her lover, are privy to her anger and frustration while she lives and works in an environment overtly hostile to women, share in her fear when she is violently attacked and raped and then later knows her life to be in danger, are ever more conscious of her growing attraction to her childhood friend, and are cognizant of her exhaustion and the resignation with which she routinely oversees Mafia business. For these reasons, without doubt *Galantuomini* "attempts to engage female subjectivity," but also "incorporate[s] female subjectivity *for* a female subject-spectator," which are vital attributes of the woman's film as detailed by Mary Ann Doane.[4]

Galantuomini is a Mafia melodrama, but with one fatal flaw, as I will later discuss. The film unfolds primarily from Lucia's perspective and chronicles the doomed relationship of Lucia and anti-Mafia prosecutor Ignazio De Raho, recently returned to Lecce from Milan. A contemporary Romeo and Juliet, Lucia and Ignazio, who have known each other since childhood, are separated along the lines of class, and are positioned on opposite sides of the law. Yet, Ignazio is drawn to Lucia and sacrifices his career and ethical code to protect her and hopefully, as the film makes clear, to spend his life with her. Thus, she is constructed as a femme fatale who lures a "galantuomo" to his moral downfall. In this way, *Galantuomini* is in line with the classical Sirkian melodrama as detailed by Laura Mulvey.

Mulvey argues that the narrative thrust of melodrama stems from a deep-seated "ideological contradiction" that is overt in its critique of dominant ideology, in this case the family, the preferred locus of melodramatic action. In such films, narrative pleasure derives "from conflict, not between enemies, but between people tied by blood or love."[5] In *Galantuomini*, such conflicts are apparent in both the Sacra Corona Unita's Mafia brotherhoods and the illicit romance. Mulvey tells us that melodramas that privilege a female point of view appeal to the female spectator because they offer "a fantasy escape for the identifying women in the audience." Melodramas hinge upon a discernible contradiction, which is, in this case, the incompatibility of female desire and agency in the Mafia.⁶

Galantuomini is unique in its exploration of the limits of female empowerment in a Mafia context, and furthers Roberta Torre's take on the liminal status of women in the Cosa Nostra in her film *Angela* from 2002. (Donatella Finocchiaro plays the lead character in both films.)⁷ And yet, in that Lucia's story is recounted within the generic confines of the woman's film, it follows that she must suffer the consequences of her emancipation. In her position of power over men of the Sacra Corona Unita, Lucia is endlessly the target of sexual innuendo and implied and enacted violence: she is threatened on several occasions, men of honour proposition her and continually intimate that she slept her way to the top, and she is brutally raped in front of her young son Biagio. "For in films addressed to women," writes Doane, "spectatorial pleasure is often indissociable from pain."⁸ However, Lucia is the only member of the clan to survive a turf war. She also routinely acts like other male members of the crime syndicate: she gives orders with precision and insight, effortlessly lies to the authorities, negotiates arms deals with Montenegro, swiftly and aggressively avenges her rape, oversees the murder of Infantino, who is the father of her son, and is quite dexterous with a gun.⁹

In short, she seems to have "made it" as a woman of power in the Mafia, something unthinkable in the Cosa Nostra, for example, with its strict policies regarding the limitations of women in the organization. Unlike in Italy's largest Mafia, women have substantial roles in the function of the Sacra Corona Unita, and work as messengers, money collectors, administrators, and "consigliere."¹⁰ Indeed, a study of eighty-three victims of the Sacra Corona Unita between 1980 and 2000 revealed that "although there were more males, they were mostly of the lowest rank whereas the females were almost always important, high-ranking members. This phenomenon is new in mafia societies, and underlines the rise of the 'ex-weaker sex' in criminal organizations."¹¹ As a Mafiosa of substantial rank, Lucia has achieved a sort of post-feminist empowerment, but one that comes with the high price tag associated with the position, such as personal and familial security, lack of autonomy, and limited life choices. But also, in that she *is* a woman entrenched in what by no means can be considered a post-patriarchal culture, her status is at least doubly precarious, as is made clear when rape is chosen as the means par excellence to advise her clan to cease in its attempt to expand its territory. Lucia blatantly told Barabba, boss of a rival clan, to capitulate to her demands. His response is to send one of his men to rape her.[12]

At first glance, it appears that *Galantuomini* is in line with other post-feminist rape revenge narratives that, in the words of Sarah Projansky, link "rape to women's independence"[13] while expressing, as stated by Lisa Coulthard, "a postfeminist discourse of individualistic, 'have it all' feminism that yokes violence to individual, personal, and financial success."[14] Like many of the women in the films studied by Projansky and Coulthard, Lucia is autonomous, and she attempts to usurp power from a warring (male) clan boss. It follows that her behaviour attracts the violent attentions of the hostile family, who use her body to send a message to her boss, Carmine Za'. In many post-feminist rape films, "a woman begins the narrative as self-determined, resists an early romantic union, faces potential rape as a result of her determination to remain independent, and then recognizes her own latent desire for romance at the end of the film."[15] This summary is decidedly fitting to *Galantuomini*, but with one small twist: in the end, Lucia abandons Ignazio, and turns her back on the possibility of a happy ending. This is because, I will argue, her transgressions are unforgivable according to the generic classifiers of the melodramatic woman's film when played out in a Mafia context. Lucia has sinned too much, has desired too much, and has usurped too much of the camera's gaze to be reinscribed into any sort of domestic family or Mafia Family. I will show that Lucia is explicitly analogized to Eve, a comparison that suggests that she is not only responsible for Ignazio's fall from grace, but for that of the entire sub-region of Salento.

Salento Then and Now

Although *Galantuomini* opens in the late 1960s when Ignazio, Lucia, and their friend Fabio were children, narrative action mainly takes place in the early 1990s in Salento (the southeastern area of Puglia) and Montenegro, during the Sacra Corona Unita's most traumatizing, bloody, and fractured, yet financially lucrative, period. The past, which erupts into the film through flashback and a dream sequence, is depicted as idyllic. Sepia tones imbue these earlier years with a sense of melancholy, and the film is overexposed so as to bring out golden shades in the landscape, which is warm and pastoral. The film opens on a tobacco farm, where a group of women sing in dialect as they prepare the leaves to dry in the radiant sun. The film's emphasis on the "honest woman's work" of tobacco farming, a mainstay of Puglia's economy, underlines a series of differences between then and now: for one, Lucia's rebellion, in that she refuses to respect traditional gender norms both as a child (she undermines her boss at the tobacco plantation) and later in life, but also the change in the region itself, whose economy will switch from dependency on tobacco farming to the heroin trade. Notwithstanding a bit of childhood bullying, 1960s Salento appears unspoiled, and free from organized crime. Lucia is clearly the leader of the group, and wields particular influence over Ignazio, who is captivated by her. She is an instigator and moments into the film baits Ignazio and Fabio into breaking into the storeroom of Pasquale Precamorti, convincing them that they must rescue a schoolmate named Antonio as Precamorti abducted him, along with other neighbourhood children, so as to almost starve them to death before selling them to the gypsies. In this way, she tests their masculinity. Fabio is unafraid, but Ignazio hesitates, and does not enter the storage room, an early indication of his unsuitability for a life in organized crime.

Absent from childhood recollections are parental figures. Although Precamorti identifies Lucia as "the daughter of Cosomino Rizzo" and warns her that he plans to tell her father about her transgression, which will warrant a beating, Lucia's mother and father have no place of import in her memory. Instead of expressing fear, she laughs and runs away, which suggests that she has already internalized the law of the father and has disregarded any potential identification with the mother. Her repudiation of her mother is underlined when, as an adult, Lucia drops her son off at her mother's house and waves goodbye to her child, but does not address or glance at the woman dressed in black. The camera affirms the mother's devaluation by momentarily capturing an out-of-focus shot of the woman's body with her head not visible. In the flashback, Lucia's disobedient behaviour goes unpunished by her father; she is fashioned as independent and in control of the males in her circle, and we view the world through her eyes.

The representation of Lucia's childhood can be informed by Freud's analysis of the masochistic fantasy, "'A Child Is Being Beaten,'" which has come to be a seminal text in feminist film theory for discussions of spectatorship and identification. The film suggests that Lucia does not experience, and literally sidesteps, in Constance Penley's words, "the multiple and successive identificatory positions taken up by the host of the fantasy" apparent in the case study.[16] The first position is active in that the child identifies with the father, *"my father is beating the child,"* the second is "of an unmistakably masochistic character," when the child looks through her own eyes, "*I am being beaten by my father*,"[17] and finally, she can identify with herself as a spectator of the abuse, "I am probably looking on."[18] In her discussion of the woman's film, Doane explains that in the fantasy, "simultaneous with her assumption of the position of spectator, the woman loses not only her sexual identity in the context of the scenario but her very access to sexuality."[19] She does this, as, in Freud's words, she "escapes from the demands of the erotic side of her life altogether. She turns herself in fantasy into a man, without herself becoming active in a masculine way, and is no longer anything but a spectator of the event which takes the place of the sexual act."[20] Instead of evading sexuality through "safely" positioning herself on the side of passive masculinity and looking on at a drama that is primarily concerned with masochism, Lucia assumes an active role in her erotic development. After tricking them, Lucia runs with Ignazio and Fabio across the rooftops of the town. She feigns injury to trick Ignazio into staying behind with her and then dominates him by pushing him down atop a bed of red peppers drying in the sun, where she holds him down and kisses him. The camera is positioned from Ignazio's perspective to show Lucia's face claustrophobically hovering above him. Following the kiss, she runs away and leaves him spent in the sun, his eyes closed and lips parted out of nascent desire. Lucia's gaze is far from "de-eroticized," and instead of laying bare a "masochistic fantasy," the flashback foregrounds Lucia's "sexuality."[21] Even as a child, Lucia is an active sexual agent.

The Puglia of Lucia, Ignazio and Fabio's youth is represented as a young adolescent's playground and the future is figured as ripe with promise. Present day Puglia, however, is overrun with drug and arms dealers, junkies (one of them is Fabio), and warring clans vying for control of the region. Mafiosi and bystanders are shot in the street in broad daylight, "guinea pigs" such as Fabio overdose and die from bad heroin, narcotics and weapon deals are made in idyllic seaside settings and lifetime loyalties are tenuous as people switch sides without much forethought. The soft and warm tones frequent in the flashback sequences are replaced by bright, sun-drenched landscapes. Instead of presiding over a small group of children, Lucia oversees a lucrative and deadly crime syndicate. In short, the age of innocence has come to an abrupt end. The opening scene when Lucia kisses Ignazio is followed by the title sequence, accompanied by a shot of a blue sky peppered with clouds. A cut takes us to another geography, as Lucia and her crew (as we learn later) race across the Adriatic in a speedboat towards Montenegro to procure illegal firearms. Hence, both the coming of age of the three childhood friends and the development of the Sacra Corona Unita, which was founded in 1983, are eclipsed from the film, which underscores the contrast between the two periods and inaugurates a cause and effect narrative that positions Lucia as both a source of knowledge and a temptress. Lucia is the film's ego ideal, she was at the helm in childhood and remains so as an adult. In this way, it is suggested that the Sacra Corona Unita is born simultaneously with Lucia's coming of age sexually.

On the "newness" of the organization, Winspeare writes:

> La nascita della Sacra Corona Unita ha determinato la perdita della verginità della nostra terra. Fino ad allora, parliamo degli anni Ottanta, il Salento non era corrotto dal cancro della criminalità. Poi è esplosa e io stavo lì e sentivo parlare di morti, di droga, di traffico d'armi, e mi chiedevo il perché di tutto questo. La cosa straordinaria è che la SCU è l'unica mafia che sia stata per ora sconfitta.
>
> The birth of the Sacra Corona Unita brought about the loss of our land's virginity. Until then, during the 1980s, Salento was uncorrupted by the cancer of criminality. Then, it exploded and I was there and I heard talk of killings, drugs, arms trafficking, and I asked myself "why?" The extraordinary thing is that the Sacra Corona Unita is the only Mafia as of yet to be defeated.[22]

Two details are of interest in Winspeare's description. The first is the director's insistence that the war against the Sacra Corona Unita was won on the part of the state, a position that he brings up in interviews.[23] Although it is true that the organization, whose power structure was weakened in the 1990s, is Italy's least cohesive Mafia, it is far from being in total decline. In a recent case study put together by *Jane's Intelligence Review*, the status of the Mafia of Puglia was classified as "active," with a threat level of "medium," an identical ranking to the Sumiyoshi-Kai, the second largest group of Japan's Mafia, the Yakuza.[24] In fact, the assessment concludes with a warning: "If [the Sacra Corona Unita] were to establish a unifying leadership and hierarchical structures it could become a major criminal factor,"[25] two outcomes that are not inconceivable given the organization's youth and the Mafia's adaptability at large.

But, according to Winspeare, contemporary Puglia is free from Mafia influence, and was only momentarily the locus of Mafia corruption.

The second significant point in the citation above is that Winspeare imbricates female sexual initiation with corruption. The land is eroticized when the director allegorizes Puglia as a female body that has lost its honour (keeping in mind the cults of male virility and female chastity embedded in southern Italian culture at large but magnified in the Mafia). This is significant considering the trope of temptation in *Galantuomini*, and the director's construction of Lucia as a seductress. Somewhat early on in the film, Ignazio is in a crowded auditorium passively listening to a presentation called "Criminalità organizzata e territorio: La Sacra Corona Unita in Puglia [Organized Crime and Territory: The Sacra Corona Unita in Puglia]." When the speaker states, "Of course, this criminal organization called the Sacra Corona Unita is still in its early stages. It's a criminal organization, not really petty crime, but a group of people that is organized," a flashback brings us to Ignazio's childhood. The singing from the first youthful memory is again present, but is now non-diegetic as Ignazio looks off-screen, fixated on something that evades our gaze. A cut to a point-of-view shot from Ignazio's perspective reveals that Lucia is offering him a snake. A medium close-up follows of the two, who stare wordlessly at the serpent, while Ignazio slowly leans towards it. A disorienting cut follows to an extreme close-up and then a dramatic low-angle shot of a colossal tangled tree. The sequence resolves with a sombre long shot of several similar trees in a stony field. Ignazio is brought back to the present as the speaker declares: "Salento is no longer a happy island and is no longer a territory immune from the criminal phenomenon, from the phenomenon of the Mafia."

The serpent and the tree (of knowledge) in Ignazio's memory, together with the comment that the region of Salento is contaminated, undoubtedly evoke the biblical metaphor of the Fall. In Ignazio's memory, Lucia is a siren who invites him towards sin. In this way, she is also likened to Lilith, the "original Eve," who is commonly referred to as a seductress.[26] In fact, later on in the film, Lucia herself lays bare her own fall from grace. After she oversees Infantino's murder, and as she tucks her son (also his son) into bed, she tells him a story which begins: "In Heaven, there was a beautiful angel, with wings as white as the snow and one day this angel decided to come down to Earth, and while falling he dirtied his wings. He tried to clean them, but they were never white again. All of the other angels in Heaven teased him, calling him 'the angel with the black wings, the angel with the black wings.'" Her narrative is cross-cut with two other events: First, we see Lucia, whose name of course recalls Lucifer, overseeing the organization of weaponry. Then, a man is shown entering a car that immediately bursts into flames. The explosion takes us back to Lucia and Biagio, where Lucia attempts to neutralize the potential trauma that such a fatalistic tale might cause her son by concluding that "Jesus loved [the angel] more than the others, he was his favourite." Thus, Lucia can also be read as a tragic Medea figure in that she symbolically murders her child through her involvement in the Mafia. In particular, she orders the death of her son's father, but also, we can imagine that Biagio is traumatized after he was forced to watch his mother's rape. Ultimately, Lucia's "masculine" power compromises Biagio, who, like the swan from Lucia's story, irrevocably loses his innocence. This scene, together with Ignazio's flashback, which significantly takes place during a lecture that gauges the extent to which the Sacra Corona Unita exerts influence in the area, universalize Lucia's transgression. Hence, the film suggests that Lucia is responsible not only for Ignazio's decline, but for that of the entire region.

Moreover, it is possible to read Lucia as a Medusa figure who, as Adriana Cavarero argues, "freezes and paralyzes" her victims.[27] The snake stands in for Medusa's severed head, which signifies castration while simultaneously representing, according to Freud, "a mitigation of the horror, for [the snakes] replace the penis, the absence of which is the cause of the horror." Ignazio is transfixed by the proffered snake, but he is far from terrorized, a common reaction according to Freud in his study on the mythical figure as she relates to the castration complex.[28] Instead, Lucia's power over Ignazio is betrayed in his eventual return to Puglia. He moves to Milan, but he cannot stay away, as he makes clear in a discussion with Fabio, and is drawn back to her and to his birthplace. In this way, Lucia is positioned as an enigma to be solved, as is the femme fatale of film noir. Like the Medusa, the femme fatale has the power to draw the man's gaze and to alter the course of his quest. Doane discusses the femme fatale as a place of signification which makes manifest "the imbrication of knowledge and sexuality," an equation that reminds us of Eve. But also, the figure is something that must be "revealed, unmasked, discovered," which makes the femme fatale "fully compatible with the epistemological drive of narrative," in that she becomes a text to be read. And this is also the case for Lucia.[29] Indeed, Lucia derails Ignazio's Oedipal trajectory and usurps narrative control. More to the point, when her misdeeds are revealed to Ignazio, instead of punishing her, he protects her.

Lucia is a castrating figure who wields an actual gun at work and exerts substantial influence over a man whose life was dedicated to the eradication of her profession. As such, she is doubly threatening to the male inscribed viewer and will pay dearly for her lapses. Akin to the femme fatale, Lucia is punished and is "situated as evil."[30] We will see that "her textual eradication involves a desperate reassertion of control on the part of the threatened male subject. Hence, it would be a mistake to see her as some kind of heroine of modernity. She is not the subject of feminism but a symptom of male fears about feminism."[31] Although Lucia has risen through the ranks in the Mafia, the film does not suggest that power is "there for the taking," a post-feminist argument put forth by power feminist Naomi Wolf. Sarah Gamble questions, "But is it, can it ever be, as easy as that?" Of course not, when one considers race, class, education, and context, in this case in that Lucia is subject to an oppressive Mafia system.[32] In Doane's words, "the power accorded to the femme fatale is a function of fears linked to the notions of uncontrollable drives, the fading of subjectivity, and the loss of conscious agency." The femme fatale, like Lucia, threatens the male subject position, a gesture that has as a consequence a series of punishments, the first of which for Lucia is rape.[33]

The Rape-Revenge Scenario

Ignazio learns of Lucia's double life and instead of issuing a warrant for her arrest, he immediately contacts her to set up a meeting, a decision that demonstrates the indomitable pull that she has over him. Lucia responds to Ignazio's allegations by reminding him of the disparity in their socio-economic status, and the two fall into a heated argument. While Ignazio, who was born into a family with money, had choices and could leave, she had none and stayed behind. Ignazio hits Lucia hard on the face and tells her that violence is the only thing that she knows. She counters by emasculating him through belittling his virility: "The only thing that you wanted was to screw me but you couldn't even do that." Realizing that her cover is blown, she takes her son to the seaside to evade the authorities and steer clear of the escalating violence associated with the turf war. While swimming in the ocean, Lucia experiences a tender moment with her son as she reassures him after he is separated from her and becomes frightened, which foregrounds her status as a mother. That night, however, two men enter her room, fire a gun and then one man pins her down and rapes her as another silences her son, who is forced to watch in terror. The sexual assault is brief, lasting less than forty seconds, and takes place in a space that is barely illuminated. The assailant, who we later learn is named Claudio, warns Lucia, "Listen, bitch, get this in your head, you are not giving orders all over Puglia, tell that to your boss," and then takes his leave. After the two depart, Lucia embraces her son and both scream and sob uncontrollably.

It is striking that the rape is not mentioned at all in discussions of the film in newspaper reviews and in blogging sites, although commentators regularly bring up other moments of violence in the film, such as explosions, scenes of torture, and murders.[34] Yes, the scene is obscured by minimal lighting, quick cuts, and chaotic and rapid camera movement, but several elements of the mise-en-scène convince the viewer that the rape took place: primarily, Claudio tells Lucia right away, "Watch what I am going to do to you," and then, as he violently gyrates atop her in a pattern consistent with penetration, he tells her, "You are making me hard," while he grunts out of what appears to be pleasure. She fights him to no avail, screaming at him to stop and to go away while repeatedly spitting at him in the face. It is telling that one commentator (whose remarks were later removed from the site) states that Lucia "non ha il coraggio di ammazzare il tipo che a momenti la stupra davanti al figlio [is not courageous enough to kill the guy who *nearly* raped her in front of her son]."[35] "Nearly" ("a momenti"). Lucia's rape is even more disturbing as it takes place in front of her son; cross-cutting shows Biagio's fully opened eyes five times during the assault and his muffled wails pervade the diegesis. The contrast between the oppressive darkness during the rape sequence and the small shaft of light over Biagio's eyes heightens spectatorial anxiety. But, as the representation of the rape is not graphic or clear cut, it has as of yet been overlooked and repressed in the critical reception of the film.

This is an interesting elision considering that the rape scene shares several cinematographic elements with other scenes of sexual violence that intend to convey to the spectator, in Alison Young's words, "the message that rape is a serious crime, with terrible effects on the victim." Techniques such as "distorted camera work, ... dark lighting, [and] ... rapid editing ... convey the trauma" of Lucia's experience of rape, a trauma that is no doubt intensified by her son's witnessing of the event, as Biagio is implicated in the scene by "point of view shots from the position of a bystander." What is missing, however, are various other devices that position the viewer to identify with the attacker, such as extreme close-ups which divide up the body of the woman, "point of view shots from the perspective of the rapist," and shots of the victim's body before or after the assault "which construct her as something to be looked at."[36] Thus, although we know we are looking at something violent, and are the witness to a crime, we have no clear point of identificatory entry into the scene. In this way, the film downplays the trauma of rape and troubles traditional modes of spectatorship and identification, which will be problematic considering the subsequent revenge narrative and Lucia's place within it.

The representation of rape in *Galantuomini* underlines Lynn A. Higgins and Brenda R. Silver's assertion regarding "an obsessive inscription – and an obsessive erasure – of sexual violence against women" in the cinema. Such a "rhetoric of elision" – the title of the second section of their collection – implies that rape is a crucial structuring device of narrative that is later repressed. "Rape and rapability," write the authors, "are central to the very construction of gender identity."[37] And yet, rape narratives are ultimately erased or elided, which then naturalizes "the cultural pervasiveness of sexual violence against women."[38] Up until her rape, Lucia is frequently the target of sexual innuendo and threatened violence. Infantino assaults her twice in an effort to coerce her into sexual activity, while attempting to negotiate with Barabba, his soldiers call Lucia's men "froci [faggots]" as they work for a woman. These men counter by declaring that they regularly use her body for sexual gratification, "even for free," and Infantino and others remind her of all the men she slept with, including her uncle Carmine Za', in order to secure her power position. As such, the verbal abuse that Lucia suffers during the first two-thirds of the film builds up to the sexual assault and the maltreatment of Lucia exposes, in Clovers words, "the power dynamic between men and women that makes rape happen in the first place," and suggests how "the dynamic of males in groups" can lead to rape.[39]

With the rape, this pervasive tone of sexual violence comes to a dramatic end, and is replaced by a revenge narrative that is meant to neutralize and contain earlier acts of brutality. After the conclusion of the rape-revenge cycle, the narrative is then focused on the love story between Ignazio and Lucia, a plot twist that works to rewrite her previously aberrant behaviour as a retributive Mafia boss. Not too long after the rape, a prolonged and disorienting chase sequence ensues, at the end of which Lucia's men catch the rapist Claudio and deliver him to her in a warehouse. As Lucia asks in a seductive voice if her men were too hard on him (he has been badly beaten), she gently touches his face and apologizes for their violent behaviour and then licks his lips and kisses him. Completely in control of her attacker, she then reaches down to grasp his penis, which she then forcefully squeezes and inquires, "What happened, don't you like me anymore … You can't get it up?" which specifically recalls Claudio's wording during the attack. Her men press her to "kill the animal," but instead, she pushes him to the ground and shoots him square in each knee, and, as he howls in pain, they all walk away. Her vengeance then consists in not only emasculating Claudio in front of a group of his peers, but also ensuring that he will have a life-long physical reminder regarding the consequences of his actions. While the viewer is somewhat challenged to find a pleasurable viewing position during the attack, several point-of-view shots of Claudio from Lucia's perspective position us to identify with Lucia as avenger during the second half of the rape-revenge cycle.[40] She is once again cast as a controlling and fatal woman.

In filmic time, Lucia takes her revenge just about two minutes after the rape, which underlines a cause-and-effect relationship between rape and retribution. Revenge, writes Young, "is imperative in the wake of sexual violence … [and] is governed by the *lex talionis*, or principle of retribution: when the law is broken, punishment must be carried out no matter what, since the force of law cannot be restored unless punishment takes place."[41] The rape revenge film demands retribution on the part of the victim to set things right in the world. Thus, the revenge scenario transforms Lucia from a threatened, terrified victim into, once again, a controlling and autonomous actor while eclipsing any potential trauma caused by the rape. Therefore, *Galantuomini* is in line with other rape-revenge films that open up gaps between, according to Jacinda Read, "the (feminine) victim and the (feminist) avenger."[42] However, such a subversive model of female agency cannot go unchecked and is frequently tempered by a narrative structure that privileges the traditional love story familiar to the melodrama. Hence, although *Galantuomini* exposes the prevalence of rape in patriarchal culture, like other post-feminist rape films it maintains "a relationship between rape and women's independence"[43] that ultimately tempers what could be radically different perspectives on a Mafia woman in a men-only society.

Post-feminism and Post-Mafia?

Towards the end of *Galantuomini*, Lucia's clan is completely wiped out, and she is left alone and unprotected. She makes her way to Ignazio's apartment in Lecce, and the two finally consummate their passion. Ignazio is ecstatic, and, in between moments of romance, jokes with Lucia and discusses a common acquaintance. Lucia, however, is more guarded and has no memory of the man from Ignazio's story. Later, he tells her of a dream that he just had in which someone who sounded like his father told him to never stop dancing, and that he must be happy (in an earlier scene he told Lucia he had never thought about dancing). Lucia counters by telling him that she never remembers her dreams. Ignazio has let go of his repressions and learned how to follow his instincts while conjuring up a paternal figure who encourages and supports his life choices. However, Lucia, who was raised according to Mafia values, represses past traumas. Indeed, the only time that she loses control is when she is alone, hiding in the mountains following the mass killing of her Mafia family. When she hears what sounds like a gunshot, she is startled and looks towards the sky. Her face soon registers instant relief and we see through a point-of-view shot that the noise is caused by fireworks. As the noises escalate in pace and in volume, Lucia breaks down and violently sobs and cries out while hitting the boulder behind her. The blast has her return to the scene of the crime, but which one? It sounds quite similar to the gunshot fired before her rape, but could easily bring to mind the other murders that she recently witnessed.

"In the rape revenge scenario," writes Coulthard, "the violence is narrationally 'used up,' such that the narrative closure erases its existence after the fact and threats of socially, politically, or ideologically disruptive, radical, or revolutionary acts of female violence are not only contained but ultimately expunged from the text itself."[44] The sexual encounter between Lucia and Ignazio feminizes Lucia and further downplays the earlier violence of the rape. What's more, the experience purifies Lucia, and renders her desirable again. The rape took place in an underlit space and was characterized by jarring editing. However, the staging of Ignazio and Lucia's second sexual encounter includes a high-angle shot of the couple focusing on Lucia's face as she has a lengthy orgasm. The scene is accompanied by an emotive score and the room is brightly lit, and the take, lasting more than a minute, is uninterrupted. In this way, the subversive potential of the revenge drama is neutralized through a heteronormative bourgeois resolution. Lucia, like other female protagonists of the rape-revenge cycle, "recognizes her own latent desire for romance at the end of the film," to cite Projansky for a second time.

Lucia, however, refuses the requisite happy ending inherent in the melodrama. When they run out of food, Ignazio leaves to go grocery shopping and to purchase some clothing for Lucia. Cross-cutting reveals that while Ignazio is a beloved member of his community, Lucia is clanless: He walks in the bright sun and happily greets friends, watches a wedding procession, smiles into the sunlight, and gazes wistfully at the advertisements for beach vacations at a travel agency. Lucia, instead, paces in his apartment nervously while clenching her hands. When the phone rings, she listens to a message from Ignazio's colleague Laura, who tells him of the recent massacre, saying that everyone was killed and Lucia is the only "survivor," and then asks him to call her if he knows of Lucia's whereabouts. When Ignazio returns home, he sees Lucia on his doorstep, looking anxiously into the street. She briefly meets his gaze and then the film concludes with a prolonged fixed close-up on Lucia's face as she walks steadily away from him with her eyes averted from the camera.

Galantuomini stands out from other Italian Mafia movies made during the last century in its depiction of a desirous woman in the organization who holds a significant position of authority and who maims her enemies and orders the deaths of those who double-cross her clan. And yet, as the film follows the generic qualifiers of the melodrama, it conforms to the workings of the dominant ideologies of patriarchal culture. Mulvey tells us that in the melodrama centred upon a male protagonist, narrative frictions are generally resolved in the service of affirming the master narrative. When a woman looks excessively, however, reconciliation is more challenging, and is frequently impossible: "It is as though the fact of having a female point of view dominating the narrative produces an excess which precludes satisfaction."[45] Such films resist narrative closure and fail to "settle all of the dust" raised during the diegesis. Mulvey puts forth Douglas Sirk's *All That Heaven Allows* (1955) as an example par excellence of the consequences of a commanding female perspective. In Sirk's film, the male romantic lead is ultimately incapacitated, which disallows a happy ending for Cary (the female lead), who, it is suggested, is forced to tend to him in perpetuity. While films dealing with male fantasy are easily resolvable, those that centre upon the look of the woman suggest that female desire represents a transgression that cannot be easily reconciled.

Projansky argues that war films (a genre with which Winspeare's film shares several characteristics) "have often used representations of women's rapes to tell stories about men."[46] Although Lucia is the focus of narrative action, her plotline is ultimately left at loose ends, while this is not the case for most of the "galantuomini" implied in the film's title. Such a phallocentric finale recalls the conclusion of *Le conseguenze dell'amore* in that Titta's memorialization comes at the expense of Sofia, who is violently effaced from the narrative. In *Galantuomini*, Fabio's death is rendered through a fantasmatic eulogy: an oneiric projection of Fabio, Lucia, and Ignazio as children on a boat accompanied by Ignazio's mother and a Charonesque boatman celebrates his passing, mourns him, and lends closure to his story. Just before Lucia oversees Infantino's death, she relives a memory of their childhood when he stood up for her and protected her from neighbourhood bullies. Thus, we remember him as a heroic figure. And, although Lucia abandons Ignazio, the film implies that he has achieved a balance in life and has a community to fall back on to help him recover from his loss. Lucia, however, is alone and without options (although at one point in the film it is implied that she can move to Montenegro). She leaves, it is implied, to not further implicate Ignazio. But where does she go? The film does not tell us, and her narrative has no resolution, a melancholic finale that recalls the conclusion of *Angela* in that both main characters are exiled and alone, without a community that might help them work through their losses.

In depicting a powerful woman who has achieved economic emancipation in the Mafia, *Galantuomini* is in line with other texts that presume, according to Tania Modleski, "the advent of postfeminism." However, in that Lucia is regularly victimized, and is eventually subsumed into a bourgeois romance, the film is "engaged in negating the critiques and undermining the goals of feminism – in effect, delivering us back into a prefeminist world."[47] Lucia, like Eve before her, is positioned to take the blame for the fall from grace and is constructed as a scapegoat for male anxieties about female agency and empowerment in a traditionally patriarchal association. *Galantuomini* suggests that the Sacra Corona Unita begins and ends with Lucia. Moreover, keeping in mind the director's comments regarding the organization's subsequent downfall, the film suggests that the Mafia of Puglia has been defeated and positions Mafia-related trauma as belonging to the past. In *Horrorism*, Cavarero puts forwards the Gorgon as the ultimate incarnation of horror: "a woman, the hideous Medusa, has always been the mythical face of horror."[48] In *Galantuomini*, Lucia, a temptress and a femme fatale, embodies the Sacra Corona Unita. Lucia is then both the first woman and the last (Mafia) woman, who belongs nowhere and to no one.

7 Melancholia and the Mob Weepie: Davide Barletti and Lorenzo Conte's *Fine pena mai: Paradiso perduto*

The ideology of melancholia appropriates from women's subjectivities their "real" sense of loss and, in Lacanian terms, recuperates that loss ... as a privileged form of male expression, if not as an expression of male privilege. In turn, that recuperation legitimates the male in his "excessive" suffering, even in his "femininity," but leaves women as an oppressed and nameless (or generic) other.

Juliana Schiesari, *The Gendering of Melancholia*, 13

In many male weepies (or male melodramas), real men do not cry, or at best they shed only a few hard-wrung tears; others do the crying for them – usually women and people of color.

Tania Modleski, "Clint Eastwood and Male Weepies," 136

Dear Lela, I know that this letter will hurt you, I know that you need to forget it all, but I need to remember to continue living, to understand how it all happened. How did I end up here, to be who I am?

Fine pena mai: Paradiso perduto (Davide Barletti and Lorenzo Conte)

The Mafia Melancholic

Davide Barletti and Lorenzo Conte's film *Fine pena mai: Paradiso perduto* (*Life Sentence: Paradise Lost*, 2008) begins in the dark. We first see a prologue including text that details the Italian state's swift and aggressive response to the murders of Falcone and Borsellino in 1992. After the Mafia's attack on the "core of the state," the government decreed a "hard prison regime," entitled "41bis," and reopened the high security prisons on the islands of Pianosa and Asinara, where 250 of the most dangerous bosses of the Cosa Nostra, the Camorra, the 'Ndrangheta, and the Sacra Corona Unita were placed in solitary confinement. As the script appears on the screen, the non-diegetic sound of several newscasters whose voices are jumbled and overlapping increases in intensity and is then mixed with the sound of a helicopter that serves as a sound bridge to the opening scene of the film. Here, the viewer is plunged into a chaotic milieu that is barely illuminated, save for a few flashes of light originating from a helicopter that is edited in rapid and disorienting takes. At times, the camera appears to be inside of the helicopter, at others, it is positioned at various extreme angles around it as it lands. The jarring montage, together with barking dogs, sirens, machine guns, and shouting men who quickly usher another blindfolded man from the helicopter to an awaiting boat, create an atmosphere akin to that of a war zone. When the same man is transferred to a speedboat, a slow-motion shot begins that inaugurates the voice-over narrative: "I didn't know where they were taking me, I thought that they were going to kill me, maybe that's what I wanted. It was the end, the end of my youth, the end of all hope. And I just stood there watching, incapable of feeling anything as I was faced with my ruin." Then, as the opening credits appear onscreen, the camera races atop a jet-black and surging sea towards, we eventually discern, a dark mountain island under a gunmetal sky. A cut follows to an aerial shot of a mass of buildings and a script tells us that we are on the island of Asinara and are looking down at the Fornelli maximum-security prison. At this point, the voice-over returns and takes the form of a letter to a woman, which begins "Cara [dear] Lela." Although, as the narrator tells us, such a letter will hurt its recipient as she wants to forget, he must write so that he can remember, continue living, and understand what brought him there. As we enter the abandoned cellblock, he asks the age-old question, "How did I arrive here, to be who I am?"

The remainder of the film is an elaborate flashback that answers this query through recounting the exploits of Antonio Perrone, a heroin addict and former boss of the Sacra Corona Unita. Perrone began as a small-time criminal who, while serving time in the prison of San Francesco in Lecce for robbery from 1983 until 1987, joined the Sacra Corona Unita and moved up its ranks. He was arrested in 1989 on drug charges and was condemned to forty-nine years in prison, fourteen of which he spent under 41bis (following the assassinations of Falcone and Borsellino in 1992 until 2006). The harsh 41bis prison regime, much criticized by human rights groups, suspends "the rules that govern prison treatment" and prohibits or greatly limits, among other things, visits with family, communication with other prisoners and the outside world, and involvement in any cultural or athletic activities.[1]

In *Fine pena mai*, Antonio's journey towards deliverance engages the viewer, who is meant to identify with him. The recipient of the letter, we will find out, is Lela, Antonio's high-school sweetheart and later wife and mother of his son Alessio (Daniela Piccinno, who goes by Lela, is Perrone's wife).[2] In the film, Lela is crucial in rendering Antonio sympathetic as she, the perennial listener and unwavering partner, lends pathos to Antonio's story and humanizes him. Thus, we are asked to show compassion for someone who spent most of his (pre-incarceration) adult life as a hardened criminal. The structuring device of the voice-over is critical in establishing the melancholic tone of Antonio's story. Antonio writes from a position of distance as he seeks to understand what he has lost. Thus, *Fine pena mai* is structured around lack. This absence is not only the loss of Lela. Instead, it will become clear that Antonio is more distraught about a series of other losses which include his youth, his male companions, his freedom and, most important, a hedonistic playground that was his earthly paradise until the Sacra Corona Unita contaminated his native soil.

Tania Modleski's work on the male weepie is fruitful for helping us understand the mechanics of identification at work in *Fine pena mai*. In particular, she looks at how melancholia functions in Clint Eastwood films so as to privilege the male subject position and "perpetuat[e] the patriarchal order."[3] The male weepie genre, Modleski argues, features stoic characters who, contrary to the protagonist of the woman's film, rarely externalize their grief. Instead, they are "wept over by other characters and by the audience."[4] This cinematic process is nothing new, and Modleski turns towards the work of Juliana Schiesari to understand why men's suffering in the male melodrama or weepie is "culturally privileged," while women's anguish onscreen is often "dismissed as sentimental drivel."[5] Schiesari notes that the suffering of the melancholic (male) artist is restorative: the loss is recuperated "in the name of an imaginary unity" that confers to him "a privileged position."[6] Schiesari is discussing Renaissance authors, but her analysis is particularly applicable to the cinema, which is a system structured around absence, and here I recall Christian Metz, who argues that cinema is an arrangement wholly based on lack: "the absence of the object, replaced by its reflection."[7] For the melancholic (and, I would add, the male protagonist of the classical cinema), the originary lack is recuperated "as a privileged form of male expression" at the expense of the female subject, who is oppressed and her suffering belittled.[8]

As is clear in the initial voice-over, the entire film takes the form of a love letter from Antonio to Lela. It is significant, however, that Antonio seeks self-fulfilment, mastery, and longevity regardless of Lela's pain ("I know this letter will hurt you," he writes. "I know that you need to forget it all, but I need to remember to continue living, to understand how it all happened"). In this way, the depiction of women in *Fine pena mai* as potentially salvific places the director in a long literary and iconographic tradition dating back to Dante and Petrarch. Antonio's loss is thus productive, and writing is a way to achieve redemption. However only he, and not Lela, will be saved.

As Claire Johnston explains, the female protagonist in the cinema is frequently represented as a fetish object; she "represents not herself, but by a process of displacement, the male phallus ... Despite the enormous emphasis placed on women as spectacle in the cinema, woman as woman is largely absent."[9] As we will see, Lela is a fetishized projection of voyeuristic fantasy. Throughout the film, she inhabits a series of roles that change according to Antonio's frame of mind. In the end, to return to Schiesari, Lela's mourning is devalued and prolonged (he will not let her move on). Antonio's epistolary expression not only recuperates his lack as expressed in the incipit of the letter to Lela, but, more crucially, it helps position the viewer to forgive him for his criminal past. Nefarious Mafiosi do inhabit *Fine pena mai*, but their conduct is far from ambiguous. The film constructs the Mafia of Puglia as defeatable and its members, save Antonio, come off as a scourge that belongs to Italy's past. Instead, the future as it is ultimately envisioned in the film is not a paradise lost (as is implied in the film's title), but one that is regained in Antonio's reconstituted ego that is finally unencumbered by the sins of the past.

Fine pena mai: Paradiso perduto and *Vista d'interni: Diario di carcere, di "scuri" e seghe, di trip e di sventure*

Barletti and Conte's film is very loosely based on Perrone's memoir *Vista d'interni: Diario di carcere, di "scuri" e seghe, di trip e di sventure* (*Interior View: A Diary about Prison, Members of the SCU and Handjobs, Trips, and Bad Luck*, 2003) that he wrote between 1997 and 2001 while travelling between several Italian prisons.[10] The film is clearly structured as a male melodrama, although critics have a hard time categorizing *Fine pena mai* in terms of genre.¹¹ Antonio is unwilling to "fulfil society's expectations of male adulthood"¹² and he "is in danger of extinction from his murderous and castrating father" (reading the father as the Mafia). In his paternal absence, he also metaphorically "fails in his duty to reproduce (the family)" while "fail[ing] his family" altogether.¹³ In line with the work of Janet Staiger and her theorizations on the male melodrama, Antonio lacks self-discipline and is thus tempted down the wrong path, but he is eventually redeemed and rewarded "in moral heaven."¹⁴

The memoir could not be more different from the film, in terms of both tone and content. Take, for example, their titles. The title of Perrone's memoir, *Vista d'interni: Diario di carcere, di "scuri" e seghe, di trip e di sventure*, is descriptive and accurate: the narrator alternates chronicles of prison life with fourteen "Commas" that are printed in italics and recount memories of his party days, life of crime, and association with the Sacra Corona Unita. Instead, *Fine pena mai: Paradiso perduto* evokes a fall from grace and is allegorical of a spiritual journey. In the memoir, Perrone describes the insufferable conditions of prison life in real time and in exhausting detail: we read of Perrone's torture during his interrogation, miniature cell sizes (some measure only seven by fourteen paces), beatings of prisoners by the guards, one prisoner's act of protest that involves sewing his mouth shut, regular suicides of inmates, lack of ventilation in the cells, frequent prison transfers, and complete isolation notwithstanding very brief monthly visits from family members with whom detainees can only communicate through Plexiglas. Perrone also suffers from claustrophobia, anxiety, and panic attacks.

In the words of Barletti and Conte, *Vista d'interni* represents "il punto più profondo dell'inferno carcerario [the deepest point of prison's hell],"¹⁵ while another reviewer writes that Perrone is "detenuto nell'inferno di un carcere [detained in a hellish prison]."¹⁶ The memoir represents prison life as an infernal and monotonous existence without end. Instead, in the film, the prison is likened not to Hell, but to Purgatory. Thus, it is implied that Antonio is far from wholly damned as he will, according to the Dantean logic of contrition, eventually expiate his sins and reach Paradise. The mountain present in the credit sequence is evocative of the summit glimpsed by Ulysses in the famous Canto 26 of *Inferno* ("There appeared to us a mountain dark in the distance, and to me it seemed the highest I had ever seen"; ll. 133–5). However, the moment that the king of Ithaca catches site of the mountain of Purgatory, a whirlwind causes his ship to sink, killing all aboard: "We rejoiced, but soon our joy was turned to grief, for from the new land a whirlwind rose and struck the forepart of the ship. Three times it whirled her round with all the waters, and the fourth time it lifted the stern aloft and plunged the prow below, as pleased Another, till the sea closed over us" (ll. 136–42).[17] While Ulysses is damned because he misuses language and his thirst for "virtute e canoscenza [virtue and knowledge]" (l. 120) is not ordained by divine grace, it is implied that Antonio transcends the infernal confusion inherent in the representation of his prison transfer, reaches the island, and begins doing penance for his sins. Like the souls in Purgatory, Antonio lives in a state of exile and nostalgically recounts and relives his tale in the hopes of achieving absolution. Indeed, Ulysses is a melancholy hero because Penelope, the wife that he leaves behind, is the pretence for his crusade to return to his homeland.

It is revealing that, in the film, we never visualize Antonio on site during his internment under 41bis. Twice, however, the narrative is interrupted and we return to the prison milieu. As in the beginning of the film, in both instances the prison is deserted, the grounds are overgrown with weeds, cell doors are open, gates are blowing in the wind, paint is chipped, and walls are decaying. The prison is represented as an otherworldly and oneiric non-space. In that it is uninhabited, the film implies that Antonio has transcended its perimeters and has reached a state of enlightenment. During most of the flashback sequences, Antonio's voice-overs are more upbeat in describing his escapades. When giving us a supposed "insider's view" of the penitentiary, Antonio's voice softens and he becomes nostalgic, introspective, and melancholy. In the first voice-over, after describing his loneliness and despair, Antonio seems to go so far as to abdicate moral responsibility for his crimes:

> It's been 15 years without you, fifteen years without anyone nearby, fifteen years of complete isolation. Every day I hope that I can make it, until evening comes, and then night, and then the next day when all begins again and ahead of me, months, years, without end. Ever [senza fine. Mai]. Lela, I feel like I never lived, that I was always running, that, in fact, I'd never had another choice.

In the second voice-over, however, Antonio is more aware of the consequences of his actions, and acknowledges the pain inherent in recall: "We were unstoppable, time flew by, while now, it suffocates me and forces me to remember. Here, remembering is dangerous. If you remember, you feel sick." Thus, for Antonio, the journey of remembrance is a painful return to the past and to all that he has lost, referring to the etymology of "nostalgia" itself, which implies a painful process of returning home.

Although Antonio begins his first voice-over by pointing out that he has been without Lela for fifteen years, she is not the only loss that he laments. He, like Freud's melancholic as described by Schiesari, "is dependent on loss as a means through which [he] can represent [him] self." His loss becomes "idealized," as it "empowers the ego," which focuses not on the lost object per se but on "the condition of loss *as* loss."[18] In representing Antonio's losses, *Fine pena mai* casts Antonio "as a legitimate, if not privileged, participant in the Western tradition,"[19] which is problematic given Antonio's criminal past. In the film, Antonio comes off as, in the words of the directors, "un apostolo dello sballo e dell'edonismo in un periodo di sbando, droghe e condivisione … Non è un vero criminale, ma finisce per restare ingabbiato in un personaggio da cui non sa più uscire [an apostle of getting high and of hedonism in a period of chaos, drugs and sharing … He is not a real criminal, but he ends up trapped in a personality that he does not know how to leave behind]."[20] Thus, the historical Perrone is rewritten as a pleasure seeker and a victim of chance who is unduly punished for his crimes and will be worthy of our forgiveness. The idealization of Lela in the film is pivotal in assuring that Antonio will be pardoned. Akin to Petrarch's Laura, Lela is "a representational place of loss,"[21] and "a mere pretext for a melancholic voice that needs her ensconced in the far away" so that Antonio's losses can be "monumentalized" as artistic gain.[22]

"La mia dolce Lela [my sweet Lela]"

In *Vista d'interni*, Perrone mentions Lela in eighteen different diary entries. For the most part, he writes of her heroin addiction, their conversations during her visits, her arrest and imprisonment for possession of marijuana (for which he blames himself as she is punished for being his wife), their two sons (she was pregnant with their second son Ruben at the time of Perrone's last arrest), and the cards and telegrams that he sends to her for her birthday or on the occasion of the death of her father. On a few instances, he is more sentimental and describes her smile and her laugh and a dream that he had about her in which they meet for the first time or he recounts how she has invented stories to tell Ruben so that he will love his father. However, Perrone implies that he is no longer in love with her and he states that "il nostro diventa sempre più un rapporto di amicizia ormai [our relationship is becoming more and more like a friendship]," something that he explains is "inevitable" given his prolonged incarceration.[23] The first time that Lela is mentioned, Perrone omits her name and simply calls her "mia moglie [my wife]" before describing her consumption of heroin.[24] He finally writes her abbreviated name "Lela," from Daniela, several entries later: "La mia dolce Lela ... sentì il bisogno, anche lei, di un buon nepente: il bisogno di eroina [my sweet Lela ... also felt the need for a good Nepenthe: the need for heroin]," an evocation that fundamentally unsentimentalizes their rapport.[25] Moreover, when he does describe masturbation (which references the "seghe [handjobs]" of the memoir's title,) his objects of fantasy are the flight attendants that he spied during prison transfers or old friends such as "la bella ninfomane di taglio quasi boteriana [the beautiful nymphomaniac with a body akin to a subject of a Botero painting]," and never his wife.[26] In short, unlike in the film, in the memoir Perrone's wife is anything but idealized. Instead, Perrone's descriptions of Lela are friendly and informative and frequently border on the banal.

One instance from the memoir does share affinities with the film. Perrone states that he is only capable of perceiving Lela (and another woman named Marcella, who was the girlfriend of a friend of his) "soltanto a livello mnemonico [only on the mnemonic level]," and that it is their "assenza (il non esserci, qui e ora, davanti a me) [absence (their not being there, here and now, in front of me)]," that ties the two together.[27] Akin to the tenor of this entry in the memoir, the narrative of *Fine pena mai* is structured around the absence of Lela. In the film, Lela is represented as a *donna angelicata* or "angel-like woman" who is incredibly desirable precisely because she is distant and unattainable. The *donna angelicata* is a key figure in the work of poets of the "Dolce stil novo" from the twelfth and thirteenth centuries that later surfaces in the writings of Dante and Petrarch. As explained by Cinzia Sartini Blum, she is "disembodied as she is idealized and transformed into a goal whose pursuit elevates the poet to new spiritual and intellectual heights." Her body becomes idealized and is "reduced to a composite of ... parts." Fragments of Laura's body are scattered in Petrarch's verses. As a result, we never see a "portrait of the whole individual interacting as a subject in an interpersonal love experience."[28]

In *Fine pena mai*, Lela is far from being an autonomous subject and her personality and representation morph quite frequently and dramatically. Lela is evoked as Bonnie to Antonio's Clyde, a femme fatale and a heroin addict. But she is also depicted as a traditional wife and mother and loyal companion who pre-emptively (and, as the film implies, perpetually) grieves the loss of her husband. She approximates the Lacanian *objet petit a*, the object cause of desire that sets Antonio's narration in motion. *Objet petit a* is a "symbol of lack" insofar as it is "something from which the subject, in order to constitute itself, has separated itself off as organ." Lacan insists that *objet petit a* "be an object that is, firstly, separable and, secondly, that has some relation to the lack."[29] Paradoxically, as Elizabeth Cowie argues, in signifying lack, the *objet petit a* makes something present and is in this way a *"monument* to lackingness."[30] In *Fine pena mai*, several different Lelas emerge according to the turns in Antonio's narrative. While in the memoir she is fairly "ordinary, everyday," in the film she functions similarly to the *objet petit a* as described by Žižek: she is "a kind of screen, an empty space on which the subject projects the fantasies that support his desire."[31]

For example, when Antonio's exploits take a more daring turn in the film, so too does the representation of Lela. Antonio and his partner's ascent to power in the area is represented through a rapid montage of short sequences that alternate between Lela dancing in a disco and Antonio and his friend Gianfranco, who is a wanted man, as they intimidate local gangsters and business owners with violence and threats. The sequence resolves after the pair, together with Lela, blows up a statuary factory (which we assume is punishment for refusing to pay protection money), then drive recklessly into the night while Lela shoots a gun several times into the distance. While in the past she was somewhat cautious about Antonio's criminality, here Lela takes on a central, active, and potentially lethal role in her husband's criminal activity. Techniques in the sequence such as the use of a slow-motion camera, loud music, and rapid cuts evoke Arthur Penn's *Bonnie and Clyde* (1967), another film that foregrounds violence as spectacle. This is, however, the only time that we see her active in her husband's illegal ventures (although she is shown doing drugs several times in the film).

Fine pena mai film constructs Antonio's initiation ceremony with the Sacra Corona Unita as a direct betrayal of his wife. After his first arrest in 1983, Antonio is incarcerated at the Lecce prison, where he realizes, "once inside, I needed family, something to belong to, a God." This is a crucial year for the evolution of the Mafia in Puglia, as the Sacra Corona

Unita was founded during the same year of Antonio's incarceration within the prison system of the region. While Perrone's initiation ceremony is not discussed in the memoir, it is depicted in intricate detail in the film. Antonio swears to three men, Nasino ("Vangelo [Gospel]"), L'africano ("Il Santo [the Saint]"), and Il bello ("Sgarro [slang for 'breach of the criminal code']"), that he will be "forever loyal to the righteous family of the Sacra Corona Unita." While Antonio swears "on this dagger tip drenched in blood to betray father, mother, and children up to the seventh generation and, as Saint, to be faithful forever to this Society that is composed of active, free determined men," the scene fades out three times and into a shot Lela lying on a distant floor and writhing in what appears to be agony. The sequence concludes when Antonio states, "They would be my family, forever. I became a member of the Sacra Corona Unita, Italy's fourth Mafia." Thus, when Antonio chooses his ritualized Mafia Family over his supposed soulmate, he imagines her suffering as a result of his betrayal.

Antonio's affiliation with the Sacra Corona Unita marks a dramatic turn in how Lela is depicted. The initiation ceremony is followed by a cut to Lela, who is smoking and wearing all black, with dyed black hair. She is heavily made up and is driving Antonio's red convertible and receiving money from Daniele, who is one of Antonio's friends and underlings. In earlier scenes, she is mostly dressed in white or red, her hair hangs loose around her shoulders, and she wears little make-up. In this scene, Lela's stylization is akin to that of the femme fatale and she becomes a potentially castrating character in that she is fully in control of her husband's business dealings while he is in prison. According to Mary Ann Doane, "the power accorded to the femme fatale is a function of fears linked to the notions of uncontrollable drives, the fading of subjectivity, and the loss of conscious agency."[32] This scene signifies the only occasion in the film when Antonio is not present in a flashback. Here, Lela is pure semblance, she is a projection of Antonio's fantasy at a time when he has lost all autonomy due to his affiliation with a group of men who, as we will see, will subsequently be portrayed as evil incarnate.

After Daniele takes his leave, Lela and her son Alessio become enveloped in a religious procession while seated in the convertible. During the scene, which is filmed in slow motion, numerous hooded men peer at Lela, as she grows increasingly uncomfortable. Thus, the threatening potential of Lela's representation as femme fatale is neutralized as she once again becomes the object of the collective male gaze.

In her discussion of the look and the gaze in the classical cinema, Kaja Silverman argues that the look is the most typical mode by which the male can "disburden himself of lack."[33] Woman, the object of the gaze, becomes the "site at which male insufficiency is deposited." In this signifying system, woman is a projection of male fantasy that guards against castration anxiety.[34] Antonio's anxieties regarding his alliance with a new Mafia family manifest in this novel portrayal of Lela as a fatal woman. However, and in line with the femme fatale's storyline, her traumatic potential is neutralized when she is subsumed to the look of the male. Ultimately, with the vagaries in Lela's representation, we see how, in the words of Perrone, "il ricordo è per buona parte invenzione: è un ricordare che ricordando revisiona le storie, revisiona se stessi [memory is for the most part invention: it is a type of remembering that, when remembering, revises stories, revises the self]."[35]

The Sacra Corona Unita, an "absolute evil"

Antonio's reminiscences in *Fine pena mai* can be divided into two time periods: before and after his association with the Sacra Corona Unita. While the mood of the first grouping of recollections is for the most part cheerful and adventurous, the tone of those belonging to the second is disheartening, bitter, and sarcastic. Up until his first arrest, Antonio's life of crime, and that of his associates, is glamorized. The film initially presents a romanticized view of criminality: there is minimal bloodshed and Antonio, Gianfranco, and his two unnamed companions, who are possibly based on Perrone's childhood friends Pinuccio and Alfredo, are depicted as good-natured, generally non-violent, and pleasure seeking. To be sure, there are only two deaths in the film, the significance of which I will discuss shortly. Antonio, a self-described "guru of high pleasure," is addicted to life in the fast lane and spends his time doing drugs and celebrating small-time heists in local clubs. After the group watches *Scarface* (Brian De Palma, 1983), they internalize the film's moral lesson "the world is ours," take to the streets, and take over in an attempt to emulate Tony Montana, an imitative strategy that we also see at work in Garrone's *Gomorra* (I go into more detail on this in the following chapter). Gangsters in both films look towards Hollywood for models upon which to base gangsteresque behaviour. In fact, in *Fine pena mai*, Gianfranco calls Antonio "Tonio montagna di coca [Tony, mountain of coke]," a clear reference to De Palma's protagonist. Antonio is similar to Henry Hill in Martin Scorsese's *Goodfellas* (1990):

like Hill, Antonio is, to quote Fulvio Orsitto, "only capable of basing his actions on purely hedonistic impulses."[36] During their ascent to power, both characters lack in insight. As Antonio conveys in the voice-over discussed earlier, he felt that his life was speeding by and that he did not have any choices. Essentially, Antonio's drug addiction made him greedy, but the film never implies that he was intrinsically a bad person. On the contrary, he comes off as a man with a moral code and an ingrained sense of guilt.

Antonio's humanity is primarily foregrounded through the development of his friendships with Gianfranco and Daniele, who are notably the only people killed in the film. In *Vista d'interni*, Perrone notes that with the former he had developed an "amicizia virile che cresceva con l'aumento del rischio [virile friendship that grew stronger with higher risks],"[37] and the homosocial undercurrents of their relationship surface in the film when Antonio watches with fascination as Gianfranco swims in the ocean. Perrone explains that Gianfranco is shot, arrested, incarcerated, and eventually dies from a drug overdose after his release. Once out of prison, Perrone writes that "la nostra vecchia amicizia si era già inaridita da tempo, per una lunga serie di ragioni: troppe cose fra me e lui non erano andate come dovevano andare [our old friendship had already dried up a while ago for several reasons: too many things between us did not go as they should have]," and that Gianfranco's body was eventually found "gonfio e livido, in fondo a un canale [swollen and bruised at the bottom of a canal]."[38] Nowhere in the memoir does Perrone express despair at his friend's premature death.

In *Fine pena mai*, Gianfranco is gunned down by the police off-camera in broad daylight in the empty train station of the imaginary town of Solino.[39] An extreme aerial long shot of what appears to be his lifeless body is followed by a sequence that is meant to convey Antonio's sorrow at the death of his friend. First, he sits in his car looking despondently out to sea. He then races up a lighthouse tower staircase and gazes out the window. Then, a shot of the moon glistening on the waves transitions to three shots of Gianfranco swimming deep in the dark ocean with his body illuminated. All of a sudden, he extends his arms and goes limp, at which time his body, in the form of a cross, begins to float upwards towards a bright light that pierces the ocean's surface. We then return to Antonio, who appears grief-stricken.

The rewriting of Gianfranco's death is telling. In an interview, Conte explains that Gianfranco has "una grande voglia di vivere che poi però la vita, il destino, quello che lui si è costruito in qualche modo glielo impedisce. Intanto che arriva al momento della morte in qualche modo quasi consapevolmente [a strong will to live, but then life, destiny, what he made for himself, will not let him. The fact is, he approaches death almost consciously]."[40] In fact, in an earlier scene, Gianfranco is shown on a rooftop, his arms extended so as to recall Christ on the cross, under a brooding sky, as we hear the non-diegetic sound of a policeman questioning Antonio about Gianfranco's whereabouts. As the policeman talks, there are two jumpcuts of low-angle shots of Gianfranco as he looks skyward, each from a slightly different angle. The effect is disorienting, but also works to draw our attention to Gianfranco's Christ-like pose, which alerts us to his eventual death and, it is implied, martyrdom. Antonio mourns Gianfranco, and implicit in Antonio's requiem is an iconography of redemption; in Antonio's phantasmatic projection, his friend will be saved.

This move towards commemoration is telling in that it speaks to Antonio's melancholia. Schiesari writes that "for those who see themselves as disempowered, loss is imbued with nostalgia." For the male melancholic, the articulation of loss is an "aesthetic ... project that continually derealizes the feminine by recasting loss in terms of a golden age."[41] The rewriting of Gianfranco's death underlines the phallocentrism of Antonio's recollections while further humanizing Antonio and lending a note of tragedy to his story.[42] According to Conte, Gianfranco represents "un pezzo di generazione che è caduta [a part of a generation that has fallen]" due to the onslaught of criminality in Puglia during the early 1980s.[43] Thus, his death is universalized. What's more, we do not see him being shot and are led to believe that he was gunned down at point blank range (in the memoir, Perrone writes that he was "sparato a vista [shot on sight]" by a policeman).[44] Like Antonio, Gianfranco is cast as a victim of destiny who merits absolution, and as we will see, his death signals the end of Antonio's "golden age."

If, in the film, Gianfranco is meant to represent Puglia's corrupted youth culture, the members of the Sacra Corona Unita, save Antonio, are portrayed as "archetipi del male [archetypes of evil]."[45] Antonio's induction into the Sacra Corona Unita marks a shift in the film's tone. Once he is released from prison in the fall of 1987, Antonio has retractable grilles installed on all his windows, which makes his home appear carceral and claustrophobic. Gone are the earlier ebullient bacchanalias complete with drugs, dancing, and male bonding. Instead, Antonio and Lela do drugs in their darkened home, and social gatherings between Antonio, Nasino, L'africano, Il bello, and their female companions are tense and rivalries run high. In earlier memories, the evocation of the film *Scarface* occasioned a raucous adventure. However, when Antonio tells a story that includes mention of the film to Nasino, the latter becomes incensed, as he assumes that Antonio is belittling him.

Fine pena mai implies that Antonio and his cohorts' adventures in small-time crime are certainly enjoyable and essentially harmless (recall that they are not responsible for any deaths in the film), which is not the case with the Sacra Corona Unita, whose membership is almost exclusively beyond redemption, as is made clear in the staging of Daniele's murder. In the memoir, Daniele let it be known throughout Mafia circles that Nasino's power was in jeopardy and, as a result, Nasino was at risk of being eliminated. As punishment for spreading those rumours, he is murdered by two of Nasino's men, named Tizzone and Giorgio. Both shoot him in the face at night in front of Perrone who was not expecting the assassination and responds by leaning against a tree and vomiting. He adds: "ero così preoccupato per la mia pellaccia da non essere neppure in grado di provare il benché minimo dispiacere [I was so worried about my own skin that I wasn't able to feel even the smallest amount of grief]."[46] And this is not the only time that Perrone admits to his lack of compassion. Later, when contemplating the suicide of an inmate in his ward, which consists of only thirty cells, he says that he is unable to love his neighbour as he loves himself. Perrone finds the suffering of others "banali [banal]" and "grottesche [grotesque]" and states that the one time that he attempted to imagine universal suffering as a means to become "un mostro d'amore come il Cristo in croce [a monster of love like Christ on the cross]" he only rediscovered "la pochezza del [suo] cuore [the smallness of (his) heart]."[47]

In *Fine pena mai*, Daniele attracts Nasino's wrath as the former paid for Antonio, Nasino, L'africano, and Il bello's dinner, a gesture which Nasino finds disrespectful and prompts him to invent a story that involves Daniele stealing hundreds of thousands of lira. So, hoping to save Daniele, Antonio tells him to sell all the drugs provided by Nasino or to make good on the debt. During this encounter, Antonio is emotionally distraught, and after Daniele takes his leave, Antonio covers his face with his hand and sobs for the first and only time in the film. This reaction recalls Modleski's point that, in the male weepie, "real men do not cry, or at best they shed only a few hard-wrung tears; others do the crying for them – usually women and people of color."[48] Antonio's tearful response to his friend's portended demise renders him vulnerable and elicits our sympathies.

Daniele is murdered by Il bello in broad daylight in the middle of a large whitewashed quarry in front of L'africano and Antonio. Il bello shoots him first in the head and then twice in the stomach at close range. Antonio is visibly distressed and yells "What the fuck are you doing," then, as Antonio nearly collapses against a nearby car, Il bello points the gun in Antonio's direction and feigns shooting him. This sequence consolidates Antonio's relatively higher ethical ground, while further vilifying the Mafia. Earlier in the film, Daniele is described by Antonio as "il migliore [the best]," and his death, the only one that is visualized in *Fine pena mai*, is meant to stand for, in the words of Conte, "tutte le morti che ci sono state in questa terra [all the deaths in this land]." Il bello, L'africano, and Nasino are constructed as "il male assoluto [absolute evil]," and the film proposes a binary model that positions Antonio on the side of not necessarily the just, but certainly as endowed with compassion, introspection, and remorse.[49]

"Castellare" – Paradise Regained

In the scene following the murder, the group attends a birthday party for Nasino's wife Rosaria at the same discotheque frequented by Antonio and his friends more than a decade earlier. Antonio appears inconsolable as he watches a group of three teenagers playing pinball, an interaction that recalls an earlier moment in the film when Antonio and Daniele are playing the same game while celebrating the gang's successes at what appears to be the same club. This parallel foregrounds Antonio's nostalgia and reveals how much he has lost due to his affiliation with the Sacra Corona Unita. When Rosaria blows out her candles, Nasino makes a toast: "cento di questi giorni [may you live a hundred years]," which inaugurates Antonio's voice-over: "We were gods, we were immortal, we were finished." His words allude not only to Antonio's arrest in the subsequent scene, but also to the supposed end of the Sacra Corona Unita, which, according to Conte, is a thing of the past:

> Oggi è quindi possibile raccontare quelle vicende ... dopo anni di omertosa rimozione, alla ricerca della dolorosa memoria collettiva di quella parte di generazione colpita senza senso dall'eroina e dalle stragi, dai lutti familiari e dalla dissoluzione degli affetti. Proprio la capacità di ricordare è il percorso che tenterà di capire e dissociarsi dal proprio passato per rinascere [Today it is possible to recount those events ... after years of

them being repressed by *omertà*, so as to search for a painful collective memory of that part of a generation struck senseless by heroin, massacres, mourning of family members and the dissolution of affection. The capacity to remember is the path towards understanding and disassociating oneself from the past in order to be born again.][50]

In *Fine pena mai*, the Sacra Corona Unita comes across as a momentary blight on the Apulian landscape, much like, as discussed in the previous chapter, it does in Winspeare's *Galantuomini*. The key difference between the two films that treat the Mafia of Puglia, however, lies in how they gender blame. In Winspeare's film, Lucia is far from absolved and she is positioned as the scapegoat for the sins of an entire region. However, in the post-Mafia landscape espoused by Conte above, the faculty of memory is redeeming, and *Fine pena mai* certainly insinuates that Antonio understands his wrong doings and will be "born again" at the film's finale.

Depicting a criminal in a sentimental light in the cinema is nothing new, especially in the Hollywood gangster tradition, where American filmmakers tend to, as I have argued elsewhere, "glamorize organized crime, and create sympathetic mobsters that many of us would like to invite over to dinner."[51] Such a poignant representation of Mafia perpetrators, however, is anomalous in the Italian tradition, especially in films made since the year 2000, in which compassion is usually aligned with those fallen in the battle against the Mafia, and this is the case of *I cento passi*, Placido Rizzotto, *L'uomo di vetro*, or *Fortapàsc* (*Fort Apache*, Marco Risi, 2009). As we saw in earlier chapters, women perpetrators in Italian new millennium Mafia movies are far from redeemed: in *Angela*, the title character's melancholy is "pathological." She is similar to female melancholics, "who by lack of a husband" (and I would add Mafia family) "are more alienated from the phallic economy." As we see at the film's end, the protagonist lapses "into inarticulateness and can no longer find a place in the symbolic order's prime system: language."[52] In *Galantuomini*, Lucia is constructed as a castrating figure who is punished through rape and is then absorbed into a conventional love story before finally leaving for an unknown destination. In the end, and similarly to Angela, it is implied that she will live in a state of exile.

The melancholic described by Freud experiences a "delusional expectation of punishment,"[53] and this is certainly the case with Angela, who is incapable of moving beyond her losses. (Recall that instead of engaging with the potentially productive process of mourning, she internalizes a series of losses that she cannot work through, such as those of her lover, her husband, her daughter, and her Mafia kinship group.) Instead, Antonio's melancholy is restorative, which recalls the redemptive pith of Milton's *Paradise Lost*, a shared ethos that evokes the full title of Barletti and Conte's film: *Fine pena mai: Paradise perduto* (*Paradise Lost*). The historical Perrone, however, is still imprisoned, and will be for quite some time, and has long ago lost all hope for an eventual release and, at least while writing the memoir, for a reprieve of 41bis.

Several times in the memoir, Perrone mentions the prison pastime "castellare," which is a neologism deriving from "castello [castle]." He explains that the expression means "I) stare ... in desiderosa attesa di un qualche risultato o evento favorevole (spesso improbabile) II) raffigurare, rappresentare con la mente, con la fantasia qualcosa d'irreale III) bramare, desiderare ardentemente, vagheggiare ritorni da favola [I) desirously awaiting some favourable result or event (that is, frequently improbably); II) to depict, to represent in the mind and in fantasy something fantastic; III) to long for, to ardently desire, to yearn for a comeback]."[54] For quite some time, Perrone is incapable of daydreaming, and of seeing himself in any type of future, and he concludes the memoir by declaring that he has been unable to transcend the prison walls in his mind's eye for some time now, not even while dreaming.

If *Vista d'interni* presents prison life as a regulated system of discipline that represses Perrone's vision, *Fine pena mai* suggests that Antonio's confinement is spiritually rehabilitating. The film concludes in September of 2007 with Antonio's final voice-over. As he speaks – "This was my end, ours, our children's. Because you are all still there today, far away, and you're still paying the price of this end with me" – we see footage of the real-life Daniela Piccinno, Alessio Perrone, and Ruben Perrone driving in a car at night.[55] As Antonio explains the terms of his punishment, we enter into an abandoned cell one last time before the camera moves outside to follow a country road that leads us to the seaside. Antonio tells us that, although he is no longer a member of the Sacra Corona Unita, he never became a *pentito* and is still imprisoned under 41bis (his tenure under 41bis actually ended in 2006 and he will be released from prison in 2018). We then see aerial shots of horses running in a field, the sun setting over the ocean, and, finally, when we cut to a lighthouse on the horizon, Antonio finishes his letter in voice-over: "Dear Lela, writing to you gave me the illusion that one day I'll be able to hold you in my arms again. Once I made a promise to you: that I would never leave you alone. I couldn't keep it." As he speaks, the camera gradually approaches the lighthouse before leaving the coastline and travelling across the ocean towards the setting sun.

In this regenerative finale, Antonio departs the island prison and travels towards Paradise. Unlike Perrone in the memoir, he is able to "castellare" and his privileged and final object of fantasy is the lighthouse, a structure that is present in two other scenes: once in the sequence following Gianfranco's death and also, quite early in the film, when Antonio and Lela discuss their future while atop a lighthouse. In this scene, Antonio is disconsolate and appears somewhat envious as he tells Lela that a group of his friends from college are leaving for India, a place, he explains, that is "beyond the sea." "Instead, we're here," he states with resignation as an eyeline match reveals a boat heading eastward. Lela counters, "And here what's missing, Tonio?" His response, "nothing," implies that he stays in Puglia for her. Thus, while later in the film the lighthouse is associated with Antonio's grief and Gianfranco's salvation, here it is linked to Antonio's sacrificial gesture that leads to his life of crime and eventual imprisonment.

At the film's conclusion, Antonio, like Gianfranco before him, is finally able to journey past the lighthouse and leave behind his criminal past and association with the Mafia so as to start anew. Antonio's reminiscences contribute to the "painful collective memory," in Barletti and Conte's words, that is born out of the supposed defeat of the Sacra Corona Unita. Hence, the organization's traumatic potential is neutralized while its activities are confined to a specific historical period, which again recalls the Sacra Corona Unita as it is represented in *Galantuomini*. Ultimately, all of Antonio's losses are recuperated when, quoting Schiesari, his "desire for a transcendent relation with the world" materializes at the film's close. And, while *Fine pena mai* legitimates Antonio's "'excessive' suffering, even in his 'femininity,'" woman remains "an oppressed and nameless (or generic) other,"[56] much like she does in the story of Ulysses: both men depart the island (Asinara and Calypso's) in an effort to consolidate the male self at the detriment of the feminine. In the end, and to recall the plight of Angela in Torre's film, Lela is an empty vessel who (both on and offscreen when we consider that Daniela Piccinno and her two sons make a cameo appearance at the film's close) will pay the price in perpetuity for Antonio's transgressions.

8 Mourning Disavowed: Matteo Garrone's *Gomorra*

Women are always a part of clan power dynamics.

Robert Saviano, *Gomorra*, 137

We don't touch women.

Gomorra (Matteo Garrone)

How does the prohibition on grieving emerge as a circumscription on representability, so that our national melancholia becomes tightly fitted into the frame for what can be said, for what can be shown? This derealization of loss ... becomes the mechanism through which dehumanization is accomplished. The derealization takes place neither inside nor outside the image, but through the very framing by which the image is contained.

Judith Butler, *Precarious Life*, 148

The Liminal Status of Mafia Women

Matteo Garrone's internationally acclaimed hit *Gomorra* (2008) signals a new direction in Italian Mafia movies, in terms of both generic approach and style. *Gomorra* is unlike most other Mafia movies from the new millennium that frequently conform to the genre of melodrama, broadly considered. Instead, *Gomorra* presents an "anthropological gaze"[1] at mob life. The film's rough and crude exposé of the Camorra's violent underworld in and around Neopolitan clan strongholds of Scampia and Secondagliano departs from Roberto Saviano's best-selling and eponymous book from 2006, which sold more than ten million copies worldwide and has been translated into over fifty languages. Unlike Saviano's overt work of denunciation or other recent films that treat the Mafia of Campania, such as Antonio and Andrea Frazzis' *Certi bambini*

(*A Children's Story*, 2004) and Vincenzo Marra's *Vento di terra* (*Wind of the Earth*, 2004), Garrone's film is almost entirely without judgment. The church, various social services, and the military are presented as viable, yet not necessarily lucrative or desirable, options to mob life for the young characters in the two other films. Such institutions are absent in *Gomorra*, as the pull of the Camorra and all that it offers in terms of respect, community, and alternative Family is too strong.

Garrone lived on site in Scampia for three months before he commenced filming. He looked at the inner workings of Camorra clans from within their own homes, he cast Camorristi both as extras and in more central roles, and he turned to them for advice on how to properly film a drug deal. Furthermore, Garrone frequently uses a handheld camera that follows characters at close range, to then suddenly veer off track, a technique that allows the spectator to glimpse a drug deal, a wedding procession, or a woman walking with her children. The representation of these slices of life emphasizes the mundane regularity of quotidian existence in a community that, by most standards, would be considered a war zone. We learn at the end of the film that the Camorra is responsible for 4000 deaths in the last three decades, or approximately one mortality almost every three days. In short, Garrone presents a snippet of Mafia life *in medias res*, and the viewer is left with the idea that things have been this way for quite some time and that mob business will only continue to develop and grow stronger. Despite governmental efforts in 2008 to wage a war on the Camorra by sending some 500 soldiers to the region, the general panorama of criminal activity will no doubt remain unchanged.[2] The city of Naples does not feature in the film at all and the peripheral Campanian locales where much of the narrative unfolds seem surreal lands lost in time. Hence, Garrone suggests that, despite its recent moment in the media spotlight, the social, economic, and political underpinnings of Camorra ethos and practice will be unaffected, and soon, like Cosa Nostra before it, business will be back to normal with the public eye directed elsewhere.

Gomorra consists of five interwoven stories that are loosely based on Saviano's book. These narratives offer a dark and troubling denunciation of the daily goings on and international reach of the Camorra. Garrone adapted storylines that expose the diverse means by which the organization turns a profit, while simultaneously disclosing patterns of violence and corruption that have allowed the Camorra to flourish for hundreds of years.[3] The first story focuses on Don Ciro, "the submarine," who is responsible for delivering weekly payments to families of imprisoned or murdered Camorristi. Maria, one of his clients and friends, is cut off when her young son becomes a *scissionista*, meaning he defected from the local clan and is involved in waging war on the home front. In the conclusion of this second storyline, Maria is mercilessly murdered after being tricked by Totò, a boy who looks to her as a mother figure but betrays her trust in order to move up the mob hierarchy. The next story involves Marco and Ciro, two teenage renegade boys who are obsessed with and attempt to emulate Hollywood images of the Mafioso. Their repeated disregard for the local mob boss results in their brutal murder that closes the film. The story of the "stakeholder" Franco, who for a pittance buys land in the region which he then systematically and illegally fills with toxic waste, and his young and eventually rebellious protégé Roberto (a clear reference to Saviano) sheds light into the eco-Mafia and its ties to international politics and big business (the term "eco-Mafia" refers to organized crime networks that engage in activities that harm the environment such as toxic dumping). The final story focuses on Pasquale, a master-tailor who labours extended hours in sweatshop conditions, yet who is never credited for his sartorial creations that end up in haute couture salons. This narrative touches on the Camorra's international control of and penetration into legitimate business.

In its almost entirely male cast, *Gomorra* might seem an unlikely subject of study regarding how female characters render problematic the national grieving process with regards to the Mafia. In fact, Maria is the only female character who has any substantial dialogue in the film (meaning more than just a few lines total). In a movie lasting 130 minutes, women characters, most of whom are extras, occupy only twenty minutes of screen time. It is striking that out of the film's eight more central protagonists, Maria is the only one completely invented by the director. All the others, to varying degrees, appear in Saviano's exposé. Moreover, she is the only character in the film who connects two of the five subplots, that of Totò and Don Ciro. Why did Garrone invent her? And, more to the point, why did he kill her off in such a violent and abrupt manner? Is her death purely sensationalist, or is it meant to function in metonymic fashion for the state of Mafia women at large? I will show that, despite her limited screen presence, Maria perfectly encapsulates the condition of a *donna di mafia* [Mafia woman]. Her life and the staging of her death allow insight into several aspects of ritualized violence in a Mafia milieu, such as initiation ceremonies, mourning rites, the price of life, and the symbolic import of *lupara bianca*, which is a type of Mafia-related killing where the body disappears. Maria's death towards the end of the film is shocking and powerful, but also peculiar as her execution is staged so as to be quickly forgotten and is then displaced onto other narrative threads and other international traumas. In consequence, the viewer is not invited to contemplate her death, which, to borrow from Judith Butler, proves ungrievable. Butler writes: "One way of posing the question of who 'we' are in these times of war is by asking whose lives are considered valuable, whose lives are mourned, and whose lives are considered ungrievable."[4] As a woman with ties to the Mafia, Maria's status is ambiguous. As such, the film suggests that it is unnecessary to mourn her passing, which is a process that, if undertaken, could lead to an understanding of her precariousness and potentially to a national awareness of the endemic Mafia problem. Here, I recall Butler's discussion of how the release of images of children "burning and dying from napalm" during the Vietnam War prompted an understanding in the United States of the precariousness of life which led to civil resistance against the war.[5]

Maria lays bare and throws into question the authority crisis, itself a symbolic identity crisis, that all inducted Mafiosi are presumed to undergo. That is, the paternal father, representative of civilization and charged with keeping all socially unacceptable drives in check, foremost in the case of the Mafia the death drive, is cast aside in favour of a symbolic father who not only encourages but outright demands that the son break social taboos. This is a symbolic rite of passage accepted in the community at large that is not to be questioned, let alone mentioned. Divided between a new Mafia Family and a symbolic mother in Maria, Totò chooses the former, and his matricidal gesture ensures his status as a made man. We will see that, in the words of Teresa De Lauretis, "cinema works for Oedipus" and Maria's death assures narrative closure and completes Totò's Oedipal trajectory.[6]

The Law of Mafia Fathers

In the chapter "Women," Saviano tells us that "women are always a part of clan power dynamics."[7] This is true with Maria, although she is only present in six very brief scenes, and takes up about five minutes of screen time. Entrenched in darkness, kept under surveillance, and confined to a small, dark, and dilapidated apartment in the crumbling 1960s era housing project "le Vele" in the Camorra stronghold of Scampia, Maria's condition in many ways encapsulates the sense of incarceration felt by women who live daily under the Mafia's shadow (e.g., as voiced in Rita Atria's diaries).[8] Maria aptly embodies the ambiguous status of many Mafia women's "submerged centrality."[9] She is not necessarily innocent, as she is obviously aware of the daily ins and outs of Mafia commerce in le Vele and her husband is an imprisoned Camorrista. However, she cannot be categorized as a perpetrator, as is the case with many other women involved in the Camorra. Whereas, with few exceptions, the Cosa Nostra and the 'Ndrangheta specifically exclude women from overt involvement in mob business, this is not true for the Camorra and the Sacra Corona Unita. As Felia Allum argues, women "take on active, formal roles" in the Camorra. Some women have leadership roles and others are involved in everything from drug running to murder.[10] In *Gomorra*, women are active in various criminal activities such as being present at the clan murder that opens the film, counting money, or working as drivers for local bosses. Maria, like many women with family ties to the clan, knows, but does not, and cannot, reveal mob secrets. She is intrinsically invisible, and must pledge silent and blind obedience to an organization that by nature excludes her yet upon which she is completely dependent.[11] Therein lies her precariousness: once her son violates Mafia codes, her life becomes meaningless, and she is murdered even though she has done nothing wrong. What's more, her killer will be rewarded instead of punished for the crime. Maria's condition approaches Giorgio Agamben's definition of *Homo Sacer* – someone who is excluded from the state yet is at its mercy as he or she may be done away with without penalty. Agamben argues: "The fundamental categorical pair of Western politics is not that of friend/enemy but that of bare life / political existence, *zoe/bios*, exclusion/inclusion."[12] At the whim of the Mafia, human, qualified, political life (*bios*) in *Gomorra* is transformed into bare life (*zoe*).

When Maria is introduced in the film, she appears to be one of several residents of le Vele with an ordinary life, complete with family and friends. She is first shot in a light-filled kitchen surrounded by several people who are pleasantly enjoying the afternoon. Her friendship with Totò is quickly established when he brings her groceries and the two engage in jovial conversation. This is one of the few cheerful moments in the film, and the upbeat mood is furthered by a cut to an aerial shot of a group of children playing in an inflatable pool on one of the building's terraces. The macabre, however, looms large over the community, as evidenced by a zoom out that reveals the presence of several armed Camorristi soldiers who patrol the rooftops in order to alert clan members if the carabinieri enter the neighbourhood.

However, any sense of ease present in the earlier scene dissipates when an anti-parallel is established between Totò and Maria. Totò's attraction to and involvement with the Camorra take him outside, in the streets, and more than with any other character, the viewer is positioned to see the world through his eyes: he is routinely shot with a handheld camera that pursues him at close distance on his journey through the Campanian wasteland, and frequent eyeline matches and point-of-view shots reveal his keen interest in gang life on the streets. Totò's gaze is undoubtedly privileged in *Gomorra*. For example, Totò takes part in a shocking and archaic recruitment ritual to prove his manhood during which a group of boys watch as, one by one, each potential recruit dons a worn and ragged bulletproof vest and is then led into a dark cave. There, each boy is shot square in the chest at point-blank range. Garrone stages the scene so that the gun aimed at the twelve- and thirteen-year-old recruits is also directed towards the viewer: we are meant to feel Totò's fear, anxiety, relief, and, eventually, his pride when he examines the bruise left by the bullet and realizes that his passage to manhood is well under way. Totò is on the way to passing through the Lacanian mirror stage, and the ritual implies "the assumption of the armour of an alienating identity, which will mark with its rigid structure the subject's entire mental development."[13]

By contrast, Maria is mainly filmed in her dimly lit apartment, where she appears trapped and is enveloped by shadow and darkness. The few times that she does look out the window, the camera does not follow her gaze and we are not positioned to identify with her or see the world through her eyes. Totò's increased activity is countered by Maria's festering captivity. For example, when Totò recovers drugs for the local clan and thereby earns the trust of its members, we see him climbing walls, running across the street, and entering and exiting buildings. During the following scene, which marks Maria's second appearance in the film, Don Ciro delivers her weekly stipend and helps her with a plumbing problem. Unlike in her earlier encounter with Totò, here her face is barely visible and her apartment is cast in shadow. Soon thereafter, her son abandons both his mother (his blood family or agnatic kinship group) and his father (his Mafia Family) and he joins with the scissionisti (who are his blood brotherhood established through ritual friendship).[14] At this point, Maria is further ostracized and is eventually condemned to death as she is loyal to her son, and hence chooses "family" over "Family," even though her own son already made the opposite choice. Garrone suggests early on, then, that Maria's growing ostracism is inversely linked with Totò's absorption with and acceptance into gang life. Thus, as is de rigueur in mob life, masculine values and the male viewpoint are consolidated at the expense of the feminine. Totò's greater visibility renders Maria invisible, and as she fades into the shadows, her life is deemed less important.

Within the economy of the film, Maria is an easy target to avenge the death of low-ranking Camorrista Gaetano, resident of le Vele whom her son presumably killed. She lives alone, is unprotected, and refuses to abandon her home, a decision that leaves her at risk in the lion's den. In an earlier scene, however, Garrone suggests that it is not only Maria's vulnerability that facilitates her murder, but also her ambiguity and resistance. At first glance, it appears that she conforms to the gender roles demanded by Mafia culture, such as silence, subservience, and the inculcation of a Mafia ethos in her children. However, in a discussion with Ciro regarding the Mafia feud and her son's role in it, she subtly critiques blind obedience, ritualized murder, and clanship, all central to the Mafia hierarchy. In this, the third scene where Maria is present, she beseeches Ciro to help her to comprehend her son's recent betrayal. Here, she is shot almost entirely in the dark, and her unlit profile stands in dramatic opposition to the bleached-out walls of the only other of le Vele's buildings still standing that are visible from her window. When Ciro confidently attempts to assure Maria that her son will come back into the fold, she is not convinced, and asks him: "Do you see what's happening? There are killings every day." When Ciro brings up her husband, she wonders: "When he gets out, what'll he do? Father and son will kill each other?" Maria's viewpoint stands in opposition to the frequent discussions in *Gomorra* that are infused with wartime rhetoric such as, "We're at war, people are dying every day," "We were friends and now we're not," or "This side is the right one." Maria also condemns the oversimplified us versus them taxonomy at the heart of Mafia turf wars. In fact, this exchange represents one of the only two moments of resistance in the film. The other, which is much more blatant, comes near the film's end when Roberto stands up to Franco, and denounces his exploitation of local farmers and the resulting toxic pollution that is overtaking the countryside. However, as one critic notes, this "hopeless, romantic, quixotic gesture" comes off as more of an appendix than a coherent part of the film's diegesis.[15]

Maria brings up potential patricide and filicide, and thus makes overt and even hyperbolizes the traditional process by which a man is made in the Mafia: he must repress all feminine qualities within himself and rebel against the law of the father in order to enter into an organization that is essentially female in nature, dubbed the "mammasantissima" or the "most holy of mothers," and ruled by its own law, the "law of the lupara."[16] In voicing the unsayable and verbally rebelling against her proscribed gender role, Maria stands out, becomes dangerous, and must be contained. In sum, Totò is compelled to eradicate one mother figure who might have acted as a positive role model so as to serve another who blatantly encourages the death drive.

Once her son deserts her, Maria becomes a prisoner in her unlit apartment that resembles a bunker. She only briefly steps outside her doorway twice: first to beseech Don Ciro for help and then to answer Totò's fatal call. Both times, she is shot in shallow focus (both Don Ciro and her killer are in focus), a technique that underlines her liminal status. Maria refuses to leave her home, as she imagines doing so would mean abandoning her son, and she overtly and publicly denounces Camorra politics by screaming to Ciro just outside of her house in plain view of everyone, "Tell those friends of yours I'm not leaving, tell those nice people I won't betray my son and I'm not leaving from here!" Thus, her fatal flaw is choosing her son (consanguinity) over her ritualized Family, the Family that governs over le Vele and upon which she is financially dependent and, more to the point, upon which her life depends.

Maria's liminality is underlined when she is depicted as in an animalistic state through a parallel that is created between her and her pet monkey Silvana. The first few times that we enter into Maria's apartment, Silvana is in a cage in the foyer, and Totò plays with her. Later, however, Maria locks her away in the storeroom in the dark, which puzzles Totò, who claims that she is "just an animal," a comment whose irony only becomes apparent after Totò's deception. To be sure, many Mafia neophytes are asked early in life to kill animals, as the act declares their ruthlessness and proves their suitability for a gangster lifestyle. For example, Roberto Faenza's *Alla luce del sole* (*In the Light of the Sun*, 2005), which narrates the life of Father Giuseppe Puglisi, who was murdered by the Mafia on his fifty-sixth birthday, opens on a disturbing scene in which young Mafia recruits feed kittens to dogs soon to be entered in dogfights and thus establishes the Mafia as diabolical. Instead, Totò is asked straightaway to orchestrate the execution of a woman who is a mother figure to him. Targets of Mafia violence are frequently made inhuman by assailants for two central reasons: for one, to further the punishment, depriving the victim of any human rites before death; and, on a more practical level, to alleviate any potential sense of guilt that might plague the assassin. Anton Blok discusses how ritualized violence, such as creating "special" animal names for victims, sets "them apart from ordinary people and remove[s] them from the moral community." The dehumanization of victims is a way for the assailant "to avoid moral responsibility for killing 'fellow' human beings."[17] The animalization of Maria foreshadows her cold-blooded execution and gives prominence to her precariousness and new clanless state.

Narrative Fetishism

Although Maria's murder is staged as an intricate negotiation between Totò and four senior members of a small gang belonging to the local district clan, it is actually a fait accompli. Eager to shed blood and to "rack up corpses," the group decides to take matters into its own hands and thus breaks with the typical protocol that would demand that they wait for orders from those higher up in the gang hierarchy. Their decision also reflects contemporary attitudes regarding who is fair game in vendetta killings. Up until the 1980s, women and children were for the most part off-limits. Maria's murder demonstrates the Mafia's attitude towards what Siebert defines as "the price of life." She explains: "The amount of money in circulation, which has been hugely increased by drug trafficking, has meant a dizzying drop in the price of life."[18] Maria's murder demonstrates how death warrants are quickly dispersed without much negotiation or forethought in a lucrative climate that has benefitted from a booming drug trade.

When one member brings up Maria's possible complicity with Gaetano's murder, another Camorrista counters "le donne non si toccano [we do not touch women]," a phrase that another man quickly repeats. One man is constructed as the obvious leader of the group: after the camera pans to his cohorts' apprehensive faces, it repeatedly captures his head, which is positioned on the right side of the frame, in a low-angle close-up. This man quickly convinces the others to follow his lead, and he demands Totò's assistance. They explain to Totò that he is the only one Maria trusts, and that he is the only one capable of luring her out of her apartment. Totò, who is primarily shot in shallow focus during the majority of this exchange, is now on centre stage, forced to choose between his symbolic mother and his larger symbolic Family. The scene is staged so as to heighten viewer involvement in Totò's plight and to foreground his moral dilemma. The boy is delivered a back-handed death threat by his new leader: "Either you're with us or against us. One or the other. If you're against us, you can't leave from here because we don't trust you." However, his established relationship with Maria together with his obvious reticence to carry out his part in the execution instils a sense of hope in the viewer and we are prompted to believe that Totò might break from what appears to be his tragic destiny. Totò is then shown walking towards Maria's apartment and banging on her door, imploring her to open because he has something important to tell her. At this point, we are still unsure as to Totò's motivation: will he warn Maria of the upcoming attempt on her life, or is he complicit with her assassins? Totò hastily walks away, and a moment later, Maria exits the apartment and is immediately gunned down from behind. In sum, Totò has made his choice and his passage to manhood is complete.

The staging of Maria's death is quite telling for several reasons. Her murder, although powerful in its condemnation of Totò, is downplayed in the film. Her shooting in the head is immediately followed by a cut to an extreme aerial long shot of the apartment building, where, a few seconds later, we see police and passersby scoping out the crime scene. This take is remarkably similar in composition to the earlier aerial view of le Vele that follows the first interaction between Maria and Totò. We do not see Maria fall and die; we are not allowed to contemplate her death. And I would suggest that the same is true within the economy of the film. In the end, Maria was essentially clanless, and no one can mourn her; not her son, not her neighbours, and least of all not her husband. Maria's death then is symbolically in line with death by *lupara bianca*, one aim of which is to humiliate the family by depriving its members of the basic rite to bury, and therefore to properly grieve, the dead. Anton Blok discusses the *lupara bianca* as "the elimination of opponents without leaving any traces. This more recent and rather unceremonious form of liquidation still permits mourning but excludes funeral rites and, therefore, underscores desecration and humiliation."[19]

The shot following Maria's murder is perfectly composed, with the two remaining buildings of le Vele in deep focus and the structure on the left framed to resemble a cruise ship that eerily dominates the Scampian badlands.[20] Such balanced and surreal arrangements in terms of space and colour palate are recurrent in *Gomorra*. Other examples include when Roberto and Franco arise from the bowels of the abandoned gas station as if from the dead, the aerial shot that depicts children who are recruited to drive the trucks full of toxic waste to the dump site, and the Dali-esque composition following the attempt on Pasquale's life.

In fact, Garrone was trained as a painter and when writing the script "worked from images."[21] *Gomorrah* has been discussed in terms of a "return to reality,"[22] and Mauro Gervasini put the film forth with Paolo Sorrentino's film *Il divo* (2008) as cinematographic examples of the New Italian Epic, a genre that has at its core ethical commitment.[23] Still, the staging of Maria's death is far from non-realist, which, as Maureen Turim explains, is the most effective mode to represent trauma on film. Trauma cinema, she explains, features "vivid bodily and visual sensation [and is] characterized by non-linearity, fragmentation, non-synchronous sound, repetition, rapid editing and strange angles." Such cinema disorients the viewer and speaks to the difficulties inherent in both representing and remembering the past.[24] However, in *Gomorra*, scenes that heighten visual pleasure frequently follow unsettling and violent episodes. As a result, potentially trauma-inducing events are stylized.

The representation of Maria's death can be read in light of Eric Santner's discussion of narrative fetishism in Edgar Reitz's epic series *Heimat* (*Homeland*, 1984), which is a response to the eight-hour American mini-series *Holocaust* (1978). Santner argues that in *Heimat*, the national trauma of the destruction of European Jewry is sublimated into a sentimental love story. Santner addresses how then recent events in Europe influence what he calls the altering of the "German historical imagination" of the Holocaust. Santner distinguishes two possible representational modes of trauma, what he names narrative fetishism and mourning:

> Both narrative fetishism and mourning are responses to loss, to a past that refuses to go away due to its traumatic impact. The work of mourning is a process of elaborating or integrating the reality of loss or traumatic shock by remembering and repeating it in symbolically and dialogically mediated doses ... Narrative fetishism, by contrast, is a strategy of undoing, in fantasy, the need for mourning by simulating a condition of intactness ... In narrative fetishism the "post" is indefinitely postponed.[25]

Far from the potentially productive outcome of mourning, narrative fetishism obliterates traces of the past traumatic event, and, in effect, is a mode of denial through a highly formal narrative. In its stylized representation of Maria's execution, *Gomorra* fits in with those films discussed by Margaret Bruder in which violence is aestheticized and is presented "so as to call attention to the cinematic apparatus." Such films highlight the self-reflexive nature of the cinema-going experience and foreground viewing pleasure.²⁶

The killing of Maria inaugurates the conclusion of *Gomorra*'s five narrative threads. During the last thirty minutes of the film, each story, one by one, comes to a close. As narrative is swiftly propelled forward, the spectator is disinclined to ponder Maria's death and the reasons for it. As such, her murder is sublimated to other diegetic concerns and she is swiftly forgotten. Ultimately, we will see that Maria's murder is the first step towards bringing the film to a conclusion that further displaces national Mafia-related grief out of Italy and onto the victims of 9/11.

"The world is ours"

Of course, Maria is not the only person killed in *Gomorra*. Her death, however, stands in stark contrast to the violent episodes that open and close the film. Whereas Maria's murder comes off as abrupt and even unnecessary, both bookend assassinations further two of the film's central thematic concerns: the meta-cinematic nature of the Mafia movie genre and the Mafioso's obsession with onscreen mobsters and their penchant for all-out violence. In his pursuit of a thwarted ego-ideal, the Mafioso actively and aggressively confronts death head on a regular basis. Thanatos dominates the Mafia milieu, and whenever a member successfully overcomes it, he further confirms his masculinity. Indeed, Renate Siebert discusses what she calls the Mafioso's "cinematographic image of life as brief but intense" in terms of this schizophrenic mentality – that of a quest for wealth and respect in the looming presence of death.²⁷ Mobsters mimic Hollywood gangsters, and find in them an ego ideal to emulate to the point of maximum identification. As Saviano explains:

> Young Spartans went to war with the feats of Achilles and Hector in their heads, but around here you go to kill and be killed thinking of *Scarface*, *Goodfellas*, *Donnie Brasco*, and *The Godfather* … There's no real difference between movie audiences in the land of the Camorra and elsewhere. Cinematographic references everywhere create mythologies of imitation. If elsewhere you can be like *Scarface* and secretly identify with him, here you can *be* Scarface, but you have to be him all of the way.²⁸

In *Gomorra*, we see that the slaughter in the tanning salon that opens the film evokes several onscreen mass ritual killings such as the baptism sequence in *The Godfather* (Francis Ford Coppola, 1972), Michael's wiping out of all his enemies in *The Godfather: Part II* (Francis Ford Coppola, 1974), and Lucky's ascension to power in *Lucky Luciano* (Francesco Rosi, 1973). In *Gomorra*, the Camorristi are murdered in the bright light from the tanning beds, and are likened to movie stars in their own ill-fated film. Their "star persona" is furthered by the mise-en-scène: after the murders, the diegetic Neapolitan neo-melodic music escalates to announce the abrupt appearance onscreen of the film's title in garish hot pink. "Lights, camera, action" is the tone evoked in the opening sequence.

Both Garrone's film and Saviano's novel point out how Camorristi ape Hollywood stereotypes in order to lend themselves legitimacy. In the chapter entitled "Hollywood," Saviano discusses Walter Schiavone, who is the brother of long-standing Casalesi clan boss Sandokan, and describes his mega-mansion, which Schiavone dubbed "Hollywood" and modelled after Tony Montana's villa in *Scarface* (Brian DePalma, 1983). The once opulent villa is now a rotting, burnt out, and empty skeleton, as after his arrest Schiavone ordered it dismantled and destroyed, since, in the words of Saviano, "If he couldn't use it, it shouldn't exist."[29] In the same chapter, Saviano details how Mafiosi revere gangster characters and model themselves on the protagonists of mob classics such as *Pulp Fiction* (Quentin Tarantino, 1994), *Donnie Brasco* (Mike Newell, 1997), *The Godfather* trilogy, *The Crow* (Alex Proyas, 1994), and *Il camorrista* (*The Professor*, Giuseppe Tornatore, 1986).

In the media age, Saviano argues, it is only natural that mobsters turn towards Hollywood prototypes and mimic mob behaviour. These Mafia mise-en-abymes came full circle when Bernardino Terracciano, who plays a mob boss in Garrone's *L'imbalsamatore* (*The Embalmer*, 2002) and clan boss Zi' Bernardino in *Gomorra*, was arrested together with six other suspected Camorristi in October of 2008 on suspicion of arms dealing, murder, and extortion. One of the most striking mise-en-abymes in Garrone's film is the scene shot on location in "Hollywood," when Marco and Ciro act out the famous fatal sequence from De Palma's film. Marco reclines in the empty and abandoned pool, another replica from the movie, and tells Ciro "the world is ours," a mantra originally borrowed from Howard Hawks's *Scarface* (1932). In Hawks's, De Palma's, and Garrone's films, such an impulsive and dominating motto leads protagonists Tony Camonte, Tony Montana, and Marco and Ciro to their bloody ends. Ultimately, these and other onscreen mobsters live out the fantasy life (and death) that they had signed up for.

"The derealization of loss"

Gomorra concludes on the story of Marco and Ciro, who have been lured to the beach and to their deaths in a scene evocative of Nanni Moretti's journey to Pier Paolo Pasolini's memorial in Ostia in *Caro diario* (*Dear Diary*, 1993). If Marco and Ciro are meant to represent Italy's youth, they are far from Pasolini's vital and invigorating "ragazzi di vita [boys of life]," the sub-proletariat Roman street kids who populate his films and novels. Indeed, *Gomorra* is peppered with allusions to Pasolini, Michelangelo Antonioni, and Federico Fellini. Fellini's *La dolce vita* (1960) is referenced several times: a statue of Padre Pio lowered in the inner courtyard of le Vele recalls the opening scene of Fellini's film, when a gilded statue of Christ is carried over Rome by helicopter. Also, the representation of the seaside locale where Marco and Ciro celebrate after a drug heist and where, later in the film, they are shot dead evokes the eatery on the beach in *La dolce vita* where Marcello first meets Paola and where the film concludes. In *Gomorra*, however, the beach, Fellini's locus of redemption and conversion, made clear in the finale of *La strada* (1954), is transformed into an apocalyptic landscape that substitutes Saviano's concluding chapter "Land of Fires," an epilogue that presents a cataclysmic vision of mountains of garbage burning in the Campanian countryside. In the memoir, Saviano imagines Marco's and Ciro's cadavers picked over by gulls, their "lips and noses nibbled up by wild dogs," and reminds the reader, "But that's something the movies never show. They end just the minute before."[30] Garrone picks up where Saviano left off and concludes his film with an image of Marco and Ciro as they are carried away in a tractor as if they were toxic waste.

The fatal outcome of local clan wars, however, is quickly redirected to a more global Mafia concern and Garrone concludes the film by waking up the spectator. As Slavoj Žižek's points out, "When confronted with the Real in all its unbearable horror, the dreamer wakes up; i.e. escapes into 'reality.'"[31] The film ends by presenting a list of facts regarding the Camorra's international reach – the number of people killed, the extent and profitability of the drug trade, the vast expanse of toxic waste and dramatic increase in cancer, and the script is accompanied by Massive Attack's song "Herculaneum," which imparts a catastrophic tone to the finale:

> In Europe the Camorra has killed more than any other terrorist or criminal organization: 4000 deaths in the last thirty years. One every three

days. Scampia is the largest open air drug trafficking market in the world. Just one clan makes about 500,000 euros a day. If the toxic waste handled by the clans was all lumped together, it would create a mountain that is 14,600 metres tall. Everest is 8850 metres tall. Cancer rates in poisoned areas have risen twenty per cent. The proceeds from illicit activities are reinvested in numerous legal activities all over the world. The Camorra invested in the reconstruction of the World Trade Center.

The final message regarding the Camorra's international penetration of legal business and post-9/11 rebuilding efforts speaks directly to the American viewer, and suggests that the Mafia is all about self-presentation, re-messaging, and repackaging. Indeed, most US reviews of the film begin or end with a reference to this "fact."[32]

This resonant final evocation of the victims of 9/11 overshadows the other deaths in the film, certainly those of the several "made" or aspiring Camorristi, themselves criminals or murderers. And most certainly that of Maria, whose entanglement with the system precludes her from being categorized as entirely a victim. Judith Butler's work on grief, precarity, and representation offers a useful way of thinking about disavowed mourning in a Mafia context. In discussing suppressed public grieving as it relates to typical US news coverage of war footage, Butler asks:

> What is the relationship between the violence by which these ungrievable lives were lost and the prohibition on their public grievability? Is the prohibition on grieving the continuation of violence itself? And does the prohibition on grieving demand a tight control on the reproduction of images and words? How does the prohibition on grieving emerge as a circumscription on representability, so that our national melancholia becomes tightly fitted into the frame for what can be said, for what can be shown? The derealization of loss … becomes the mechanism through which dehumanization is accomplished. This derealization takes place neither inside nor outside the image, but through the very framing by which the image is contained.[33]

Butler explains that graphic images of "US soldiers dead and decapitated in Iraq, and then the photos of children maimed and killed by US bombs," were not used by mainstream media, which instead preferred footage "that took an aerial view," a technique that privileges the dominant perspective of state power but also, and more germane to my argument, creates a distancing effect that encourages passive observation.[34] And here I recall the specific "framing" of Maria's death as it compares to other murders in the film: that is, unlike with the slayings that open and close the film, with Maria's execution we are immediately physically distanced from the scene of the crime. Essentially, the demise of several male characters helps ground the film in a gangster tradition, and, in the case of Marco and Ciro, occasions a moment of mourning for the victims of international terrorist attacks. The staging of Maria's death, however, hints at a sense of national melancholia in Italy with regards to the Mafia. I am suggesting that *Gomorra* represents another case in which the hierarchy of grievability is laid bare: some lives, such as anti-Mafia martyrs Peppino Impastato and Placido Rizzotto, are acceptable to mourn. Others, in particular those who are ambiguously connected with the system, are not and their deaths will not be worked through.

In many ways, Maria is the perfect embodiment of life at its most precarious in a Mafia context insofar as she allows insight into the dehumanizing conditions under which tens of thousands live daily. The film is structured in such a way, however, as to reduce her death to a plot twist and to disavow mourning for her and those like her. It is interesting that in the film's final moments, narrative focus is dramatically shifted from the local to the global and from smaller to much bigger and distant families. My intent is by no means to belittle or downplay the import of Garrone's film. Yet ironically, in attempting to wake us up, to remind us of the international grasp of the Camorra, *Gomorra* returns to a more real, yet very displaced, and "derealized" reality.

9 Recasting Rita Atria in Marco Amenta's *La siciliana ribelle*

No one will ever understand the void inside me, that overwhelming void that everyone, little by little, has made even greater. I don't have anything anymore, all I have are crumbs. I can't tell good from bad, everything is so dark and gloomy. I thought that time would cure all wounds, but no, time opens them up more and more until they slowly kill you. When will this nightmare end?

Rita Atria's diary entry, 12 January 1992

No one will ever understand the void inside me, that overwhelming void that everyone, little by little, has made even greater. I thought that time would cure all wounds, but no, time opens them up more and more until they slowly kill you.

La siciliana ribelle (Marco Amenta)

In melodrama, the spectator is introduced to trauma through a film's themes and techniques, but the film ends with a comforting closure or cure. Such mainstream works posit trauma (against its reality) as a discrete past event, locatable, representable and curable.

E. Ann Kaplan, "Melodrama, Cinema, and Trauma," 204

Rita Atria: Anti-Mafia Martyr par excellence

For many, the name Rita Atria is synonymous with the women's anti-Mafia movement in Italy.[1] Atria was born into a family of Mafiosi in Partanna, Sicily, and after her father Vito Atria and her brother Nicola Atria were murdered by rival clans in 1985 and 1991, respectively, she followed the example of her sister-in-law Piera Aiello and became a collaborator of justice. As her life was in jeopardy, Atria was transferred to Rome, where she lived under police protection as she worked with the authorities, in particular with Paolo Borsellino, until his assassination on 19 July 1992. Precisely one week later, Atria committed suicide by throwing herself from the terrace of her seventh-storey apartment. Almost instantly, Atria became a martyr, and her name, according to Robin Pickering-Iazzi, was transformed into a "name symbol" standing for "courage, the struggle for truth and justice, and female rebellion against mafia violence and death," and this symbol "resonated particularly amongst women."[2] Atria's martyrdom snowballed no doubt in part because of the writings she left behind: diary entries, testimonies, initial attempts at crafting an autobiography, and a note left on her nightstand stating "Adesso non c'è più che mi protegge, sono avvilita, non ce la faccio più [Now there is no one left to protect me, I am discouraged, I can't take it any more],"[3] and another written in block letters in pencil on the wall of her apartment: "Ti amo, non abbandonarmi, il mio cuore senza di te non vive [I love you, don't abandon me, without you my heart is lifeless]."[4] Most who write on her suicide tie her death unambiguously to that of Borsellino, and note the time frame – one week later, at just about the same hour of day – and even reference the similar street names, Via d'Amelio and Via Amelia, where the two met their ends. Thus, together with that of Giovanni Falcone, who was assassinated by the Mafia less than two months earlier, Borsellino and Atria's deaths would come to inaugurate an intense, albeit short-lived, period of anti-Mafia mobilization in Sicily that was marked by hunger strikes, public demonstrations, and the famous sheet protest whereby citizens hanged either bleached clean or slogan-painted bed sheets from their window as a sign of resistance to Mafia oppression.

Marco Amenta's film *La siciliana ribelle* (*The Sicilian Girl*) from 2009 depicts Rita Atria (named Rita Mancuso in the film) as unambiguous in her quest for justice. The film is a follow-up to Amenta's 1997 documentary on Atria's life called *Diario di una siciliana ribelle* (*One Girl against the Mafia*). The feature film represents Rita's journey from a wilful *figlia di mafioso* seeking vendetta for the loss of her beloved father and brother (named Don Michele and Carmelo in the film) to a civic-minded, more or less uncomplicated, young woman. Early on in the film, the village of Balata (Atria actually lived in Partanna) is seen through Rita's eyes: point-of-view shots of sun-drenched fields of wheat, a religious procession, and her father in profile as he calms local farmers or threatens corrupt Mafiosi conjure up the oneiric Sicily represented by Coppola, where *uomini d'onore* are represented as family men tied to the soil and to traditional customs who protect the peasant class from various oppressors. Don Michele is portrayed as both Rita and the spectator's ego ideal. The child has clearly repudiated her mother, who is authoritarian and stone-hearted, and idealizes her father, bestowing upon him nothing but positive qualities: he is a peacemaker, a problem solver, and a man of justice. Fundamentally, as she tells the nameless judge based on Borsellino later in the film, her father was the "best man on earth." Later on, however, her repressed memories return, and she is able to see, with some difficulty, her father for the murderous Mafioso he really was. At this point, she hands over to the court as evidence the gun first used by her father and then by Carmelo as she tells the judge: "I realize that my father and my brother were no better than these killers. It's true, I came here seeking revenge [per avere vendetta]. Now I am asking for justice. I realize that it is not the same thing." In Amenta's rendition of Atria's life story, Rita's odyssey is complete when she commits suicide. She does so, the film makes apparent, in order for her testimony to stand so that all those against whom she gave evidence will receive lengthy prison sentences. Rita then sacrifices herself in the name of justice, a thesis that works well with the predominant interpretation of her motivations in life and in death. *La siciliana ribelle* sets out to tell the life story of Rita Atria. But, as I will argue here, it in fact only tells the side of the story that is stripped of any of the ambivalence that is part and parcel of Italy's ongoing and complex negotiation with the Mafia.

Atria's diaries reveal a much less unitary moral than that which is presented in the film, as Pickering-Iazzi has deftly argued. In particular, she considers the usefulness of looking at Atria's identity formation as "an ongoing process requiring the constant negotiation of oppositional psychological, affective and ethical pulls"[5] instead of assuming that she has "a coherent, stable antimafia identity."[6] Atria never accepted that her father and brother were murderers and idolized them until the end. In her writings, she wishes that she could live with her deceased father and brother, and yearns to have Nicola Atria beside her "to feel his loving touch" and believes that if her father were alive, he could easily prove the guilt of Vincenzo Culicchia, the former mayor of Partanna. She describes Don Vito Atria and Nicola Atria as her stars, "her two great loves" who await her in infinity. Her writings reveal that, up until the end, her self-world view was anything but cohesive and instead was fragmentary and marked by several earlier traumas including growing up in a Mafia stronghold that witnessed over thirty deaths in a few short years, her mother's physical and emotional abuse, and the death of her father and brother. In the months before her death she writes about "the emptiness inside [her], that immeasurable emptiness that everyone, little by little, has made even greater" and in poems asserts "what was stolen from you can never be returned ... No one will listen, no one will understand you / instead they will judge you" and "nothing will protect you from a world that can never be yours." She also describes a "sliver of deep darkness" that makes one "die inside."[7] Atria's writings evinced her schizoid condition as someone both inside and against Mafia code and culture.

Melodramatic versus Traumatic Memory

Rita's destiny as martyr is announced early on in the film. *La siciliana ribelle* opens with series of shots detailing a conversation between Rita and Bruni, a sympathetic police officer later murdered by the Mafia, about Don Michele's gun. The sombre mood is furthered by the solemn musical score and dark, oppressive lighting. After hearing that the gun is all that Rita has left by which to remember her father, Bruni lets her keep it, telling her, "It will be our secret." Thus, Rita is introduced as tied to her father's memory and by extension to the world he embodies. After the title appears, a close-up reveals a hand writing in a journal. A zoom out quickly follows to a medium close-up of a teenaged Rita who looks towards what is assumed to be a window or a door (light enters the screen from that direction) as a church bell chimes. Her memory triggered, a flashback takes us to another act of writing in her youth. We are transported "seven years earlier" to Sicily in 1985 to an image of most likely the same door, now closed, accompanied by a sound bridge of the same church bell. Rita's mother opens the door that reveals the cathedral in the background, partially obscured by white sheets put out to dry. Her mother calls for Rita, asking if she stirred the tomato sauce, and immediately discovers another white sheet soiled by dark orange handprints. The culprit, we soon learn, is Rita, who has used the sauce to write a salutation ("Ciao papà") to her father, who is due home at any moment. Her mother is furious, but her father counters, "That is a good thing. Do you want her to be as ignorant as us?"

The flashback weds the two acts of writing and champions her father for his enlightened thinking, which stands in stark contrast with Rita's mother, who is represented throughout the film as ignorant and tied to the politics of honour. More to the point, the sheet begs to be read together with the image that closes the film. Before cutting to the credits, a documentary still of a sheet reading "Rita per te nel ricordo [Rita, we will never forget you]" appears on the screen for a few brief moments. The colour of the lettering is not unlike the deep orange-red of the tomato sauce that Rita used as a child to welcome her father home. The banner preceding the one dedicated to Rita includes the faces of Falcone and Borsellino and reads "Non li avete uccisi: le loro idee camminano sulle nostre gambe [You did not kill them: Their ideas live on in our hearts]." This parallel suggests that Rita's intelligence and literacy are intimately entwined with her death and subsequent martyrdom. Also, the flashback neatly ties a national trauma to an act of childhood whimsy encouraged by a violent Mafioso masquerading as a benign paternal figure. To the Italian viewer, the sheet stained with a blood-like colour present at the beginning of the film will no doubt conjure up media images of the thousands of sheets hung to commemorate Falcone and Borsellino during the summer of 1992. The film opens by presenting four distinct time periods from Rita's life: (1) when she is transported to Rome to begin collaborating with the authorities, (2) her late adolescence at home in Balata, (3) her childhood, and (4) her death (reading the sheet as suggestive of the aftermath of her demise.) Hence, from the outset, the film is interested in constructing Rita's subjectivity and universalizing her personal familial story through positioning her as a central part of the national trauma discourse with regards to high-profile Mafia-related murders in the 1990s.

The structure of the flashback minimizes the traumatic potential of this association, however. Joshua Hirsch defines as "posttraumatic" a type of flashback that is capable of transmitting "to the spectator a series of experiences that were, in turn, analogous to a series of characteristics of psychological trauma."[8] These types of flashbacks deny any mastery over the past and shock the viewer, who is confronted with painful, fractured, involuntary, and anxiety-producing memories.[9] Hirsch juxtaposes the post-traumatic flashback with what he calls the "classical flashback," which "works to promote spectator mastery" of narrative in its constructing of a historical memory that is pleasurable.[10] The spectator is prepared for the classical flashback by such narrative devices as plot, dialogue, sound, camera movement, and other elements in the mise-en-scène. Rita's flashback can be defined as "melodramatic" in that it helps develop her character, explains her motivation in her present conflict, and clarifies what steps need to be taken for narrative resolution. Although the flashback speaks to a series of traumatic memories, they are mediated by Rita's recollection of her father and lead, as is the case with the typical melodramatic flashback, "directly to the resolution of plot."[11]

Moreover, the initial flashback makes evident the Oedipal scenario apparent in the father–daughter relationship. Rita is dressed in a colourful and short dress with bright red tights, her hair is braided, and she applies lipstick while her father announces that the two of them are going out. Immediately enraged, Rita's mother snatches the lipstick out of her hand and tells her daughter that she should be ashamed of herself and that she will not permit her to leave the house dressed as she is. Don Michele counters that he told his daughter to dress that way for an important errand that is, as Rita precociously tells her mother, her and her father's secret. In the beginning of the film, we are privy to two secrets revolving around Don Michele and his daughter (this outing and the earlier discussion of the gun) which foreground the primacy of the positive Oedipus complex with regards to the father–daughter relationship. "The positive Oedipus complex," writes Kaja Silverman, "represents the primary vehicle through which the subject affirms the 'reality' of the family and the phallus, as well as the other ideological elements with which they are intertwined." These elements constitute the "dominant fiction," which is the "stable core around which a nation's and a period's 'reality' coheres."[12] Silverman also argues that, ideally, the Oedipus complex inducts "the female subject into desire for her father and identification with her mother."[13] Rita has not identified with her mother per se, but with what she represents: the cult of honour and familial memory. Meanwhile, Rita acknowledges her father as the bearer of the phallus; he is the incarnation of Law and the signifier of desire. Her image of him must remain intact so as to not rupture the dominant fiction. And throughout most of her life this is the case: her memory is subjective and incomplete, filtered by her father, who shelters her from images of violence. Indeed, the pair's secret destination is revealed to be a Mafia massacre: a house in flames, with one man burnt to death on the ground. As Don Michele shields Rita's eyes from the spectacle, the camera cuts to her point of view as his fingers obscure her (and our) vision of the world.[14]

Throughout the film, young Rita is witness to various Mafia-related atrocities, including murder and rape. But she chooses to look away or to go on with her childhood adventures. The only act of violence that shocks her is that of her father's murder, which she witnesses first hand in the town square on the day of her first communion (Vito Atria did not die in front of his daughter, however). According to Hirsch, the cinema engages in the act of witnessing "both the outer physical reality of historical events and the inner, psychological reality of the effects of those events on people." The problem with historical films, he maintains, is that they make manifest a tension between "the witnessing of reality and the witnessing of fantasy."[15] In Amenta's film, fantasy wins out. Or, more precisely, what is affirmed is the ideological fantasy of the supremacy of the patriarchal family and of normative masculinity. According to Silverman, "The dominant fiction … solicits our faith above all else in the unity of the family and the adequacy of the male subject."[16] This is not to say that the film completely ignores the representation of Atria's traumas as expressed in her memoir. Just after a meeting with the judge, Rita is shown exiting her gloomy apartment and a voice-over conveys her deep-seated angst: "No one will ever understand the void inside me, that overwhelming void that everyone, little by little, has made even greater. I thought that time would cure all wounds, but no, time opens them up more and more until they slowly kill you." This passage comes from Atria's last diary entry with a specific date, 12 January 1992; all those following are marked "Roma, … 1992." Of note is what is left out from the original, which I quote in its entirety:

> No one will ever understand the void inside me, that overwhelming void that everyone, little by little, has made even greater. I don't have anything anymore, all I have are crumbs. I can't tell good from bad, everything is so dark and gloomy. I thought that time would cure all wounds, but no, time opens them up more and more until they slowly kill you. When will this nightmare end?

Here, Atria feels completely alone and admits that she cannot distinguish between right and wrong and inhabits a grey zone that is absent in the film. This is telling as, while in Rome, Atria was far from isolated: she lived with her sister-in-law Piera Aiello, had a serious relationship for a series of months with a boy named Gabriele, and had established a close circle of friends. Of this entry, Pickering-Iazzi writes that Atria seems to be speaking "from the grave." She continues: "From the position of abject solitude, Atria creates a discourse of loss, of her brother, possibilities for happiness and the void that is herself."[17] Thus, as Pickering-Iazzi argues, Atria's diaries give voice to her profound trauma and implicate "everyone" in her suffering, and not just those who harmed her family. Furthermore, her writings engender a "testimonial body" that demands a reading and creates an interlocutor who is meant to bear witness to her pain long after her death. Pickering-Iazzi reads the note written on the apartment wall, "I love you, don't abandon me, without you my heart is lifeless" not as a direct address to Borsellino, but as a way of committing "herself to others" in the hopes of bearing "a testimony that may survive her death."[18]

The "Post-Mafia" Melodrama

The normalization of Atria into a unifying martyr figure is helped in large part by Amenta's choice to craft the *La siciliana ribelle* as a melodramatic woman's film with a twist. Elements of high melodrama abound: emotional excess, mother-daughter conflict, love stories, social and moral injustice, the creation of the classic villain in Don Saro, the man who ordered Don Michele's death, and a heroine in peril. For example, Rita is almost victim to a shoot-out in a cemetery, but is saved by a police helicopter at the last moment. What's more, the film includes the requisite "situation," as Leah Jacobs describes it, by which Rita is confronted in court by a woman who testifies that Don Michele raped her in her youth. The protagonist must then examine her conscience and decide if she can go forward in her role of *collaboratrice di giustizia*.[19] In this way, *La siciliana ribelle* strives to be a woman's film as it unfolds from Rita's perspective, and attempts to "conceptualize female subjectivity" only to subsequently destroy it, as I will later elaborate. Furthermore, the film is primarily concerned with female desire and has an "insistent address to the female spectator." In her exploration of the woman's film, Mary Ann Doane touches upon the problematics that "accompany the concerted effort to engage female subjectivity within conventional narrative forms" and make apparent "certain contradictions within patriarchal ideology."[20] That Rita ultimately sacrifices herself for justice to reign obliterates her difference and reinforces "the impossible position of women in relation to desire in a patriarchal society."[21] And this is particularly the case for someone like Rita who stands on the threshold of two diametrically opposed patriarchies: the Mafia and the Italian legal system.

Throughout much of the film, Rita is out of place in both worlds and frequently masquerades as a man: she carries her father's and then her brother's gun since the latter's death, swears that she will avenge her family members' murders, and repeatedly upsets the gender paradigms at play in Mafia culture (and patriarchal culture at large) through her many public outbursts. Until she comes out against her family in court, Rita is uneasy in her role as both harbinger of vendetta and avatar of an impartial legal system because she was cast out of the Mafia by her mother and remains an outsider to the latter.

In a subgenre of the woman's film that, as Doane points out, mobilizes a "medical discourse," female subjectivity is tied to pathology. These films, in which women suffer from a physical or psychical illness, "manifest an instability in the representation of female subjectivity"[22] and strive to convince "the woman that her way of looking is ill."[23] In the film, Rita is routinely referred to as "mad": Rita herself, her boyfriend Vito, and her mother describe her as "pazza [crazy]" and the opposing counsel at the trial depict her as an adolescent with a "psiche turbata [troubled psyche]." Her metaphorical transvestism and aberrant behaviour, however, cannot go unpunished according to the traditional logic of classical cinema.

As Rita begins to comprehend the moral implications of, in the judges' words, the difference between those who respect the law and those who do not, the film works to normalize and domesticate her. Rita's coming of age as an Italian citizen in her role of *collaboratrice di giustizia* is shown as parallel to her coming of age as a woman. She discovers her femininity in Rome just after watching a mass arrest on television that includes the mayor of Balata and Don Salvo as a result of her testimony. Moments later, she adjourns to the bathroom and admires herself in the mirror for what appears to be the first time. As she provocatively applies lipstick, a gesture that recalls her earliest memories of her father, the film implies that Rita's new position of empowerment within the law has allowed her to move on past the past, to let go of her trauma and to embrace a new sensual self that would not be possible in her native village. Amenta equates emotionality with femininity when he claims: "Maybe her growing femininity allowed her to put aside her pride and to accept emotionally the fact that her father was guilty. This is something that a man, with a big sense of honor, couldn't do."[24] Thus, in the film, mature femininity is unequivocally equated with justice and enlightened thought, while masculinity is tied to moral ignorance.

What is problematic about this representation is the simple collusion between sacrifice, gender, and unified national identity inherent in the film's anti-Mafia message. "In melodrama," E. Ann Kaplan writes, "the spectator is introduced to trauma through a film's themes and techniques, but the film ends with a comforting closure or cure. Such mainstream works posit trauma (against its reality) as a discrete past event, locatable, representable and curable."[25] Amenta's film, as one reviewer notes, attempts to espouse a "post-mafia" mentality that I find problematic.[26] In her final journal entry, Atria famously wrote of the need to resist and combat the "mafia dentro" that exists in all of us: "Before fighting against the Mafia you have to examine your own conscience and then, after you have defeated the Mafia inside yourself, you can fight the Mafia that's in your circle of friends. We ourselves and our mistaken way of behaving are the Mafia."[27] Atria's proposition is anything but straightforward and suggests that a Mafia mentality has taken up residence in the collective imagination. Yet, this message, similar to Atria's diary entries which make manifest her fractured psyche, does not find a place in Amenta's film, which instead positions Mafia-related trauma as a "past event" that is "locatable, representable and curable."

Peter Brooks and others have proposed that melodrama and realism should not be considered antithetical.[28] Melodrama taps into a collective unconscious and engages everyday scenarios. It gives voice to the emotional life of its characters while staging age-old battles between good and evil that ultimately find narrative closure and thus reassure the audience. The true stakes of melodrama, Brooks proposes, are "to make the 'real' and the 'ordinary' and the 'private life' interesting through heightened dramatic utterance."[29] But the challenge posed to melodrama, as Christine Gledhill has shown, is representing the world as it should be, and not simply tackling the status quo. This is because, she argues, melodrama operates "within the framework of the present" and thus has trouble positioning narrative dénouement in a "revolutionary future." Instead, it is much more plausible that the melodrama will come to a close on how things should have been rather than how they "ought to be."[30] Most melodramas conclude on some sort of heartening moral note that reinscribes masculinity within the traditional framework of home and hearth. The happy ending frequently takes the form of a marriage which neatly, and swiftly, restores the social order and privileges a tempered masculinity that acts "in the interests of civilization, law, and culture."[31]

Laura Mulvey, however, points out that in some melodramas that are centred around a female protagonist, conclusions are all but conclusive and instead blatantly reveal the crisis of masculinity previously apparent throughout the entire film. A female point of view that dominates the narrative, she claims, "produces an excess which precludes satisfaction." In such films, narrative structure is incapable of neatly managing all of the over-determined Oedipal and ideological conflicts brought to the foreground during the film which "put up a resistance to being neatly satisfied in the last five minutes." Amenta's film includes a series of unsettled Oedipal scenarios that demand resolution: for one, Rita's unresolved libidinal attachment to the father and her instant exchange of one (Mafia) father for another in the judge, who stands for justice. But also, her complicated relationship with her mother who, we find out, only bore her daughter because she was tricked into it by her husband. She tells Rita: "I was right not to want to have you. I sensed it.

I wanted to get an abortion. Your father stopped me. If you're here, if you were born, you owe that to him. And now you are soiling his name in public. He'll be pleased with his little darling." Hence, Rita's betrayal, her symbolic killing off of her father in the courtroom, can be read as a pre-emptive suicide in that she effaces the memory of the one person responsible for her existence.

Rewriting Suicide: Rita as Antigone

The finale of *La siciliana ribelle* conforms to the traditional climax of the melodrama in its privileging of a "beneficial sacrifice of unrestrained masculine individualism" in the interest of a cohesive national identity.[32] For example, Rita is able to let go of her thirst for vendetta, obsession with familial honour, and arrogance, all typical of a gangsteresque hyperbolic masculinity, and embrace and speak to the law of the state. Ironically, this unified ethos is only possible with Rita's suicide. Atria's diaries are so radical in their challenge to patriarchy that female perspective must be first domesticated in *La siciliana ribelle* and then violently and abruptly repressed at the film's close. The staging of Rita's suicide is, however, problematic. Bereft after the judge's death, Rita telephones her mother, who rejects her, and then calls a boy named Lorenzo whom she met at the Coliseum and had been dating. His mother answers and implores her to stop calling. Finally, she reaches out to her Mafioso boyfriend Vito and asks him to visit. He arrives that day and after they sleep together, Rita jumps to her death, arms outstretched like Christ.[33] This, a completely invented plot twist, will shock any viewer familiar with Atria's story. Why in the film is Rita's suicide staged directly after what is suggested to be her first sexual experience? More to the point, why does she take her life in front of a witness, in particular one with loyal Mafia ties?

In filling in the holes in her testimony, *La siciliana ribelle* attempts to lay Atria's memory to rest through recasting her as an anti-Mafia martyr par excellence. Peppino Impastato, Placido Rizzotto, and Leonardo Vitale were killed because they resisted and spoke out against the Mafia. In the film, however, Rita consciously chooses death and makes a martyr of herself rather than renouncing her beliefs, that is, letting the Mafia win. As befits the etymology of "martyr," Rita is cast as a true witness for her faith, which in *La siciliana ribelle* is undeniably the anti-Mafia struggle. What is implied here is that Rita's belief system was fully formed and hermetic, and that her past traumas were completely healed at the time of her death. Amenta claimed that he wanted to make a movie with a universal message. When asked how her story is universal, he replied: "It's the story of resistance against oppression. The story of a young girl's rebellion against the system, against oppressive and macho power. It's about the mafia, but it could just as well be about Nazism or a South-American dictatorship. Rita's destiny is a tragic one, similar to the tragedy of Antigone, who places morals above social law."[34] It is true that the historical Atria did "resist oppression" through her collaboration with the criminal justice system. Amenta implies here, however, that Rita's suicide, her "destiny," like that of Antigone, is motivated by a sense of right and wrong and civic duty.

Moreover, the director suggests that the Mafia is readily comparable with other historical traumas such as the Final Solution or any number of totalitarian regimes throughout history. In his discussion of whether the Holocaust should be considered a unique or a comparable event, Dominik LaCapra agrees that comparing can facilitate understanding, but cautions, "The greatest danger at the present time, at least in the context of the historians' debate, is that certain comparisons function as mechanisms of denial that do not enable one to 'work through' problems ... The seemingly balanced account of an unbalanced situation," he argues, can in fact embody a "mechanism of denial that seeks normalization ... through an avoidance or disavowal of the critical and self-critical requirements of both historical understanding and anything approximating 'normality.'"[35] In Amenta's words, the story of a girl who resists the Mafia is equivalent to that of anyone who has fought against any tyranny. The trouble with such a straightforward message is its assumption of resistance and history as absolute, intelligible, and rational. Such a take on Atria's story allows no place for the "mafia dentro" with which she was at odds until the end. Instead, Rita as depicted in Amenta's film worked through her past horrors quite swiftly while in court. Thus, the film universalizes both Atria and the Mafia, and in doing so effaces any ambiguous or conflicting narratives associated therewith.[36]

One of the most effective positions for a viewer of trauma films is when, as Kaplan argues, "the spectator is addressed as a witness," as is the case, she argues, with *Night and Fog* (Alain Resnais, 1955). This is accomplished most readily in films that in deferring from the classical model are not obligated to adhere to traditional narrative structures and plotlines. Non-realist films that utilize techniques that "show paralysis, repetition, circularity – all aspects of the non-representability of trauma and yet of the search to figure its pain"[37] can directly engage the viewer in the crisis of representation of a traumatic event. Hirsch defines such a cinema as "posttraumatic," which he explains is not determined by specific images of atrocity but by "the attempt to discover a form for representing that content that mimics some aspects of posttraumatic consciousness itself, the attempt to formally reproduce for the spectator an experience of suddenly seeing the unthinkable." Such films can produce within the viewer a "traumatic afterimage" which "formally repeats the shock of the original encounters with atrocity" and leaves the viewer feeling helpless in the face of an unmasterable event.[38]

While the diaries implicate the reader as witness to Atria's trauma, the same is not the case for the film. In *La siciliana ribelle*, Rita's boyfriend Vito is addressed as the true witness to her death and is the privileged recipient of her parting message regarding her quest for justice. Rather than attempting to depict an event that is "radically out of joint with one's mental representation of the world,"[39] as is the case with trauma, the film imparts "a sense of mastery over the past"[40] that is in accordance with classical realist cinema. In a heroic speech that implies that Rita is a coherent speaking subject who has faced up to and tackled her demons, she tells Vito that she is aware that Don Salvo does not want her dead. "If I die," she recognizes, "the evidence will stand, the trial goes on, and he gets life imprisonment. You know something? This time, the Mafia loses. This time, I win, my love. Rita wins. Crazy Rita, Rita the bitch, the fixated little girl." Hence, the film makes swift meaning of her suicide and leaves no room for dissension. It is telling that her message is conveyed to the viewer through a perpetrator who, in the film, murdered her own brother, a plot twist that amplifies the film's straightforward anti-Mafia and good-guy/ bad-guy message.

In her analysis of authorial suicide, Elizabeth Leake argues that the death of an author by suicide changes how their work is read while also making their life "into a text to be read."[41] The example of Atria as put forth in *La siciliana ribelle* is extreme in its commemoration of Rita for her extraordinary courage. Her suicide is rewritten as a monumentalizing gesture that is dangerous because, as Pickering-Iazzi has pointed out with regards to other public discourses around Atria, this revision makes her an "exception" to the anti-Mafia struggle.[42] What of the countless women who live within the system with no viable method of resistance, whose precarious condition might help us understand Italy's national melancholia as I discussed in the introduction? Or those who attempt to rebel in any number of ways yet are completely ignored in public discourse? In a moment of high melodrama, Rita makes the ultimate sacrifice in order to protect the Italian people from further subjugation by the Mafia and jumps to her death in front of her lover.

The Master Narrative and Memorializing Gestures

La siciliana ribelle comes to a close with a montage of documentary footage of Atria herself, her funeral, and various anti-Mafia protests contemporary with her death, most of which was also included in Amenta's earlier documentary. The film is dedicated "to Rita Atria and Judge Paolo Borsellino who sacrificed their lives in the fight against the Mafia." Thus, *La siciliana ribelle* puts forward the final word on the motivation behind Atria's suicide. Documentary images of her funeral are accompanied by a voice-over of the actress who played Rita in the film reciting one of the most memorable sections from Atria's diary: "Forse un mondo onesto non esisterà mai, ma chi ci impedisce di sognare. Forse se ognuno di noi prova a cambiare, forse ce la faremo. Rita Atria [Perhaps an honest world will never exist, but who prevents us from dreaming. Perhaps if each one of us tries to change, perhaps we will succeed. Rita Atria]." In this way, the film concludes optimistically, a tone that is furthered by a montage of four anti-Mafia slogans painted on white sheets and a final script that reads, "The extracts are taken from Rita Atria's original diaries, admitted as evidence at the trial. Most of the Mafiosi accused by her received lengthy prison sentences. The mayor was cleared of all charges and re-elected a few years later." Documentary elements in the finale ground the film in historical fact, and, ultimately, Atria's suicide is recrafted into a memorializing gesture that tames her as she is put forward as an exemplum of resistance.

However, as is clear in her diaries, the Mafia no doubt obscured Atria's world view and profoundly traumatized her, much like, as I argue here, it has Italy at large. But, Kaplan tells us that in the wake of national trauma, societies and individual members thereof prefer to displace traumatic memory onto another part of the consciousness that is accessible by "flashbacks, phobias, and dreams." This happens, she argues, not because it is impossible to recall the traumatic event, but because, "for political and social reasons ... it is too dangerous for the culture (or powerful political figures) to acknowledge or recall, just as the 'forgotten' contents in individual consciousness are too dangerous to remember." Forgetting then becomes a performance that is enacted by a people or a culture in order to safeguard themselves from the recent past. Historically, however, the melodrama engages those breaches that trauma has made apparent in the dominant fiction, "while at the same time seeking unconsciously to repair and reveal" them,[43] and this dynamic plays out in *La siciliana ribelle*.

It is striking that a film that is centred on a female protagonist and that purportedly discloses Rita's point of view is over-saturated with deceased father figures, including several of Rita's real and metaphorical fathers: Don Michele, Carmelo, the judge and Bruni, all killed by the Mafia. Indeed, the figure of Piera Aiello, Atria's best friend, former roommate, and fellow collaborator of justice, is completely absent in the film. Thus, the narrative is primarily motivated by Rita's relationships with the men in her lives. Interestingly, Amenta dedicated the film "a nostro padre Nino" ("our father," he notes, as his sister is the film's producer). In discussing his father's death, Amenta explains that he was a smoker and died from cancer, but believes that "his professional disappointment was a contributing factor in his death."[44] He means that his father, who was a doctor, was denied a promotion as he refused to capitulate to the local Mafia and that his illness was subsequently accelerated by his dead-end career.

Ultimately, female perspective in *La siciliana ribelle* is minimized or rewritten so as to further the film's paternalistic anti-Mafia message. The film opens on a gun that represents Rita's tie to one (Mafia) father and ends on a collective memorial that acts as a surrogate for another: the nation that is newly unified against a common, and as the film suggests, vincible, enemy. Right before her suicide, Vito made an offer to Rita: she could return home, marry him, retract her statements to the authorities, and thus become a respectable citizen of Balata. Instead, she jumps. Her choice makes explicit the double bind of the woman who desires to know "more" in classical cinema. Doane writes: "The woman's exercise of an active investigating gaze can only be simultaneous with her own victimization. The place of her specularization … is transformed into a locus of a process of seeing designed to unveil an aggression against itself."[45] A desirous female gaze must be punished. Accordingly, as Rita is unwilling to return "home," she is left with only one other option: death. Rita's sacrifice in the name of the father, "our father," positions her in the memorialist tradition of the likes of Peppino Impastato and Placido Rizzotto, whose struggles, to borrow from Kaplan, "betray a traumatic cultural symptom" that must be smoothed over by a pleasurable narrative.[46] In the end, Rita is deprived of agency and reinscribed into a normative anti-Mafia discourse that consolidates the dominant fiction in its working to ensure that the story of the nation remain untainted.

10 Trauma Postponed: Claudio Cupellini's *Una vita tranquilla*

> If a community has to recognize that its members, instead of being heroes, have been perpetrators who violated the cultural premises of their own identity, the reference to the past is indeed traumatic. The community can cope with the fundamental contradiction between identity claims and recognition only by a collective schizophrenia, by denial, by decoupling or withdrawal.
>
> Bernhard Giesen, "The Trauma of Perpetrators," 114

> Italian *film noir* is politicized and the figure of the *femme fatale* is subordinated to the drive to express anxieties about power, powerlessness, corruption, and other wounds to the body politic.
>
> Mary Wood, "*Chiaroscuro*," 165

> In effect, Italian film noirs are male melodramas rehearsing shifting power relationships in Italian society.
>
> Mary Wood, "Italian Film Noir," 264

Oedipal Traumas

Towards the end of Claudio Cupellini's *Una vita tranquilla* (*A Quiet Life*, 2010), protagonist Rosario Russo gives his estranged son Diego specific instructions on how to achieve the requisite "quiet life" of the film's title:

> Tomorrow leave for Hamburg. Find Sergio at the restaurant called "Cavallino Bianco," I'll let him know you are coming. Tell him that you need a job and a new identification card. Never call anyone, and if I have to talk to you, I'll call you. Then throw away your cell phone, stay in Hamburg for a year. Shave your beard, let your hair grow, learn German

and in a year, change jobs. Never trust anyone, especially Italians. Avoid them. Don't make friends. Work, go to bed early in the evening, you have to become a ghost. Leave tomorrow morning. If all goes well you will have a quiet life.

The pair have just buried Edoardo, Diego's best friend and fellow Camorrista. Edoardo is also the son of Mario Fiore, one of the most powerful bosses of the Camorra, the Mafia of Campania. Rosario killed Diego to protect himself, as the latter just discovered that fifteen years earlier Rosario (originally named Antonio de Martino) faked his own death, abandoned his wife and son, and fled from Campania to Germany in order to save his skin and start anew. The choice to set the film in Germany is compelling. The hamlet in the subdued region of Hesse that Rosario calls home is geographically, linguistically, and culturally different from his native Campania and appears untouched by the Mafia. At the same time, however, the setting recalls the international reach of another of Italy's Mafias, the 'Ndrangheta of Calabria, which is quite active in Germany and was responsible for the murder of six men in an Italian restaurant in Duisburg in 2007.

The whole film can be read as a mise-en-scène of the complications of repressing the past: early in the film, Diego tracks down his father while executing a Mafia hit in a nearby town so as to see him again, regardless of the dangers inherent in such an act; even though Rosario has remarried, has a second son, and has become a successful chef and hotelier, he is incapable of cancelling out either his violent temper or past career as a mafia hit man and is still fully adept at the business of murder; Diego ignores his father's advice and, instead, kidnaps Rosario's son Matthias as a means to force his father into the hands of the Mafia. When the plan goes awry and Diego is shot dead, Rosario escapes his past again by deserting his second family.

Una vita tranquilla is best defined as a "male suspense thriller," which is a subgenre of film noir in which "the hero is in a position of marked inferiority, with regard both to the criminal conspirators and to the police, and seeks to restore himself to a position of security by eradicating the enigma."[1] In these films, Kutrik argues, the hero must consistently prove and consolidate his masculinity in the hopes of ultimately conforming to the dominant patriarchal model. Like most examples of film noir, *Una vita tranquilla* depicts a male protagonist with a murky past who is lacking a stable identity. Rosario is at the mercy of both his inner demons that threaten to overtake his outwardly serene and stable demeanour and also the Mafia, an external enemy that demands retribution. According to Alan Woolfolk, in the world of the noir, "existence is irremediably fractured, [and] the self can neither be integrated into a community nor find a home in the universe, ... Self-identity is itself highly contingent and subject to disintegration." One of the key tenets of traditional noir is a lack of narrative resolution whereby the hero comes to terms with his past misdoings or trauma, understands that he is a valued member of his family and community, and envisions a future ripe with promise. Although noir protagonists "are always in transit," time in the genre is characterized by a "cruel stasis" which reveals the impossibility of any sort of epiphany or revelation at the stories' end. This is because, according to Woolfolk, the noir prioritizes the past over the present and the future.[2]

Thus, as R. Barton Palmer argues, "lacking a moment of reformative turning, the film noir juxtaposes the false promise of a future with the reality of a present that, instead, turns back to the past, trapping the protagonist 'between times' and in a multiplicity of irreconcilable spaces."[3] In its insistence on such a temporal quagmire that precludes narrative resolution, the film noir illustrates the impossibility of moving beyond past traumatic injury. Fundamentally, noir protagonists are incapable of escaping their true demon: themselves. Never coming to terms with their histories, such characters cannot, and will not, relinquish "a past self,"[4] "reform their ways,"[5] and settle down into a culturally acceptable lifestyle, as is frequently the case in classical melodrama, for example. Hence, the noir rehearses, yet ultimately represses, traumatic experiences. Read this way, the film noir can be considered the genre par excellence for representing the Italian Mafia: it is an ongoing and seemingly unending wound to the nation without the cultural capital associated with national trauma. Born concomitantly with the Italian state in the 1860s, the Mafia is ever present in Italian private and public life. However, no turning point has occurred with regard to the organization that has allowed the nation to reflect and to begin to heal. For both the Mafia and the noir protagonist, it is impossible to make "a clean break" with the past; both are backwards thinking and lack a "coherent narrative."[6]

Una vita tranquilla is about the Mafia, and deals with the Camorra, Mafia-hired guns, men on the run, and the eco-Mafia. But I will argue that the film is mainly interested in staging the Oedipal traumas of abandonment, betrayal, parricide, and filicide inherent in the relationship between Rosario and Diego. The film conforms to Freud's definition of the tale of Oedipus as a "tragedy of destiny," which enacts "the contrast between the supreme will of the gods and the vain attempts of mankind to escape the evil that threatens them." Despite all his efforts to save himself and his Italian family with his vanishing act, the father ultimately brings about the son's demise; in fact, he is powerless to stop it. Freud writes that the spectator of the tragedy realizes "his own impotence" in the face of divine will.[7] The son, even having purportedly symbolically renounced Rosario in order to serve another Mafia father, is still drawn to his biological father, and thus to his death. Claire Johnston writes that "the Oedipus complex allows access to desire only through repression: it is through lack that desire is instituted."[8] The film suggests that Diego has never successfully resolved the Oedipus complex. In fact, there would be no story had he not attempted to pacify his profound sense of lack as a result of paternal abandonment. He is, in effect, caught between two fathers, one biological in Rosario and one symbolic in his Mafia brotherhood, and he is unresolved as to which signifies the Law. I will also show that, in the film, women are radically othered into a sort of quasi non-existence in order for the film to focus completely on the Oedipal drama that is, after all, concerned with "the primacy of male identity and inheritance." Neither father nor son learn the moral lesson of Oedipus's ordeal, which is, according to Krutnik, "the need to *know* and *accept* one's place under the law – or face devastating consequences."[9]

In essence, *Una vita tranquilla* is about the trauma of perpetrators, a central yet disregarded element of the national trauma discourse with regard to the Mafia. Indeed, the film stages the primal trauma of parricide that Freud maintains is at the heart of monotheistic religions. Freud explains the history of monotheism as an acting out of the repressed traumatic memory of the murder of the primal father which inaugurated the incest taboo and brought about "the beginnings of morality and justice." When the Jews murdered Moses, it triggered the repressed memory of the murder and cannibalism of the primal father. In offering them a single god, Moses reminded the people of the primordial father and thus of their subconscious role in his death.[10] According to Jan Assman, parricide is a "religion of the father" and as such appeals to the basic Oedipal structure or "archaic inheritance" of the human soul in the depths of which people have always known that "they once possessed a primal father whom they have murdered." But, the experience of murdering a parent, whether literal in the case of Moses or the primal father or symbolic in the example of the inducted

Mafioso who must renounce family for Family, is profoundly traumatic, and leaves "traces in the psyche of perpetrators" which are bound to remain until both the group and the wounded subjects acknowledge and work through the primal trauma.[11]

Like Father, Unlike Son

The opening moments of Una vita tranquilla establish the suspenseful and dark tone that permeates the film. As the anxious score escalates, a pitch-black screen gradually transitions to an extreme close-up of a lichen-covered tree trunk that dominates the frame and obscures our view of the surrounding area. Thus, the film begins in the dark, an incipit that suggests the lacunae of memory central to the discourse of repressed trauma played out in the film. A steady zoom-out reveals three trucks entering an underlit sylvan setting. Subsequently, a stationary low-angle shot captures several pairs of legs and a dog who take their exit from the vehicles. Six men are then shown venturing into the forest armed with rifles and dressed in camouflage. However, we do not see their faces, but only their backs and legs. The unsettling score, shadowy and mysterious mise-en-scène, and unexplained action confuse the viewer and prompt a question regarding narrative motivation: the men appear to be hunting, but is their target human or animal? Moments later, a lone man enters the frame and spots his prey: a wild boar. Shot in medium close-up in shallow focus, he then raises his gun and points it directly at the camera. A reverse shot reveals the boar that seems to be staring both at the camera and into the eyes of its killer. A gunshot returns us to the hunter, who fires at the boar, but also into the camera's lens. The scene resolves with a cut to the film's title in white lettering which flutters anxiously against a black screen.

Thus, Una vita tranquilla begins under the sign of death. Specifically, the film opens with the suggestion of the execution of the viewer, who is twice placed in the position of the hunted animal. Such a self-conscious breaking of the fourth wall has several implications for the spectator. For one, we begin the film in a state of post-mortem, which provokes an association with the killer, who we learn a bit later has annihilated his earlier self and is thus, too, already dead. But also, and more germane to my argument, in that we are animalized early on in the film, we are prompted to see through the eyes of the victim, yet, as becomes clear from the beginning, victim status in the film is nebulous. The viewing position is uncomfortable as we have been identified as spectators from the outset. In that we are not hidden, we cannot pleasurably look on without being seen. Thus, we are forever implicated in the film's diegesis and are wary to identify with the filmic apparatus. Christian Metz argues that cinema conveys "the illusion of *perceptual mastery*"[12] to the spectator, who becomes an all-knowing and all-seeing unified subject:

> When I say that "I see" the film, I mean thereby a unique mixture of two contrary currents: the film is what I receive, and it is also what I release, since it does not pre-exist my entering the auditorium and I only need close my eyes to suppress it. Releasing it, I am the projector, receiving it, I am the screen; in both these figures together, I am the camera, which points and yet which records.[13]

This happens, he argues, as we have already successfully passed through the mirror stage and understand that we no longer reside in the imaginary and instead have a stronghold in the symbolic. "The cinema," writes Metz, "involves us in the imaginary: it drums up all perception, but to switch it immediately over into its own absence, which is nonetheless the only signifier present."[14] Film then represents what is not currently close at hand, but what once was and can thus be recalled by the spectator. In this way, cinema acts as a mirror that takes us back to the imaginary without the anxiety of misrecognition. Our absence from the screen does not typically trouble or confuse us because we have "already known the experience of the mirror (of the true mirror)" and are capable of creating "a world of objects" without needing to place ourselves within it.[15]

Instead of foregrounding scopophilic mastery and a unified subject, *Una vita tranquilla* constructs the viewing position as fragmented, fragile, and precarious. Thus, the traumatic event that opens the film and inaugurates the investigation that is traditionally central to the film noir is the death of the viewer. Specifically, the film pushes the viewer from the beginning to acknowledge the illusion of voyeuristic mastery and to be wary of any identification with the principal character. The viewer is constantly on edge, in part because of Rosario's behaviour that grows increasingly erratic as the film progresses. But also, although Rosario is our constant point of reference, he does not conform to the active male protagonist theorized by Laura Mulvey and therefore fails to convey "a satisfying sense of omnipotence" to the viewer. Typically, the hero is "the more perfect, more complete, more powerful ego ideal conceived in the original moment of recognition in front of the mirror."[16] Rosario, however, is in a constant state of breakdown, made clear later in the film when, driving through the forest, he stops just in time before hitting another wild boar. He looks tense and apprehensive as if he were now the one being hunted, a role reversal that is underlined when the boar aggressively rams the car before taking its leave. The boar, which was originally Rosario's prey, has returned in the guise of the aggressor. Indeed, each step Rosario takes to ensure his salvation brings him closer to his downfall, which is in keeping with the narrative arc of the protagonist of film noir. Instead of embodying the ego ideal with which we are meant to identify, Rosario's ego is "under attack."[17] Instead of consolidating masculinity, *Una vita tranquilla* demonstrates that male agency is in crisis. Instead of resolving the enigma at the heart of the narrative, Rosario is ineffectual and sloppy. What's more, he is incapable of mastering his environment.

And this is the case for Diego as well, whose initial presentation suggests that he is lacking in a stable identity as a result of paternal abandonment. Towards the beginning of the title frame, a voice is heard speaking rapidly in German. A sound bridge takes us into a bathroom where, moments later, we see a young man in partial profile, his face concealed by his hands, who is styling his eyebrow with a razor. His reflection is multiplied in two mirrors; in both, however, his likeness is obscured. Cross-cutting reveals another man, who we later learn is Edoardo, snorting cocaine while watching a news program about an agreement soon to be enacted between Italy and Michael Richter, president of the central German region of Hesse, that involves the transfer of twenty thousand tons of refuse from Campania to the German city of Biebesheim, where it will mainly be recycled for use in the industrial sector. Diego enters the room and notes the smell of gas before the two watch as Richter speaks in German on the television, and his words are not subtitled. An explosion in the hotel interrupts the scene and the two men, who we soon learn are Mafiosi, make a hasty exit in search of alternative lodging. Only later in the film do we realize that the man interviewed on German television is the Mafia target. Richter must be taken out, it is assumed, to halt the contract and to return the garbage trade into the hands of the Camorra. The explosion acts as a *deus ex machina* that pushes Diego on his quest for meaning and paternal validation.

Diego's inaugural reflection establishes his ego as fragmented and suggests that he has yet to secure a stronghold in the symbolic as is typical with the successful resolution of the Lacanian mirror stage.

The trauma that resulted in his father's abandonment when Diego was a child interrupted his psychic development and created confusion regarding symbolic law. We know nothing of the particulars of his childhood, but can imagine that Diego, in search of a surrogate father, was taken under Mario Fiore's wing and eventually inducted into his clan. Thus, he became trapped between a real Mafia father who had left him and a symbolic Mafia father who acted in his stead. Lacan explains that the symbolic father and the real father are instrumental in inaugurating the child into symbolic law and aid in the process of normalization necessary for the successful resolution of the Oedipus complex. He writes:

> The boy enters the Oedipus complex by a half-fraternal rivalry with his father ... But the father appears in this game as the one who has the master trump and who knows it; in a word, he appears as the Symbolic father ... The Symbolic father – he who is ultimately capable of saying "I am who I am" – can only be imperfectly incarnate in the real father. He is nowhere ... The real father takes over from the Symbolic father. This is why the real father has a decisive function in castration which is always deeply marked by his intervention or thrown off balance by his absence.[18]

Thus, the real father stands in for the law and functions to symbolically threaten castration, a process which then allows the child to internalize the incest taboo, venture outside of the family unit, and live his own life according to the Oedipal logic of patriarchal culture. Hence, castration gives access to culture, which in Diego's case should translate into a gangster lifestyle. Instead, he is clearly at odds with his symbolic Mafia father and attempts to come to terms with his real father who deserted him. However, as Diego lacks a stable ego ideal, his Oedipus complex was never normalized and, as a result, he experiences an unconscious murderous intent towards his father that plays out in the film.

The Most Holy of Mothers

An Oedipal struggle lies at the heart of *Una vita tranquilla*. What is broadly missing from the film, however, is a physically manifest maternal component of the complex. Although Rosario's leaving resulted in a non-functioning paternal metaphor that Diego attempts to resolve, he is dispassionate about women. When Rosario asks after his first wife and whether Diego gets along with her second husband, Diego curtly responds that he never sees them and that he lives by himself. Also, although Edoardo promptly initiates a sexual relationship with Doris, a waiter at Rosario's hotel, Diego is disinterested in erotic conquests. Moreover, Rosario's wife Renate is not central to the story whatsoever. Although *Una vita tranquilla* is a noir, the film is completely lacking a femme fatale character. The role of women in the film is minimized, as is the case with the Italian political film noir, which, as Mary P. Wood argues, instead centres on relationships between men and the power structures that they represent. She writes that "the necessity to pare down the narrative in the drive to uncover unpalatable or hidden truths about the complex political situation in Italy results in a focus on the male drive to investigate and contain, and the containment of the disruptive presence by any *femme fatale*,"[19] and that "Italian *film noir* is politicized and the figure of the *femme fatale* is subordinated to the drive to express anxieties about power, powerlessness, corruption, and other wounds to the body politic."[20] Such noir narratives are "homosocial" and depict Oedipal struggles regarding power in a corrupt socio-political climate.[21]

In traditional noir, the femme fatale can be considered a projection of male fantasy. In that she signifies lack, she is both a symptom of male anxiety and a source of fascination for the protagonist, who eventually either succumbs "to her power which ends in a paroxysm of their common death" or he can repudiate her, "which changes her into mucous slime," as Slavoj Žižek explains.[22] In *Una vita tranquilla*, the role typically allotted to the femme fatale is taken over by the Mafia, which Rosario tries to escape and renounce, while it becomes clear that Diego is not fully ready to capitulate to Mafia influence. His resistance is most conspicuous when Rosario is present. For example, while carrying out the hit on Richter, Diego freezes when he catches sight of his father and Edoardo must finish the job for him. But also, after Diego contacts his clan members in the wake of Edoardo's death and they make the trip to Wiesbaden to settle the score with Rosario, at the last minute, the son decides to save the father, a decision that results in Diego's own death.

Ironically, although the Mafia is a homosocial patriarchy, the sodality achieves identity and purpose out of a common love for an archaic mother figure. The Mafia, the *mammasantissima*, or "holyholymother," is a brotherhood born out of a common desire to both possess and defend the mother, who engenders a tie to mother earth and is fabricated in the collective imaginary as pure and benevolent. Thus, the maternal metaphor unites this esoteric group while defending it from the world outside, that is, the symbolic, or the law of the state.[23] The newly inducted Mafioso receives a "psychic gain" once he becomes part of the organization as he relinquishes his previous ego-ideal and assumes that of the group.[24] He becomes obsessively attached to the new symbolic mother so much so that he "deve essere disposto a morire per la mafia, a dare il suo sangue per la mafia [must be ready to die for the Mafia, to give his blood to the Mafia]," so as to protect the fantasmatic projection.[25] In this way, the relationship between the Mafia neophyte and his surrogate mother is akin to that of the noir protagonist and the femme fatale: both men can choose to either renounce her allure in the (most frequently unsuccessful) attempt to regain autonomy or to completely identify with her as pure death drive and accept the fatalistic outcome.

Thus, although no physical fatal woman is incarnate in the film, she is metaphorically present in the minds of both father and son, so much so that, in his failed endeavour at reinvention, Rosario settles down with a woman who can be considered to be the femme fatale's antithesis. Renate is best described as a "nurturing woman," a figure that Janey Place positions against her polar opposite, whom she dubs the "spider woman" in her discussion of feminine archetypes as they appear in the film noir. The redeeming woman, she explains,

> offers the possibility of integration for the alienated, lost man into the stable world of secure values, roles and identities. She gives love, understanding (or at least forgiveness), asks very little in return (just that he come back to her) and is generally visually passive and static. Often, in order to offer this alternative to the nightmare landscape of film noir, she herself must not be a part of it.[26]

Although Renate is at times frustrated with Rosario when he is running late or forgets to pick up Matthias from school, she is generally supportive, and appears very much in love with him. She has no knowledge of his secret past, forgave him when he had an affair a few years previously, and wrongly assumes that his recent volatile behaviour might be prompted by another dalliance. Her character is quite flat and underdeveloped, and like many "safe women" depicted in the genre, she is "static, undemanding and rather dull."[27] In the words of Christine Gledhill, Renate can be considered one of several "marginal female figure[s] representing the good woman, who [are] worthy of being a wife."[28] She offers Rosario an ordinary and quiet lifestyle that is the polar opposite of his previous situation in Campania, where, he explains, he "lived in a basement like a dog." Thus, Renate's representation is in keeping with that of other female characters in the Italian political noir where, as Wood explains, the "protagonist's female companions generally remain in supportive and subordinate roles, maintaining the traditional female stereotype."[29] With Renate, Rosario aspires to cancel out his past and preserve, in one reviewer's words, "the future of his new life," which is underlined when he poisons the trees behind the hotel so as to eventually legally remove them and build a beer garden in their place.[30] In her position as supporting wife and mother, Renate stands in stark opposition to both the femme fatale and the most holy of Mafia mothers.

Male Noir Melodrama

Rosario strives to repress and rewrite his past in order to start anew. It is telling that he is watching the opening scene of Emanuele Crialese's *Nuovomondo* (*Golden Door*, 2006) when Edoardo informs Rosario that he is aware of his true identity, a gesture that precipitates Rosario's breakdown. Crialese's film begins by depicting Sicilian peasants Salvatore and Angelo Mancuso, who climb a mountain with rocks in their mouths to arrive at a shrine so as to ask for a sign regarding their potential emigration to the new world at the turn of the century. The family eventually departs and, en route to America, Salvatore meets Lucy Reed, a blond Englishwoman who is assumed to be the widower's future bride. The final shot of *Nuovomondo* shows the Mancuso family keeping afloat in an ocean of milk. A slow zoom out reveals that Salvatore, Lucy, and sons Pietro and Angelo are accompanied by some 100 other immigrants, all of whom are treading water, and going nowhere. Ultimately, however, the film suggests that they have begun the process of assimilation and purification necessary for naturalization. The milk, together with the diegetic sound of Nina Simone's "Sinnerman," reinforces the thematics of rebirth and conversion, and the film obtains a neat sense of closure.

Una vita tranquilla disallows such a restorative finale that reaffirms the power of the nuclear family through depicting the Italian emigrant who unites with a fair-haired northern European woman. Rosario will start again, but he will be alone, and trapped in a perpetual past made present that literally gets him nowhere. Wood writes that, "in effect, Italian film noirs are male melodramas rehearsing shifting power relationships in Italian society."[31] Wood's interest in the hybridity of both genres is not isolated. Krutnik considers the "tough" thriller, a subgenre of film noir, "as representing a form of 'masculine melodrama,'"[32] while Janet Staiger writes of film noir as "Male Melodrama"[33] and Elizabeth Cowie coins the term "male film noir melodrama" in her discussion of gender politics as they play out in the noir.[34]

In many ways, Cupellini's film conforms to the definition of a male melodrama as theorized by Geoffrey Nowell-Smith, who discusses the gender divide at work in the melodrama and insists that, in the genre, "patriarchal rite is of central importance." Male melodramas are tragedies of origins in which the son must "become like his father in order to take over his property and his place within the community."[35] As Diego does in the film, the child asks the fundamental question "Whose child am I (or would I like to be)?"[36] as a means to establish an identity within the family and under the law of the father and therefore secure a stronghold in the symbolic. This is only possible, however, with a sacrifice.

Although *Una vita tranquilla* most certainly focuses on male emotion and excess, and demonstrates a crisis of masculinity and meaning as a result of an outside force that upsets familial life, the film does not ultimately conform to the traditional generic constraints of melodrama. Laura Mulvey explains that, in the melodrama that revolves around familial and generational conflicts, a positive conclusion is reached when the male protagonist is capable of rejecting "rampant virility" and successfully opposes "the unmitigated power of the father" so as to finally endorse the values of the normative family.[37] Instead, Rosario is not successful in standing up to Mafia law and is left without both a nuclear family and a Mafia clan. It is significant that he abandons his second son Matthias when he is more or less the same age as Diego was at the time of Rosario's first desertion. In this way, the film suggests that the legacy of betrayal and violence will be passed down generationally. In the film, the melodramatic thrust gives way to noir conventions in which "an external enigma, a murder or theft" is interwoven with a narrative that "focuses on the personal and subjective relations between the characters." While outside forces in the melodrama generally consist of "family circumstance, wars or illness," the threat in the noir derives "from the characters' psychology or even pathology as they encounter external events."[38]

Nowell-Smith demonstrates that, in the melodrama, "a 'happy end' which takes the form of an acceptance of castration is achieved only at the cost of repression."[39] He argues that castration, the marker of sexual difference and signifier of normalization, is central to the genre and is perpetuated and "renewed within each generation" by the father.[40] Films that centre on a male protagonist generally arrive at a reasonable conclusion through the siphoning off of emotional and narrative excess into music (in the musical) and mise-en-scène. Nowell-Smith likens such a narrative substitution to the Freudian concept of "conversion hysteria," which means that "the energy attached to an idea that has been repressed returns converted into a bodily symptom." Such a "return of the repressed" takes place in melodrama when extreme emotional and psychological situations fail to be represented within the confines of conventional plotlines and instead make their way into the film's structure and diegesis. In this way, the melodrama "somatizes its own unaccommodated excess, which thus appears displaced or in the wrong place."[41] In effect, the body of the patient is akin to the body of the filmic text, both of which must be read and explained.

The Return of the Repressed

Although Cupellini's film lacks the traditional melodramatic dénouement, emotional and psychological excess as a result of latent unresolved trauma surface in a series of narrative disruptions just after Rosario kills Edoardo towards the end of the film. Immediately following the murder, Rosario orders Diego to efficiently clean up the blood that is spilling all over the floor of the walk-in freezer. After Diego lowers himself to the ground while sobbing, the film jarringly cuts back and forth between four moments in the film: Diego and Rosario as they drive at night, the two of them while the bury Edoardo, Diego in the freezer, and, finally, Diego looking very despondent in the shower. This sequence, during which the father lays out the plan for a new start to his son, embodies one of the film's only two examples of non-linear narrative. At this point, Diego must choose: to accept the quiet life and flee, thereby following in his father's footsteps, conforming to his example and letting Rosario live, or to rebel against him, which would mean turning him in to the Mafia and effectively signing his death sentence. Choosing the latter would mean the triumph of Rosario's family life at the expense of severe repression for both father and son. Parricide, however, would give Diego access to Mafia culture, and would effectively resolve his identity crisis.

Returning to Nowell-Smith, Diego's moment of truth marks a "hysterical" point of the film when "the realist representative convention breaks down."[42] Up until this time, *Una vita tranquilla* follows the conventions of cinematic realism, which include, in particular, unobtrusive editing and a linear narrative, but also, as defined by Joshua Hirsch, "omniscience and flexibility of point of view, and unself-conscious voice." When flashbacks do occur in the classical realist historical film, "they are contained within narrow formal boundaries,"[43] so as to not confuse the viewer, who is meant to feel "a sense of mastery over time."[44] This is not the case, however, during this moment in this film where time is not constructed as heterogeneous. Instead, as is the case with the representation of "posttraumatic memory," here time is "experienced as fragmented and uncontrollable."[45] At this point, stable modes of representation "break down" and the repressed traumatic content of the film, that is, the murder of a Mafioso and Diego's reaction to it, is expressed through visual excess and narrative confusion.[46]

We soon learn that Diego has chosen to reject his father and the new life that he offers him by choosing Family over family, an act that should further the resolution of his Oedipus complex. I would like to recall my earlier discussion of parricide and perpetrator trauma as proposed by Freud, whereby the primal trauma of the murder of the primordial father is repressed and then passed down transgenerationally until it resurfaces in the guise of Moses, whose act of offering the people the idea of a single god "signified the revival of an experience in the primaeval ages of the human family which had long vanished from men's conscious memory."[47] In other words, the return of the repressed father. In the film, Diego refuses his father's offer of a new life as the Jews rejected Moses's proffering of a new religion. However, the murder of Moses ultimately brought about the creation of monotheism. And the Mafia follows a similar basic structure whereby members routinely repudiate one father in order to serve another all-powerful "father religion." Thus, the film exhibits how repressed traumatic memory is transferred from one generation to the next and is then acted upon when the abandoned son vindicates the absent Mafia father. Diego is first constructed as a victim, although his involvement in the Mafia precludes his status as completely innocent (it is interesting, however, that in the film he is never shown committing any sort of illegal act.) Yet, his betrayal would classify him as a perpetrator if, at the last minute, he had not changed his mind.

On their way to what was meant to be the place of Rosario's execution, father and son speak candidly for the first time. Rosario states that he is afraid of death, which prompts Diego to finally accuse his father of the Oedipal crimes of abandonment and parental neglect, and he then demands to know why Rosario did not take him with him to Germany. Then, as they approach the parked car, Diego orders his father not to stop, to which Rosario responds, "If I don't stop, they will kill both of us." Diego repeats his command, and Rosario complies, only to provoke gunfire which hits and kills Diego and forces Rosario to crash the car. Realizing that his son is dead, Rosario flees the scene and manages to pick up Matthias and return him to the hotel before disappearing once again. The staging of Diego's death signifies the second and final occasion where narrative is non-chronological. Images of Diego slumped over and bloody recur four times, and serve to punctuate Rosario's remorse regarding both his first son's physical death and his second son's eventual symbolic demise, which is sure to follow Rosario's departure. While driving with Matthias back to the hotel, Rosario is weeping and clearly grieving a series of losses. Ultimately, however, Rosario twice saves himself at the expense of his sons, and after dropping off Matthias, he hurriedly takes off and the film comes to a close as he travels by bus to northern Hamburg to attempt to "outwit" his past once more.[48]

Fundamentally, as David Kehr asserts in his work on the "new male melodrama," the genre is no different from the classical melodrama in that both smooth "over contradictions; [and make] us feel whole."[49] It works as an "idealized mirror" that reassures us as it completes and conventionalizes our world view.[50] Cupellini's film, however, lays bare the cracks in the national ego ideal both by disallowing the spectator to embrace the imaginary plenitude of the cinematic image and by representing the deaths of two Mafiosi as traumatic ruptures in the narrative framework. At the same time, *Una vita tranquilla* demonstrates how, in the Mafia, symbolic parricide and murder are routine and traumatic knowledge is regularly repressed and then passed on from symbolic father to son without being worked through. According to Bernhard Giesen,

> If a community has to recognize that its members, instead of being heroes, have been perpetrators who violated the cultural premises of their own identity, the reference to the past is indeed traumatic. The community can cope with the fundamental contradiction between identity claims and recognition only by a collective schizophrenia, by denial, by decoupling or withdrawal.[51]

The film insists that, in a Mafia context, there is no escaping or getting over the past, even though Rosario claims to have "repented" for his past sins. Ultimately, *Una vita tranquilla* maintains that Italy at large does not acknowledge the trauma of Mafia perpetrators and suggests that, until such a time, the repressed legacy of parricide will continue unabated.

Epilogue: Why Must Caesar Die?

> We thought it was important to show the trauma inmates had lived through ... They were feeling pain and ... it should be taken into account.
> Vittorio Taviani, "Mafioso and Murderer Tackle Shakespeare in New Film"

> How many times will Caesar have to bleed on theatre stages, like here today, as well, in this prison of ours lying on the stone, no more than dust.
> *Cesare deve morire* (Paolo and Vittorio Taviani)

I started this study by suggesting that the ongoing and apparently unending nature of the Italian Mafia hinders the extent to which it can be considered a cultural trauma as is the period of terrorism in Italy known as the "leaden years." I noted that Italian cinema in the new millennium has witnessed a remarkable outpouring of feature films with a Mafia focus (I count thirty-five films released since the year 2000), the vast majority of which somewhat follow the generic conventions of melodrama (including the woman's film and male melodrama) and the film noir. I set out to study how gender is represented in recent Italian Mafia cinema, and to look in particular at female characters in, around, and against the organization, many of whom are murdered, commit suicide, die in an accident, or are the victim of sexual violence. I also discuss how the homosexuality of male characters is elided so as to consolidate their status as an anti-Mafia martyr. In the introduction, I suggested that looking at how gender is constructed in these films can help us decide if Italy considers the Mafia a traumatic and traumatizing national problem or if the country at large has yet to engage in the process of mourning work necessary for the generation of a trauma narrative, and instead inhabits a state of national melancholia.

I then looked at ten Mafia movies made since the year 2000 so as to understand how contemporary directors represent Italy's Mafias. I went into the project with a series of questions. Is the Mafia presented as a phenomenon belonging to the past, or is it still constructed as an enduring component of Italian life? How are female characters treated in these films? Is the violence enacted against women sensationalist and meant to heighten dramatic tension or might murder, suicide, accidental death, and rape occasion our contemplation of the precariousness of life and safety in a Mafia context? Is the audience positioned to mourn the deaths of perpetrators or those loosely connected with the system, or is grief only reserved for those fallen in the battle against the Mafia? How are the stories of anti-Mafia martyrs rewritten so they conform to the generic qualifiers of the biopic? Finally, to what extent does the predominantly traditional and classical nature of these ten films both influence their final message regarding the inelasticity of gender roles in the Mafia and limit the representability of potentially trauma-inducing events?

I have shown in *Unfinished Business* that the Mafia is an integral concern of contemporary Italian national cinema, and is a versatile subject with which to tell stories of heroism, resistance, corruption, romance, and family drama. In the films discussed in the preceding chapters, the Mafia looms large and we are privy to numerous assassinations, massacres, and sexual assaults. Indeed, in these films, seventeen central protagonists are murdered, one commits suicide, four are raped, two are killed in automobile accidents, and one dies of a drug overdose.[1] Six of these films (including *Gomorra*) are inspired by real events and represent the demise of eleven historical figures within, around, and against the Mafia. These films treat the Cosa Nostra, the Camorra, and the Sacra Corona Unita's very real involvement in drug smuggling, money laundering, the eco-Mafia, kidnapping, clan wars, prostitution, and racketeering as well as the Mafia's penetration into legitimate business on an international scale.[2] The preponderance of violence, criminality, and diverse anxiety-provoking events in these films might suggest that Italian filmmakers are beginning to acknowledge and engage with the latent trauma of the Italian Mafia.

In all the films treated in this book, however, I find that pleasurable narrative forms such as the biopic, film noir, melodrama, and woman's film ultimately reassure the viewer at the film's end. E. Ann Kaplan and Ban Wang discuss how the "trauma film" marks "not the cinema itself but the viewer," and propose four main positions for the viewer of trauma cinema: we might be vicariously traumatized, might be positioned as a voyeur, or situated as a witness. Also, as is frequently the case with melodrama, we might be made aware of trauma while watching a film, but will leave the theatre feeling serene as distressing narratives have been neatly resolved by the film's end. Melodrama, they write, "is a symptom of a culture's need to 'forget' traumatic events while representing them in an oblique form."[3] In the genre, trauma is safely positioned in the past and is represented as something that is readily treatable. Paradoxically, however, melodrama might "reveal what it is that needs to be forgotten."[4] Hence, in the Italian case, remnants of Mafia-related trauma momentarily surface, only to be eventually smoothed over.

All the films of my study exhibit, to varying degrees, a "closure of meaning in the representation of trauma"[5] of the Mafia. Such categorical and, I would add, frequently restorative finales take a variety of forms. Several films conclude with a commemorative gesture that celebrates the life and death of an anti-Mafia martyr. This is the case with *I cento passi, Placido Rizzotto, L'uomo di vetro,* and *La siciliana ribelle,* in which the lives and relationships of several protagonists are rewritten so as to eradicate their ambivalence and difference and to foreground the film's straightforward anti-Mafia message. In other films, such as *Angela* and *Galantuomini,* female protagonists are ultimately punished for desiring excessively and usurping or threatening the male subject position. Although at the film's close these women have no place within the symbolic (either Mafia culture or normative bourgeois society), it is implied that, in the words of Luce Irigaray, these films' "dominant phallic econom[ies]" remain intact and master narratives are unaltered.[6] Conversely, *Le conseguenze dell'amore, Fine pena mai: Paradiso perduto,* and *Una vita tranquilla* dramatize the punishments of male characters with mob affiliations. Unlike in the films that represent female perpetrators, in these three films, all of which partially fall under the rubric of male melodrama, male characters find redemption at the film's close. They are either forgiven for their crimes (as is the case in *Una vita tranquilla*) or their lives (and deaths in *Le conseguenze dell'amore*) are celebrated and idealized. Finally, although *Gomorra* is less indebted to classical models than other Italian films from the new millennium, the film's "appeal to narrative pleasure" (to borrow from Eric Santner) minimizes the impact that scenes of violence might have on the viewer.[7]

As a result, possibly trauma-inducing events are downplayed, as is the strength and destructive potentiality of the Camorra when the organization is discussed in relation to international terrorism and to 9/11 at the film's close.

My study is particularly timely in that, as I hope to have made clear, the Italian Mafia frequently appears on the big and the small screen, is routinely discussed in the print media and on talk shows, and is a deadly, lucrative, and adaptable structure. The average citizen is no doubt aware that the Mafia is a national problem. Nonetheless, it appears that Italy at large has yet to come to terms with the traumatic experiences caused by the Mafia precisely because Italy's several Mafias are far from being in decline and their revenue, power, and reach increase daily. In such a delicate climate, the films of my study serve a valuable purpose in the construction of national identity: to borrow from Eric Santner, they "reinstate the pleasure principle without addressing and working through" traumatic injury. The "narrative fetishism" at work in the films discussed in this book "directly or indirectly offers reassurances that there was no need for anxiety in the first place."[8] Narrative fetishism, as Santner explains, implies a narrative, and he is discussing the cinema, in which trauma is a main thematic concern, but is represented in such a way that denies and undoes loss by "situating [its] site and origin" elsewhere. Thus, the individual, and also the culture, is not yet obligated to "reconstitute ... identity under 'posttraumatic' conditions."[9] Such restorative and pleasurable narrative strategies ultimately disavow the creation of a trauma discourse and postpone a process of national mourning.

I would like to conclude my study by briefly discussing a film that won the Golden Bear at the Berlin International Film Festival in February of 2012 and was Italy's pick for best foreign-language film for the Oscars. Paolo and Vittorio Taviani's *Cesare deve morire* (*Caesar Must Die*, 2012) is not a Mafia movie per se, but certainly engages themes familiar to the genre, such as vendetta, loyalty, betrayal, murder, and honour in the strictly homosocial milieu of the penal institution. Primarily set in the high-security wing of Rome's Rebibbia prison, *Cesare deve morire* is a fully scripted docu-drama about a group of inmates staging a production of Shakespeare's *Julius Caesar*. The film begins by showing the last few minutes of the prison production in front of a packed house and then flashes back to "six months earlier" to represent the auditions, cast selection, and rehearsals that brought the company to the final curtain. While *Cesare deve morire* opens and closes in colour (the penultimate sequence of the film once again depicts a slightly extended version of the formal performance), the bulk of the film is shot in black and white, a technique that underlines a series of contrasts that the film both explores and undermines, which include, past and present, reality and fiction, and artifice and naturalism.[10] Indeed, dramatic camerawork and lighting, an emotive musical score, and the scripted dialogue denaturalize the rehearsal sequences and call attention to the film's constructed and artificial nature. During the rehearsals, more often than not, inmates call each other by their stage names. All these elements aid in overturning distinctions between reality and fiction.

Of the six inmate cum actors who take centre stage in the film, three are imprisoned for Mafia activity: Cosimo Rega (Cassius) is a former Camorrista serving a life sentence for murder and other crimes, Salvatore "Sasà" Striano (Brutus) is incarcerated for fourteen years and eight months for Camorra-related crimes, and Enzo Gallo (Lucius) is sentenced to life under 416bis, or the crime of Mafia association.[11] Other protagonists are imprisoned for drug trafficking and unspecified criminal activity. The film raises many compelling questions regarding the performative aspects of criminality. In this way, *Cesare deve morire* is reminiscent of *Gomorra* in that both films depict mobsters whose lives are mirrored in the characters that they either emulate, in the case of Marco and Ciro in Garrone's film, or portray, as in the Tavianis' film. Such a self-reflexive ethos is laid bare in the credit sequence at the end of *Cesare deve morire* when we learn that Sasà Striano, the inmate who plays Brutus, was pardoned and is now an actor in the theatre and the cinema. Originally sentenced in 2000, he was released from jail in 2006 and has appeared in several films; he played one of the Scissionisti in *Gomorra* and also appeared in Marco Risi's *Fortapàsc* (2009), a biopic about engaged reporter Giancarlo Siani, whose crusade against the Camorra results in his death. But while it is implied that Marco and Ciro's veneration of onscreen mobsters whose behaviour they imitate directly pushes them towards their deaths, acting in *Cesare deve morire* proves liberating and redeeming as inmates are shown to get in touch with, express, and work through what appear to be previously untapped emotions. Thus, the experience of acting is cathartic in the truest sense of the word.

The Tavianis' film no doubt humanizes the prisoners and emphasizes their individuality. For example, they recite their roles in their own dialects, and we learn of their earlier travels, adventures, hometowns, rivalries, idiosyncrasies, and families. We are privy to a range of their emotional reactions, including anger, sadness, nostalgia, and insecurity, and witness their genuine affection for one another and communal elation at the conclusion of the performance. The directors are quite open about their expectations with regards to how the film will affect the audience. When accepting the prize, Paolo Taviani said, "We hope that when the film is released to the general public that cinemagoers will say to themselves or even those around them ... that even a prisoner with a dreadful sentence, even a life sentence, is and remains a human being,"[12] while Vittorio Taviani added that the play "was a kind of liberation" for the prisoners and wished that viewers would see inmates "no matter what their crime was, as men first and foremost."[13] Prisons in Italy are quite overcrowded, with approximately 68,000 inmates in a system with a maximum capacity of 45,000. Suicides are routine and overcrowding creates several physical and mental health concerns. Over 30 per cent of those detained have not even faced their first court date.[14] In December of 2011, Pope Benedict XVI visited the Rebibbia prison and spoke of the overcrowding in the system, emphasizing that prisoners should be treated with dignity, and that space should be made for the prisoner "in our time, in our home, in our friendship, in our laws, in our cities," a sentiment that echoes that Tavianis' comments above.[15]

In staging the pathos of incarceration, *Cesare deve morire* recalls *Fine pena mai: Paradiso perduto*, another film that engages with Mafia perpetrators and renders them sympathetic. One reviewer notes that *Cesare deve morire* "might equally be called 'Shakespeare can set you free,' as prisoners mentally escape the confines of their cells, at least fleetingly," which is certainly the case in Barletti and Conte's film.[16] Like Antonio in *Fine pena mai*, inmates in *Cesare deve morire* daydream of their families, and imagine a life outside the prison walls. Such gestures are often meant to elicit compassion for the protagonists of the Tavianis' film, as happens when Enzo (Lucius) is shown gazing off-screen melancholically. An eyeline match reveals the subject of his vision to be a mural depicting a small windswept island. As the camera slowly zooms in, the monochrome hues inherent in the flashback transition to a vibrant palate of blues and greens before the idyllic image is superimposed with an aerial shot of Rebibbia in black and white – a technique that reminds us of Enzo's perennial confinement.

In *Cesare deve morire*, when inmates interpret villains, murderers, traitors, and tyrants, many are prompted to relive their criminal past and take stock of the actions that brought them to Rebibbia. Thus, performing the play becomes a type of therapy that is similar to grief work. As Santner tells us, the work of mourning involves the process of "remembering and repeating" traumatic experiences in the present within safe and controlled environments (in dreams or in therapy, for example).[17] The six-month process of rehearsing Shakespeare's play, and repeating lines that deal explicitly with murder, treachery, and corruption, moves many of the inmates emotionally.[18] Moreover, the inclusion in the adaptation of words such as "vendetta," "uomini d'onore [men of honour]," "capo [boss]," and "quaquaraquà [a windbag and parasite]" grounds the play in a Mafia context and assists in returning the men to the scene of their own crimes.[19]

Vittorio Taviani explains that the directors "thought it was important to show the trauma inmates had lived through … They were feeling pain and … it should be taken into account."[20] Therefore, unlike in *Una vita tranquilla* where the trauma of Mafia perpetrators is repressed and elided from the narrative, in *Cesare deve morire*, it is literally put on centre stage and acted out in front of a series of audiences, which include fellow inmates, guards, the director Fabio Cavalli, the audience of the prison performance, and the spectator of the film. Several times in the film, actors become visibly shaken when dialogue strikes too close to home. For example, when Decius (Juan Bonetti) attempts to convince Caesar (Giovanni Arcuri) to appear in front of the Senate on the infamous Ides of March, the latter breaks character to relate to Juan "what has been in [his] heart for years." He then tells Juan that he is two-faced and an argument breaks out between them. Also, when Brutus (Sasà) pronounces the line "If I could remove the spirit of the tyrant without tearing open his chest," he suddenly becomes angered and covers his face with his hands. Enzo (Lucius) insists that Sasà knows his lines, as he has "the character of Brutus inside of him," while Cosimo (Cassius) reminds the group of the verisimilitude of the play with respect to their own lives: "Have we never known bullying Caesars in our home? And betrayal and murder?" We then learn that the expression is so moving to Sasà as it reminds him of a friend of his, but we never hear how the story is resolved. Thus, it is suggested that acting helps these men make sense of and come to terms with their violent pasts and work through their losses.

Problematic, of course, in such an emotive representation is the absence of the voice of the victims of these men's crimes. What's more, Giovanni, Sasà, Cosimo, Enzo, Juan, and Antonio Frasca (Mark Anthony) never specifically speak to their offences. Ruth Glynn deftly argues that "perpetrator speech is never neutral,"[21] and this is particularly the case in *Cesare deve morire*, where dialogue is not spontaneous and, notwithstanding minor modifications to accommodate dialect, follows the screenplay at mostly all times.[22] Indeed, we rarely forget that we are watching a fully scripted film, a reaction that is solidified once we realize that one of the central protagonists has been a free man for years and has only returned to the prison to make the film. Such a meta-cinematic and self-reflexive motif recurs frequently and is made obvious when characters break the fourth wall so as to directly address the audience and to solicit our empathy.

Although the prisoners' outlooks are retrospective and their dialogues (both in and out of character) are frequently imbued with regret, they never express remorse for their crimes nor do they ask for forgiveness. Instead, their melancholy and despair seem to be caused by the realization of their enduring internment, and this is especially the case for Enzo and Cosimo, who will live out the rest of their days behind bars. The film concludes when Cosimo returns to his cell following the performance of *Julius Caesar*. After bitterly surveying his environs, Cosimo addresses the camera and says, "Since I have found art, this cell has become a prison," before he begins to make coffee with resignation. In staging the humanity of the inmates and omitting a specific discussion of their infractions, *Cesare deve morire* turns Mafia perpetrators into sympathetic victims of the Italian penal system.

Although *Cesare deve morire* does not strictly qualify as a male melodrama, the mise-en-abyme of the play does provide a venue in which the inmates can express their angst and tell their stories to a listener who is meant to feel concern for them (or, as we have seen, channel these stories through the characters that they represent). Thus, as happens in *Fine pena mai*, the prisoner's losses become restorative. In this way, the film engages "in the activation of the previously repressed emotions of men," a generic trait of the male weepie as theorized by Linda Williams.[23] Furthermore, the emphasis on male bonding and the complete omission of female characters, with the exception of the women who form part of the audience, recall the homosocial configuration of the buddy movie (although here we do have more than two characters on centre stage).[24] The film has a "highly emotive narrative" and depicts, "if only through fantasy, ... the possibility of reconciliation with the past through the pursuit of dreams," to borrow from John Mercer and Martin Shingler's discussion of the male melodrama.[25] In sum, like other films that belong to the genre of male melodrama, *Cesare deve morire* thematizes the loss and grief of male characters and ultimately presents them as redeemed, in this case through their encounter with the play.[26]

After Caesar is murdered, Cassius looks squarely at the camera and asks, "How many centuries to come will see actors play this grandiose scene of ours in kingdoms that are not yet born and in languages yet to be invented?" before Brutus queries, while also staring right at us, "How many times will Caesar have to bleed on theatre stages, like here today, as well, in this prison of ours lying on the stone, no more than dust?" In the prison context, art, as the film proposes, is therapeutic and potentially redemptive. In voicing the trauma of mafia perpetrators, albeit in a choreographed manner, *Cesare deve morire* stands out from other films from the new millennium that engage the Italian Mafia. The film makes plain that Caesar *must* die, over and over again, so that the inmates can begin to heal. At the same time, however, the film elides Mafia malfeasance and displaces recent acts of violence onto a distant and glorious past through a culturally acceptable art form. Ultimately, this gesture reminds us that the business of the Italian Mafia is by no means unfinished.

Notes

Introduction

1 For more on the Mafia as an esoteric "men only society," see the eponymous chapter in Siebert, *Secrets of Life and Death*, 13–27.
2 Here I am discussing the Mafia in general, which is of course made up of several Mafias: the Sicilian Cosa Nostra, the Camorra of Campania, the 'Ndrangheta of Calabria, and the Sacra Corona Unita of Puglia. Both the Cosa Nostra and the 'Ndrangheta can be dated to the period of Italian unification. The Camorra predates the Cosa Nostra and the Sacra Corona Unita was founded in the prison system of Puglia in 1983.
   It is out of the scope of my project to detail the history and expanse of the Italian Mafia. However, a substantial body of scholarship is available on the topic. See, for example, Allum, *Camorristi, Politicians and Businessmen*; Felia and Percy Allum, "Revisiting Naples"; Felia Allum and Renate Siebert, eds, *Organized Crime and the Challenge to Democracy*; Apollonio, *Sacra corona unita*; Arlacchi, *Men of Dishonor*; Behan, *See Naples and Die*; Chiarelli, *Sacra corona unita*; Dickie, *Blood Brotherhoods* and *Cosa Nostra*; Duggan, *Fascism and the Mafia*; Falcone, *Men of Honour*; Gambetta, *The Sicilian Mafia*; Parini, "The Strongest Mafia"; Ingrascì, *Donne d'onore*; Jamieson, *The Antimafia*; Lupo, *History of the Mafia*; Massari, *La sacra corona unita*; Occhigrosso, ed., *Ragazzi della mafia*; Puglisi, *Donne, Mafia e antimafia*; Reski, *The Honoured Society*; Saviano, *Gomorrah*; Jane C. and Peter T. Schneider, *Reversible Destiny*; Siebert, *Secrets of Life and Death*; Stille, *Excellent Cadavers*; and Truzzolillo, "The 'Ndrangheta."
3 See the chapter "The System" in Saviano, *Gomorrah*, 33–59.
4 Siebert, "Mafia and Anti-Mafia: Concepts and Individuals."

5 For excellent discussions of the memory of Italian political terrorism during the *anni di piombo*, see Glynn, "Through the Lens of Trauma" and *Women, Terror and Trauma in Italian Culture*.
6 Neal argues that "the test for a national trauma is that of the disruptive effects of an extraordinary event on the institutional underpinnings of a social order." *National Trauma and Collective Memory*, xi. Conversely, the Italian Mafia is far from "extraordinary," as it is a constitutive component of Italian society present since the birth of the nation. Alexander takes issue with Neal's discussion of trauma as resulting from an abrupt and catastrophic event and classifies his approach under the rubric of "enlightenment thinking." Such an understanding implies that "trauma is a kind of rational response to abrupt change, whether at the individual or social level," and that "responses to such traumas will be efforts to alter the circumstances that caused them." "Toward a Theory of Cultural Trauma," 3.
7 During the first few months of the Second Mafia War that began on 23 April 1981, hundreds of people were killed in and around Palermo (counting only the bodies that were actually found). For more on the Second Mafia War and Mafia-related deaths in the 1980s, see Dickie, *Cosa Nostra*, 259–308.
8 This, for example, from Sicilian author Vincenzo Consolo: "Palermo è fetida, infetta. In questo luglio fervido, esala l'odore dolciastro di sangue e gelsomino, odore pungente di creolina e olio fritto. Ristagna sulla città, come un'enorme nuvola compatta, il fumo dei rifiuti che bruciano a Bellolampo ... Qui Palermo è una Beirut distrutta da una guerra che dura ormai da quarant'anni, la guerra del potere mafioso contro i poveri [Palermo is rank, infected. In this fervid July, the bittersweet stench of blood and gelsomino wafts in the air, a strong odour of creolin and fried oil. The smoke of the garbage burning at Bellolampo is stagnant over the city like an enormous compact cloud. Here, Palermo is a Beirut destroyed by a war that has lasted now for 40 years, the war of Mafia power against the poor]." *Le pietre di Pantalica*, 170; my translation. Unless otherwise indicated, all translations are mine.
9 For more on contemporary Mafia tourism and the reinvention of the Sicilian Cosa Nostra, see Renga, "Introduction," 4–5.
10 Landesman, "Gomorra."
11 Several documentaries on the eco-Mafia include interviews with residents who express horror, sadness, anger, and shock regarding the "garbage emergency" and illegal toxic dumping by the Mafia. See, for example, *Biùtiful cauntri* (Esmeralda Calabria and Andrea D'Ambrosio, 2007), *La bambina deve prendere aria* (*The Baby Needs Some Fresh Air*, Barbara Rossi

Prudente, 2009), *Una montagna di balle* (*A Mountain of Lies*, Nicola Agrisano, 2009), *Toxic: Napoli* (Santiago Stelley, 2009), and *Campania In-Felix* (*Unhappy Country*, Ivana Corsale, 2011). For two excellent analyses of films on the eco-Mafia, see Angelone, "Talking Trash," and Past, "'Trash Is Gold.'" Iovino maintains that the eco-Mafia is involved in the following illegal endeavours: "Traffic in toxic waste, in protected animal and plant species, illegal gambling on exploited animals, systematic devastation of 'local' territory for abusive building developments that cause severe ecological damage." "Ecocriticism and a Non-Anthropocentric Humanism," 31.
12 Herman, *Trauma and Recovery*, 33.
13 New work done in the wake of the 9/11 attacks looks at how Americans immediately began experiencing traumatic symptoms and engaging in a discourse of trauma in an attempt to make sense of the traumatic experience of terrorism. See, for example, Kaplan's chapter "'Wounded New York': Rebuilding and Memorials to 9/11," in *Trauma Culture*, 136–47; her article "Global Trauma and Public Feelings"; and Sturken, *Tourists of History*.
14 Leys, *Trauma: A Genealogy*, 20.
15 Freud, *Beyond the Pleasure Principle*, 12–13.
16 Smelser writes that Freud's earlier hypotheses regarding traumatic memory and neuroses indicate that trauma is "not a thing in itself but becomes a thing by virtue of the context by which it is implanted." "Psychological Trauma and Cultural Trauma," 34.
17 Caruth, "Introduction," 9; original italics.
18 Erikson, *Everything in Its Path*, 154.
19 Ibid., 155.
20 Alexander, "Toward a Theory of Cultural Trauma," 5. For a discussion of the centrality of restored memory to traumatic recovery in the writings of Saul Friedlander and Cathy Caruth, see Alexander, ibid., in particular the section "Psychoanalytic Thinking," 5–8.
21 Ibid., 11.
22 Ibid., 12.
23 As Alexander explains, "It is by constructing cultural traumas that social groups, national societies, and sometimes even entire civilizations not only cognitively identify the existence and source of human suffering but 'take on board' some significant responsibility for it." Ibid., 1.
24 Ibid., 10.
25 For example, Rousso asks, "What connection is there ... between cinematic representation and collective memory?" *The Vichy Syndrome*, 239.
26 Eyerman, *Cultural Trauma*, 1.

27 See Igartua and Paez, who explain that through the analysis of film it is possible to see "how a social group symbolically reconstructs its past in order to confront traumatic events for which it is responsible." "Art and Remembering Traumatic Collective Events," 81.
28 I reference here the title of Friedlander's historical memoir *When Memory Comes*.
29 Kaplan, *Trauma Culture*, 74.
30 Smelser, "Psychological Trauma and Cultural Trauma," 53.
31 Alexander, "Toward a Theory of Cultural Trauma," 12.
32 Ibid., 13–14.
33 Ibid., 14–15.
34 Smelser, "Psychological Trauma and Cultural Trauma," 43. For more on the tie between national trauma and collective identity see the chapter "Society as Moral Community" in Neal, *National Trauma and Collective Memory*, 20–36.
35 Silverman, *Male Subjectivity at the Margins*, 55.
36 See Alexander, "Toward a Theory of Cultural Trauma," 21.
37 Ibid., 12.
38 Kaplan, *Trauma Culture*, 68.
39 Giesen, "The Trauma of Perpetrators," 116.
40 LaCapra, *History in Transit*, 119.
41 Felman and Laub, *Testimony*, xiv.
42 Specifically, Santner addresses how then-recent events in Europe influence the altering of the "German historical imagination" regarding the Holocaust. "History beyond the Pleasure Principle," 143.
43 I refer to the title of the co-authored volume by Rousso and Conan, *Vichy: Un passé qui ne passe pas*.
44 Marcus, *Italian Film in the Shadow of Auschwitz*.
45 See, for example, Antonello and O'Leary, eds, *Imagining Terrorism*; Glynn and Lombardi, eds, *Remembering Moro*; Glynn, Lombardi, and O'Leary, eds, *Terrorism, Italian Style*; Glynn, *Women, Terror and Trauma in Italian Culture*; O'Leary, *Tragedia all'italiana*; and Uva, ed., *Schermi di piombo*.
46 See, for example, Blake, *The Wounds of Nations*; Hirsch, *Afterimage*; Kaplan, *Trauma Culture*; Kaes, *Shell Shock Cinema*; Kaplan and Wang, eds, *Trauma and Cinema*; King, *Washed in Blood*; Lowenstein, *Shocking Representation*; McIntosh and Leverette, eds, *Zombie Culture*; Sarat, Davidovitch, and Alberstein, eds, *Trauma and Memory*; and Walker, *Trauma Cinema*. Blake, for instance, investigates the connection between the "bewildering array of traumatic happenings" in the last hundred years and an "escalating public interest in horror films." She feels that such an interest speaks to "a public

will to understand the experience of traumatic events while self-reflexively exploring the function of mass cultural representations of such trauma," 4; Lowenstein questions: "How does this film access discourses of horror to confront the representation of historical trauma tied to the film's national and cultural context?" 9.
47 The "special debate" consists of five essays, the first of which is an introductory piece by Radstone called "Trauma and Screen Studies: Opening the Debate."
48 Elsaesser, "Postmodernism as Mourning Work," 195.
49 Ibid., 201.
50 Kaplan, "Melodrama, Cinema and Trauma," 203.
51 Kaplan, *Trauma Culture*, 66.
52 Hirsch, *Afterimage*, 19.
53 Turim, "The Trauma of History," 210.
54 Ibid.
55 Herman, *Trauma and Recovery*, 2.
56 Quoted from Rousso's study *The Haunting Past: History, Memory and Justice in Contemporary France*, 1. The entire citation reads: "We are living in the 'age of memory,' that is, in a sensitive, affective, even painful relationship with the past."
57 Hirsch, *Afterimage*, 20.
58 Frisch, *A Shared Authority*, xxii, cited in Walker, "Trauma Cinema: False Memories and True Experience," 216.
59 Silverman, *Male Subjectivity at the Margins*, 30. She continues: "images and stories which cinema, fiction, popular culture, and other forms of mass representation presumably both draw upon and help to shape."
60 Ibid., 15.
61 Ibid., 41.
62 Alexander, "Toward a Theory of Cultural Trauma," 26–7.
63 Freud, "Mourning and Melancholia," 245.
64 Ibid., 249.
65 Butler, *Precarious Life*, xiv.
66 Ibid., 32.
67 *Contre la dépression nationale* is the original title of Kristeva's interview with Philippe Petit translated as *Revolt, She Said: An Interview with Philippe Petit*. She points out that "the incapacity to rebel is a sign of national depression. Faltering images of identity ... and lost confidence in a common cause, gives rise at the national level to just what the depressed individual feels in his isolation" (83). Although she is discussing the situation in France, such a statement is appropriate to the Italian cultural scene.

68 See, for example, Aiello and Lucentini, *Maladetta mafia*; dalla Chiesa, *Le ribelle*; De Toni, *Dolentissime donne*; di Lorenzo, *La grande madre mafia*; Fiandaca, ed., *Women and the Mafia*; Ingrascì, *Donne d'onore*; Lanza, *Donne contro la mafia* and *Ho fame di giustizia*; Longrigg, *No Questions Asked*; Lo Verso, ed., *La Mafia dentro*; Madeo, *Donne di mafia*; Masciopinto, *Donne d'onore*; Principato and Dino, *Mafia donna*; Puglisi, *Donne, Mafia e Antimafia, Sole contro la mafia*, and *Storie di donne*; Renga, "Screening the Italian Mafia"; Rizza, *Una ragazza contro la mafia*; and Siebert, *Secrets of Life and Death*.

69 The term "submerged centrality" was originally coined by Principato and Dino in *Mafia donna*, 14.

70 Siebert, *Secrets of Life and Death*, 26.

71 Cavarero, *Horrorism*, 14.

72 This is the case of Cosa Nostra and the 'Ndrangheta. Women are involved in several aspects of official mob business in the Camorra and the Sacra Corona Unita.

73 Cavarero, *Horrorism*, 33.

74 Yuval-Davis, *Gender and Nation*, 47.

75 See Hipkins's article on *In the Name of the Law*, "Which Law Is the Father's?," for a nuanced reading of the character of the Baroness.

76 Wood, "*Chiaroscuro*," 158.

77 Hipkins, "Why Italian Film Studies Needs a Second Take on Gender," 213.

78 Silverman, *The Threshold of the Visible World*, 178.

79 Silverman, *Male Subjectivity at the Margins*, 55.

1. Oedipal Conflicts in Marco Tullio Giordana's *I cento passi*

1 I would like to thank Dom Holdoway for generously sharing his research on *I cento passi*.

2 Five chapters of *Unfinished Business* are dedicated to films that represent historical figures (Giuseppe "Peppino" Impastato in chapter 1, Placido Rizzotto in chapter 2, Leonardo Vitale in chapter 5, Antonio Perrone in chapter 7, and Rita Atria in chapter 9). In chapters 1, 2, 5, 7, and 9, I will refer to historical figures by their last name (Impastato, Rizzotto, Vitale, Perrone, Atria) and will designate filmic characters by their first name (Peppino, Placido, Leonardo, Antonio, and Rita). All discussions of other historical figures and characters upon whom they are based are clearly indicated throughout the book.

3 Marcus, "In Memoriam," 292.

4 Examples abound. For instance, Bondanella labels the two films as "biopics celebrating two Sicilians who fought against the Mafia and paid with their lives" (*A History of Italian Cinema*, 480); Babini argues that both films "reviv[e] neorealism, endowing it with epic tones" and hark back to "the tradition of the political cinema of the 1970s ... [to] bring to the fore two of the many unknown martyrs in the war against the Mafia" ("The Mafia: New Cinematic Perspectives," 244–5); Small discusses how *I cento passi* "narrates a tale of exceptional courage" ("Giordana's *I cento passi*," 44); and de Stefano states that *I cento passi* is "a consciousness-raising tool for anti-mafia forces, as well as a memorial to a fallen leader of the anti-mafia struggle" ("Marco Tullio Giordana's *The Hundred Steps*," 320).

5 Here is the complete citation: "In contrast to woman as icon, the active male figure (the ego ideal of the identification process) demands a three-dimensional space corresponding to that of the mirror-recognition, in which the alienated subject internalised his own representation of his imaginary existence. He is a figure in a landscape. Here the function of film is to reproduce as accurately as possible the so-called natural conditions of human perception. Camera technology (as exemplified by deep focus in particular) and camera movements (determined by the action of the protagonist), combined with invisible editing (demanded by realism), all tend to blur the limits of screen space. The male protagonist is free to command the stage, a stage of spatial illusion in which he articulates the look and creates the action." Mulvey, "Visual Pleasure and Narrative Cinema," 20.

6 For a reading of Giordana's "epitaphic strategy" and how the photo montage that closes *I cento passi* is "proof of the historicity and credibility of [the film's] memorialist task," see Marcus, "Return of the Referent," 277. Catherine O'Rawe offers another reading of the archival footage that closes the film. She argues that the inclusion of the photographs does not, as Marcus puts forward, help us to return to the historical moment. Instead, these images evoke a sense of nostalgia for "the return to the origin ... and demonstrate an anxiety that such a return may not be possible." O'Rawe, "'A Past That Will Not Pass,'" 110.

7 It is intriguing that in *I cento passi* Luigi Lo Cascio is cast as an anti-Mafia activist killed by the Mafia and some years later plays Saro Scordia, a Mafioso (albeit an eventually repented one) in the melodrama *Il dolce e l'amaro* (*The Sweet and the Bitter*, Andrea Porporati, 2007). In Porporati's film, Saro is in love with Ada, a woman opposed to the Mafia who is interpreted by Donatella Finocchiaro. This is an interesting casting choice

given that Finocchiaro plays a woman involved with the Mafia in the films *Angela* and *Galantuomini*.
8 D'Onofrio, "Italian Cinema Revisits the 1970s," 162. In another article, D'Onofrio interestingly argues that music in *I cento passi* specifically recalls the period of the late 1960s, in particular 1968, a year that is utopistic, "familiare e innocuo [familiar and innocuous,]" and is unlike the 1970s, a much more controversial period of Italian history. D'Onofrio, "Percorsi di identità narrativa nella memoria difficile," 230.
9 O'Rawe, "More More Moro," 214.
10 O'Leary, *Tragedia all'italiana*, 225.
11 Wood, *Italian Cinema*,173.
12 See Dall'Orto, "La 'tolleranza repressiva' dell'omosessualità."
13 See the chapter "A Men-Only Society" in Siebert, *Secrets of Life and Death*, esp. 22–7.
14 Sedgwick, *Between Men*, 1.
15 Siebert, *Secrets of Life and Death*, 22. Here, Siebert is quoting the work of the French feminist Élisabeth Badinter, *XY de l'identité masculine* (Paris: Éditions Odile Jacob, 1992), 79.
16 Siebert, *Secrets of Life and Death*, 24.
17 In "Coming to Be a Man," Ferrero Camoletto and Bertone interview seventy-one men and women about male pleasure. In interviews pertaining to male group masturbation, the authors note that interviewees "avoid interpreting homosociality as having an erotic meaning, stressing instead its training function," 243.
18 Butler, *Bodies That Matter*, 112.
19 Siebert, *Secrets of Life and Death*, 60.
20 Siebert, "Mafia and Anti-Mafia," 49.
21 Creed, *The Monstrous Feminine*, 38.
22 Lacan, "The Mirror Stage as Formative of the Function of the I," 4.
23 Silverman, *The Subject of Semiotics*, 164.
24 De Lauretis, *Alice Doesn't*, 157.
25 Ibid., 145.
26 Ibid., 112.
27 Ibid., 143.
28 Ibid., 113.
29 Bartolotta Impastato, *La mafia in casa mia*.
30 Films made in the late 1960s and 1970s that treat Italian fascism, the Second World War and the partisan resistance, for example, frequently infuse the historical narrative with an Oedipal twist. In films such as Luchino Visconti's *La caduta degli dei* (*The Damned*, 1969), Bernardo Bertolucci's *La strategia del ragno* (*The Spider's Stratagem*, 1970), *Il conformista*

(*The Conformist*, 1970) and *Novecento* (1976), Liliana Cavani's *Il portiere di notte* (*The Night Porter*, 1974), and Lina Wertmuller's *Pasqualino settebellezze* (*Seven Beauties*, 1975) male protagonists confront the past head on in an attempt to liberate themselves from the hold of real and metaphorical fathers.

31 Wittman, "Pasolini's 'Inner Enemy.'"
32 Pitrè, *Usi e costumi, credenze e pregiudizi del popolo siciliano*, 294.
33 See the chapter by Siebert called "A Men-Only Society" in *Secrets of Life and Death*.
34 See Blok, "Mafia and Blood Symbolism."
35 Marcus, *Filmmaking by the Book*, 140.
36 Dickie, *Cosa Nostra*, 33.
37 Blok, *Honour and Violence*, 105.
38 Giordana, Fava, and Zapelli, *I cento passi*, 79.
39 Silverman, "On Suture," 140.
40 Ibid.
41 Ibid.
42 Ibid., 141.
43 Ibid.
44 Fiore, "La famiglia nel 'pensare Mafioso,'" 54.
45 For a discussion of the maternal role in Mafia families, see Ingrascì, *Donne d'onore*, esp. 1–45, and the chapters "A Men-Only Society," "The Family," and "Women" in Siebert, *Secrets of Life and Death*. See also lo Verso, "Per uno studio dello psichismo mafioso," in *La mafia dentro*, 23–36. Lo Verso writes that the transmission "di valori, della cultura, dei modelli relazionali, simbolici ed affettivi viene fatto, in larga parte, dalle madri [of values, of culture and of symbolic, affective, and relationship models is mostly done by mothers]," 31.
46 Ingrascì, *Donne d'onore*, 23.
47 After her son's death, together with her surviving son Giovanni Impastato, Felicia Bartolotta Impastato publicly broke off all relations with her relatives involved in the Mafia. For more on her anti-Mafia activity see Impastato, *La mafia in casa mia* and dalla Chiesa, *Le ribelli*, 39-60.
48 Pasolini, *Tutte le poesie*, 1102. Translation from Pier Paolo Pasolini, *Roman Poems*, 97–9.
49 Impastato, *Lunga è la notte*, 115–16, my translation. Note that Impastato crossed out the possessive in the sentence "non espressi mai i miei desideri, ma su questa ~~mia~~ condizione schizoide ..."
50 For a discussion of references to Pasolini in more recent Italian cinema see Renga, "Pier Paolo Pasolini and the Memory of Martyrdom in New Italian Cinema."

51 I thank the anonymous reader for University of Toronto Press for this reference. Following a screening of *I cento passi*, the reader heard Giordana admit that he had based Peppino and Felicia's relationship on that of Pasolini with his mother.
52 De Stefano, "Marco Tullio Giordana's *The Hundred Steps*," 325.
53 See the many pages of Impastato's diary, *Lunga è la notte*, esp. 115–29. See also a dissertation by Paparcone that includes an interview with Umberto Santino, who confirms Impastato's homosexuality, "Echoes of Pierpaolo Pasolini in Contemporary Italian Cinema," 108–9.
54 The citation reads: "Mi ancora una volta di un mio giovane 'compagno.' È stato forse quello il periodo più straziante e al tempo stesso più esaltante della mia esistenza e della mia storia politica. Passavo di continuità ininterrotta da fasi di cupa disperazione a momenti di autentica esaltazione creativa [I _____ once again with one of my young 'comrades.' This was possibly the most heartrending and exalting period of my existence and political life. I continually oscillated between phases of bare desperation and moments of authentic exaltation and creative ability]." Interestingly, Impastato cannot bring himself to put his feelings in writing and omits the expression "fall in love," leaving instead a blank space. Impastato, *Lunga è la notte*, 118, my translation.
55 Paparcone, "Echoes of Pierpaolo Pasolini," 109.
56 Dominic Holdaway shared this information and pages from the screenplay with me. I am forever in his debt. He is currently working on a project that looks at how cinema as industry tempers the level of political engagement in *I cento passi*. He interviewed Antonio Carella, who confirmed Impastato's homosexuality and described the reasons for which the screenplay was never produced (essentially, although Carella had support from Giovanni Impastato, RAI, and others, the appearance of the already funded script by Claudia Fava and Monica Zapelli put an end to the project).
57 Carella, *Nel cuore della luna*, 113, my translation.
58 Silverman, *Male Subjectivity at the Margins*, 2.
59 De Lauretis, *Alice Doesn't*, 153.
60 Ibid., 140.
61 Marcus, "In Memoriam," 292.
62 Di Pelo, "*I cento passi*."

2. Honour, Shame, and Vendetta

1 In the online commercial for this agriturismo, the Mafia is absent. Instead, the spot features the popular "Love Show" by Skye, which also appeared

in an episode of *Grey's Anatomy*, a Nivea commercial, and the Portuguese soap opera *Morangos con Açúcar*.
2 Smith, "Sicily Offers a Safe Taste of Mafia Life." It is not my contention that Libera Terra consciously sets out to capitalize on Mafia culture in the same way that, for example, numerous tour companies in New Jersey have by offering "tours of Sopranoland." Nonetheless, it is compelling how many pivotal events and notorious figures of Sicilian mafia history since the Second World War are bottled, as it were, and decanted into a wine glass. These include the bandit Salvatore Giuliano and the infamous Portella della Ginestra May Day massacre in 1947, the murder of anti-Mafia crusaders Rizzotto and Impastato in Cinisi in 1978, Pio la Torre in Palermo in 1982, and Giovanni Falcone in Capaci and Paolo Borsellino in Palermo in 1992.
3 See De Stefano, *An Offer We Can't Refuse*.
4 The subtitle reads "In Sicily, a woman is more dangerous than the lupara." In Italian the two are equated as equally perilous.
5 Žižek, *The Sublime Object of Ideology*, 163.
6 Boylan, "Pasquale Scimeca's *Placido Rizzotto*."
7 Dickie, *Cosa Nostra*, 260.
8 Blok, *Honour and Violence*, 113.
9 Haskell, *From Reverence to Rape*, 39–40.
10 Babini, "The Mafia: New Cinematic Perspectives," 245.
11 Marcus, "In Memoriam," 292. In addition, Boylan argues that Scimeca "creates a cinematic memorial to a previously forgotten young Sicilian man, and offers his life story as a model of behavior for future generations." "Pasquale Scimeca's *Placido Rizzotto*," 313.
12 For more on the history of the Mafia during the years of Fascism, see Duggan, *Fascism and the Mafia*.
13 Boylan, "Pasquale Scimeca's *Placido Rizzotto*." In particular Boylan argues that "Placido's witnessing and subsequent memory gives their deaths meaning" (318).
14 For a discussion of the sexual politics at work in Rossellini's film, and in particular how lesbianism is aligned with absolute evil, see O'Healy, "Politics and Sociosexual (In)Difference from *Roma città aperta* to *The Last Emperor*."
15 Marcus, *Italian Film in the Light of Neorealism*, 44.
16 De Lauretis, *Alice Doesn't*, 13.
17 Metz, *The Imaginary Signifier*, 60.
18 Rooney, "Placido Rizzotto."
19 Babini, "The Mafia: New Cinematic Perspectives," 245.
20 Nepoti, "Rizzotto, l'eroe bello contro 'Lo sciancato.'"

21 Higgins, "Screen/Memory," 307.
22 Horeck, *Public Rape*, 5.
23 Ibid., vii.
24 Ibid., 9.
25 Higgins and Silver, "Introduction: Rereading Rape," 3.
26 Dickie, *Cosa Nostra*, 263. Indeed, the film downplays her activism, as Sorisi was supposedly quite involved in the worker's movement. Fava writes that she "Lavorava con [Rizzotto], si batteva con lui, lottava con lui, occupava le terre insieme ai contadini [she worked with Rizzotto, she fought with him, she struggled with him, she occupied the land with the farmers]." Bongiovanni, "Le parole di Pippo Fava."
27 Bongiovanni, "Le parole di Pippo Fava."
28 Francesco, "Il 'Professor' del crimine che leggeva Kant."
29 Biagi, *Il boss è solo*, 237–8. Another account recounts that, at Leggio's arrest, Sorisi "non disse nulla, abbassò solo gli occhi per la vergogna [said nothing, and lowered her eyes out of shame]." Bolzoni and D'Avanzo, *Il capo dei capi*, 66.
30 Molino, *Taci infame*, 115.
31 Zermo, "A 87 anni è morto il questore Angelo Mangano, arrestò Liggio." For more on Sorisi's discussion of her relationship with Leggio, see Follain, *The Last Godfather*, 65, and Bellavia, "Fiamme, misteri, dicerie, depistaggi e sullo sfondo il business dei rifiuti."
32 Follain, *The Last Godfather*, 31.
33 Siebert, *Secrets of Life and Death*, 159.
34 Ibid., 160
35 Ibid.
36 For more on the cycle of honour, shame, and vendetta in the Mafia as it relates to women, see the eponymous section in Siebert, *Secrets of Life and Death*, 37.
37 Here is the complete citation: "Si pensi al tema del 'sado-masochismo' che sottilmente percorre tutto il suo cinema, rilevante ne *Il giorno di San Sebastiano*, ma presente pure in *Placido Rizzotto* – vedi la scena, particolarmente insistita dello stupro della donna di Placido; a quello della sessualità, si pensi, ancora, alle tematiche 'psicanalitiche' incentrate sui conflitti uomo-donna. [Think of the theme of sadomasochism inherent in all of your films that is significant in *Il giorno di San Sebastiano*, but also present in *Placido Rizzotto* – take, for example, the particularly demanding scene when Placido's girlfriend is raped. But also think of the motif of sexuality or 'psychoanalytic' thematics centred upon conflicts between men and women]." Zagarrio, "Incontro con Pasquale Scimeca."

38 Modleski, "Rape versus Mans/laughter," 304.
39 Deutsch, *The Psychology of Women*, 1: 277.
40 Ibid., 256.
41 Horeck, *Public Rape*, 141.
42 Metz, *The Imaginary Signifier*, 62.
43 Horeck, *Public Rape*, 147.
44 Metz, *The Imaginary Signifier*, 65.
45 Silverman, *Male Subjectivity at the Margins*, 164.
46 Ibid., 165.
47 Horeck, *Public Rape*, 155.
48 Boylan, "Pasquale Scimeca's *Placido Rizzotto*," 318.
49 De Lauretis, *Technologies of Gender*, 82.
50 Silverman, *Male Subjectivity at the Margins*, 15.

3. Mafia Woman in a Man's World

1 See Áine O'Healy's excellent treatment of the film for an account of Torre's interaction with the real "Angela" when preparing the project, which was originally conceived as a documentary. O'Healy also notes that Torre's decision to set the film in 1984 is interesting when one considers the women's movement in Italy. At that time, the movement had made considerable strides in northern and central Italy, but had not "fully penetrated the societies of the south." O'Healy, "Anthropological Anxieties," 94.
2 Mulvey, "Visual Pleasure and Narrative Cinema," 20.
3 See Marangi, "Mafia e legge (del desiderio)," 42.
4 Here and throughout the book, I use "Family" to designate the symbolic mafia family and "family" when discussing the biological family. Siebert states that Joe Bonanno "draws significant distinctions between 'family' and 'Family.' Despite repeated declarations of love and affection for his close relatives, his account demonstrates the unquestionable subordination of the interests of his family – with the small 'f' – to those of the Family – with a capital 'F.'" *Secrets of Life and Death*, 30.
5 O'Healy, "Anthropological Anxieties," 83.
6 O'Rawe, "Roberta Torre's *Angela*," 334.
7 Ibid., 330.
8 See many of the essays in Fiandaca, ed., *Women and the Mafia*; and Ingrascì, *Donne d'onore*.
9 Pizzini Gambetta writes: "Women in Sicily had been granted equal criminal status to the men only when civil rights were quashed," and in various periods during the mid-twentieth century, "women were taken into

custody not necessarily for their own crimes but to put pressure on fugitive male relatives." "Becoming Visible," 207.
10 Principato, "The Reasoning Behind This Research," 286.
11 Quoted in Siebert, *Secrets of Life and Death*, 49–50. See also the chapter "Garante della reputazione maschile" in Ingrascì, *Donne d'onore*, 26–38.
12 Siebert, *Secrets of Life and Death*, 49.
13 O'Rawe, "Roberta Torre's *Angela*."
14 As one reviewer notes: "Women viewers interested in mob stories but who abhor violence will find much to enjoy here." Bergmann, "Angela," 11.
15 Reviewers of the film have a hard time classifying *Angela* in terms of genre. Mitchell, for example, calls it a "romantic melodrama" and a posh "television movie" with a "weepie's fury." "A Sleeping Mafia Wife, Awakened by Some Irresistible Cheekbones."
16 Jacobs, *The Wages of Sin*, 6.
17 "In psychological terms, the female figure poses a deeper problem. She ... connotes something that the look circles around but disavows: her lack of a penis implying the threat of castration and hence unpleasure ... The male unconscious has two alternatives of escape from this castration anxiety: preoccupation with the re-enactment of original trauma (... demystifying her mystery), counterbalanced by the devaluation, punishment or saving of the guilty object ... or else complete disavowal of castration by the substitution of a fetish object or turning the represented figure itself into a fetish so that it becomes reassuring rather than dangerous." Mulvey, "Visual Pleasure and Narrative Cinema," 21.
18 Ibid., 17.
19 Mulvey, "Afterthoughts on 'Visual Pleasure and Narrative Cinema,'" 30.
20 In her discussion of *Duel in the Sun*, Mulvey concludes that "Pearl's position ... is similar to that of the female spectator as she temporarily accepts 'masculinisation' in memory of her 'active' phase. Rather that dramatizing the success of masculine identification, Pearl brings out its sadness. Her 'tomboy' pleasures, her sexuality, are not fully accepted by Lewt, except in death." Ibid., 37.
21 For more on Finocchiaro's performance, and possible correlations with that of Anna Magnani, see O'Rawe, "Roberta Torre's *Angela*," 333.
22 Mulvey, "Afterthoughts on 'Visual Pleasure and Narrative Cinema,'" 35.
23 Doane, "The Woman's Film," 79–80.
24 Ibid., 79.
25 O'Healy, "Anthropological Anxieties," 95.
26 Freud, "Mourning and Melancholia," 245.
27 Ibid., 244.

28　Ibid., 249.
29　Kristeva, *Powers of Horror*, 2
30　Ibid., 12.
31　Ibid., 2.
32　Ibid., 4.
33　Ibid.
34　O'Rawe, "Roberta Torre's *Angela*," 335. It is interesting that when I taught this film to my graduate class in 2012, all students commented that they felt quite distanced from Angela and mentioned that they had little insight into her motivations and decision-making process.
35　Kristeva, *Powers of Horror*, 26.
36　Jacobs, *The Wages of Sin*, x.

4. The Mafia Noir

1　See, for example, Wood, "Lipstick and Chocolate"; Small, "No Way Out"; Rodriguez, "Ejercicios deconstructivos"; and Morgoglione, "La tragedia di un uomo solo diviso tra la mafia e la passione." Instead, Leotta discusses the film's generic hybridity; it is at once "a thriller, an action movie, a dark comedy." "Do Not Underestimate the Consequences of Love," 286.
2　Palmer, "Moral Man in the Dark City," 203.
3　Wood, "Lipstick and Chocolate," 358.
4　De Stefano, *An Offer We Can't Refuse*, 371.
5　Romney writes that Sorrentino is obsessive "in his interest in female beauty pushed to idealisation, especially when contrasted with mortal male weakness. Olivia Magnani and Laura Chiatti [from *L'amico di famiglia*, 2006] are not just gorgeous, they embody an extreme of beauty." "Tragedies of Ridiculous Men," 42.
6　Ibid.
7　Following is the citation from the film: "Poi succeda quel che vuole, bell'affare. Il vantaggio d'eccitarsi, in fin dei conti, solo su delle reminiscenze. Puoi possederle, le reminiscenze, puoi comperarne di belle, di splendide, una volta per tutte. La vita è più complicata, quella delle forme umane specialmente. Un'avventura paurosa, non c'è niente di più disperato. A confronto di questo vizio, delle forme perfette, la cocaina non è che un passatempo per capistazione … Ma torniamo alla nostra Sophie: facevamo come dei progressi in poesia, solo con l'ammirare il suo essere tanto bella e tanto più incosciente di noi. Il ritmo della sua vita scaturiva da altre sorgenti, che non le nostre, striscianti per sempre le nostre, invidiose. Questa forza allegra, precisa e dolce insieme, che l'animava dai capelli

alle caviglie ci veniva a turbare. Ci inquietava in un modo incantevole, ma ci inquietava, è la parola." English translation taken from: Céline, *Journey to the End of the Night*, 407–8.

8 Sorrentino's film *L'amico di famiglia* (*The Family Friend*, 2006) is inspired by *Journey to the End of the Night* and reviews of his novel *Hanno tutti ragione* (*They're All Right*, 2010, finalist for the Premio Strega) frequently compare Sorrentino's writing style to that of Céline's.
9 Céline, *Journey to the End of the Night*, 407.
10 Kristeva, *Powers of Horror*, 161.
11 Ibid., 9.
12 Ibid., 154.
13 See Wood, who discusses how the diagonal composition and asymmetry of the opening shot "disturb the eye" and prevent the viewer from passively accepting narrative events. "Lipstick and Chocolate," 357.
14 Žižek, *The Plague of Fantasies*, 39.
15 In her discussion of the limits of Italian film criticism, particularly in relation to gender studies, Danielle Hipkins brings up the "much lauded films of Paolo Sorrentino, in which the female is merely a fetish object for the narration of male desire." "Why Italian Film Studies Needs a Second Take at Gender," 213–14.
16 Doane, *The Desire to Desire*, 32.
17 Mulvey, "Visual Pleasure and Narrative Cinema," 22.
18 Kristeva, *Black Sun*, 45.
19 Doane, *Femmes Fatales*, 1. See also the introduction to *The Femme Fatale: Images, Histories, Contexts*, ed. Hanson and O'Rawe. The editors make a case for the "tautological" link between the femme fatale and the film noir: "If a film has a *femme fatale* it is a *film noir*, and in order to qualify as a *noir*, the *femme* is indispensable" (2).
20 Doane, *Femmes Fatales*, 2.
21 Ibid.
22 Ibid.
23 Ibid., 1.
24 Ibid., 1–2.
25 Bach, *Marlene Dietrich*, 91.
26 Muller, "Opening Remarks to *The Woman Men Yearn for*" at the 2011 San Francisco Silent Film Festival.
27 Žižek, *Enjoy Your Symptom!* 160. For more on the femme fatale as victim, see Grossman, *Rethinking the Femme Fatale in Film Noir*.
28 Žižek, *Enjoy Your Symptom!* 160.
29 Ibid., 158.

30 Ibid., 169.
31 Freud, "Inhibitions, Symptoms, and Anxiety," 91.
32 Rodriguez, "Entravista: Paolo Sorrentino," 42.
33 The entire citation reads: "Sophie had the winged, elastic, precise gait that is so frequent, almost habitual, among the women of America, the gait of heroic creatures of the future, whom life and ambition carry lightly toward new kinds of adventure ... Three-masters of joyful warmth ... bound for the infinite"; Céline, *Journey to the End of the Night*, 408.
34 Kristeva, *Powers of Horror*, 10.
35 Ibid., 172.
36 Žižek, *Interrogating the Real*, 33.
37 Žižek, *Enjoy Your Symptom!* 155.
38 Žižek, *Looking Awry*, 66.
39 Sorrentino, however, explains that Titta does not confess and chooses death because of the missed appointment with Sofia. "D'une certaine maniere il décide de se laisser mourir à cause de cet amour qui ne s'est pas materialisé [in a certain way he decides to let himself die because of this love that did not materialize]." Codelli and Thirard, "Entretien avec Paolo Sorrentino," 38.
40 Žižek, *Enjoy Your Symptom!* 152.
41 Ibid., 151.
42 Ibid., 152.
43 Wood, "Lipstick and Chocolate," 360.
44 Žižek, *Enjoy Your Symptom!* 44.
45 Ibid., 46.
46 Small calls such a mentality regarding the persistence of the Mafia "post-political": "The films [*The Consequences of Love* and *Gomorra*] combine to offer what can be termed a form of post-political Mafia filmmaking characterized by resignation to, though not at all acceptance of, the presence of illegality deeply embedded in Italian society." "No Way Out," 127.
47 And here I reference Lacan's two notorious propositions: "Woman is a symptom of man" and "Woman does not exist."

5. Men of Honour, Man of Glass

1 For more on Tommaso Buscetta as the first credible *pentito*, see Dickie, *Cosa Nostra*, 265–8, and Lupo, *History of the Mafia*, 255–6.
2 Bongiovanni and Petrozzi, "Leonardo Vitale: La prigione della follia," 37.
3 Lo Verso, "Mafia a follia,"101.

4 Parlagreco, *L'uomo di vetro*, 31.
5 Foucault, "Madness Only Exists in Society," 8.
6 Ibid., 9.
7 And here I reference the title of a paper presented by Laura Wittman that looked at the films *I cento passi* and *Placido Rizzotto*. "Pasolini's 'Inner Enemy' and the Revisionist Mafia Movie."
8 De Lauretis, *Technologies of Gender*, 43.
9 Ibid., 44.
10 Inconsistencies arise regarding Vitale's age at the time of his father's death. Some say he was twelve or thirteen, but in a statement taken in the Ucciardone prison on 10 May 1973, Vitale reports, "Mio padre è morto e 38 anni, cioè 13 anni fa, ossia quando avevo 18 anni [my father died when he was thirty-eight, thirteen years ago, or when I was eighteen]." Galluzzo, Nicastro, and Vasile, *Obiettivo Falcone*, 97.
11 Ibid., 101.
12 Ibid., 109.
13 Ibid. Here the authors paraphrase Vitale's feelings about blood.
14 Lo Verso, "Mafia, psicopatologia, psicoterapia," 140.
15 Lo Verso and Lo Coco, "Working with Patients Involved in the Mafia," 175.
16 O'Leary, "Power as Such," 281. See also Wood, "Lipstick and Chocolate," 359–60.
17 Foucault, "Of Other Spaces," 24.
18 Ibid., 27.
19 Ibid., 24.
20 Lacan, "The Mirror Stage as Formative of the Function of the I," 4–5; original italics.
21 Foucault, "Of Other Spaces," 24.
22 Ibid., 25.
23 Parlagreco, *L'uomo di vetro*, 73.
24 Ibid., 105.
25 Ibid., 78. In response to the question "Was Leonardo Vitale crazy?" Gelso replies, "He was not, but he was made to believe that he was." *Mafia*, 148.
26 Parlagreco, *L'uomo di vetro*, 30.
27 See Cervantes, "Man of Glass," in *The Portable Cervantes*, 760–96.
28 Parlagreco, *L'uomo di vetro*, 130.
29 Ibid., 26
30 For a discussion of Vitale's possible homosexuality, his Oedipal crises, and desire to be like everyone else, see Lo Verso, "Mafia a follia," 105–17; Lo Verso, "Mafia, psicopatologia, psicoterapia," 138–41; and Galluzzo, Nicastro, and Vasile, *Obiettivo Falcone*, 100–2, 107.

31 Parlagreco, *L'uomo di vetro*, 113; original italics.
32 Galluzzo, Nicastro, and Vasile, *Obiettivo Falcone*, 102.
33 Parlagreco, *L'uomo di vetro*, 88.
34 Freud, "From the History of Infantile Neurosis," 40.
35 Ibid., 86.
36 Ibid., 42.
37 Ibid., 68.
38 Ibid., 118.
39 Ibid., 64.
40 Ibid., 101.
41 Ibid., 115.
42 Ibid., 114.
43 Parlagreco, *L'uomo di vetro*, 86.
44 Freud, "From the History of Infantile Neurosis," 40.
45 Ibid., 101.
46 Ibid., 102.
47 Galluzzo, Nicastro, and Vasile, *Obiettivo Falcone*, 106.
48 Lo Verso, "Mafia, psicopatologia, psicoterapia," 140.
49 Lo Verso, "Mafia a follia," 117.
50 Silverman, *Male Subjectivity at the Margins*, 46.
51 Silverman, *The Acoustic Mirror*, 2.
52 Žižek, "Introduction: Alfred Hitchcock," 6.
53 Ibid., 8.
54 Ibid., 6.
55 Williams, *The Erotic Thriller in Contemporary Cinema*, 56.
56 Bal, *A Mieke Bal Reader*, 44–5.
57 Anderson, "Sins of Permission," 77.
58 Parlagreco, *L'uomo di vetro*, 62.
59 I would like to thank Vlad Dima for conversations about Hitchcock's cinema and the MacGuffin as relating to the feminine.
60 At the beginning of the credits, a script appears that states: "The facts described in the film really happened and have been verified, even if, for narrative purposes, fictional elements have been included."
61 Caprara, "Vitale, pentito e martire."
62 Catacchio, "Cosa nostra, Leonardo 'morto che cammina.'"
63 Escobar, "L'uomo di vetro."
64 Catacchio, "Cosa Nostra, Leonardo 'morto che cammina.'" Citing Elaine Scarry, Richard Dyer maintains that the Pietà is "an image simultaneously of cradling and death," which is significant to the film in terms of

Leonardo's Christlike attributes. Dyer, *White*, 15. I thank Catherine O'Rawe for bringing this reference to my attention.
65 For more on the effects of electroshock and drug therapy on Vitale's memory, see Parlagreco, *L'uomo di vetro*, 135–46 and Lo Verso, "Mafia a follia," 114–15.
66 Girard, *Violence and the Sacred*, 290.
67 Bongiovanni and Petrozzi, "Leonardo Vitale," 37.
68 Custen, "Where Is the Life That Late He Led," 308.

6. The Female Mob Boss

1 Interestingly, the word 'Ndrangheta, the name of the Mafia of the southwestern Italian region of Calabria, derives from the Greek *andragathia*, a compound of "andra," meaning "man," and "agathia," signifying goodness, virtue, and nobility. The combined form implied bravery or manliness in antiquity. I am indebted to Tom Hawkins for bringing this fascinating etymology to my attention.
2 In an interview, Winspeare defines "galantuomo" as an honest, good, and an upstanding member of society. He says that Ignazio is a "galantuomo" who still believes in a land that has utterly changed. "Galantuomini."
3 For more on the history of the Sacra Corona Unita, see Apollonio, *Sacra corona unita*; Bruneli, "Italy Keeps a Rein on Smallest Mafia Group"; Chiarelli, *Sacra corona unita*; Massari, *La sacra corona unita*; and Occhigrosso, ed., *Ragazzi della mafia*, 89–93, 119–56.
4 Doane, *The Desire to Desire*, 34; original italics.
5 Mulvey, "Notes on Sirk and Melodrama," 39.
6 Ibid., 43.
7 The expression "galantdonna" or "woman of honour" does not exist in Italian, and the closest equivalent is "gentildonna," meaning "gentlewoman" or "lady."
8 Doane, *The Desire to Desire*, 16.
9 In an interview, Winspeare questions whether women had lost their femininity and had to "masculinize" themselves in order to become members of the Sacra Corona Unita. Regarding the film, he states, "Solo alla fine sapremo se Lucia sceglierà di seguire la propria femminilità o se in qualche modo, continuando a seguire il suo destino, dovrà rinunciarvi [Only at the end will we know if Lucia will choose to follow her femininity or if somehow, continuing to follow her destiny, she will have to renounce it]." "Galantuomini."

10 For more on the history and function of women in the Sacra Corona Unita, see Massari and Motta, "Women in the Sacra Corona Unita."
11 De Donno et al., "Manners of Killing and Rituals in Apulian Mafia Murders," 897.
12 The name of the rival Mafioso undoubtedly evokes the biblical thief Barabbas, who was released in the place of Christ.
13 Projansky, *Watching Rape*, 97.
14 Coulthard, "Killing Bill," 172.
15 Projansky, *Watching Rape*, 101.
16 Penley, "Introduction," 22.
17 Freud, "'A Child Is Being Beaten,'" 185; original italics.
18 Ibid., 186.
19 Doane, *The Desire to Desire*, 18.
20 Freud, "'A Child Is Being Beaten,'" 199.
21 Of Freud's remarks regarding the position of women in the fantasy, Doane writes: "Masochistic fantasy *instead* of sexuality. The phrase would seem to exactly describe the processes in the woman's film whereby the look is de-eroticized." *The Desire to Desire*, 19; original italics.
22 "Galantuomini."
23 In another interview, Winspeare explains that the Sacra Corona Unita is "l'unica mafia che è stata sconfitta dai magistrati [the only Mafia that the authorities have wiped out]." Dentice, "Cinema Padrino."
24 Bruneli, "Italy Keeps a Rein on Smallest Mafia Group," 40; Takahashi, "Capital Punishment," 1.
25 Bruneli, "Italy Keeps a Rein on Smallest Mafia Group," 43.
26 I am indebted to Julia Nelson Hawkins for the reference to Lilith.
27 Cavarero, *Horrorism*, 8.
28 Freud writes, "To decapitate = to castrate. The terror of Medusa is thus a terror of castration that is linked to the sight of something." "Medusa's Head," 273.
29 Doane, *Femmes Fatales*, 1.
30 Ibid., 2.
31 Ibid., 2–3.
32 Gamble, "Postfeminism," 49.
33 Doane, *Femmes Fatales*, 2.
34 Out of over fifty film reviews and blogging sites consulted, only one (discussed below) mentions the sexual assault, but states that Lucia is "nearly" raped.
35 The comment appears as a "cached" link in the search engine that is no longer available for viewing when clicked. I originally came across

it under the following web address: http://www.google.com/search?client=safari&rls=en&q=galantuomini&ie=UTF-8&oe=UTF-8#sclient=psy-ab&hl=en&client=safari&rls=en&source=hp&q=galantuomini+winspeare+%22la+stupra%22&pbx=1&oq=galantuomini+winspeare+%22la+stupra%22&aq=f&aqi=&aql=&gs_sm=e&gs_upl=5902159021316204111101010101011921192l0.11l10&bav=on.2,or.r_gc.r_pw.r_cp.,cf.osb&fp=1995634a4db7f5e8&biw=1190&bih=548; my italics.

36 Young, *The Scene of Violence*, 71.
37 Higgins and Silver, "Introduction: Rereading Rape," 2.
38 Projansky, *Watching Rape*, 63.
39 Clover, *Men, Women and Chainsaws*, 144.
40 For more on traditional modes of spectator identification during the rape-revenge film see Clover, *Men, Women and Chainsaws*, 137–59, and Moore, "If It Was a Rape, Then Why Should She Be a Whore?" 136–8.
41 Young, *The Scene of Violence*, 46.
42 Read, *The New Avengers*, 12.
43 Projansky, *Watching Rape*, 120.
44 Coulthard, "Killing Bill," 163.
45 Mulvey, "Notes on Sirk and Melodrama," 43.
46 Projansky, *Watching Rape*, 120.
47 Modleski, *Feminism without Women*, 3.
48 Cavarero, *Horrorism*, 3.

7. Melancholia and the Mob Weepie

1 Di Amato, *Criminal Law in Italy*, 211.
2 As Perrone calls Daniela Piccinno "Lela" in the memoir, I will also refer to her as "Lela" throughout the chapter.
3 Modleski, "Clint Eastwood and Male Weepies," 154.
4 Ibid., 136.
5 Ibid., 139.
6 Schiesari, *The Gendering of Melancholia*, 13.
7 Metz, *The Imaginary Signifier*, 74.
8 Schiesari, *The Gendering of Melancholia*, 13.
9 Johnston, "Women's Cinema as Counter Cinema," 249.
10 Perrone, *Vista d'interni: Diario di carcere, di "scuri" e seghe, di trip e di sventure*.
11 For example, Giancristofaro describes *Fine pena mai* as "un Bonnie & Clyde alla pugliese intriso di Scarface, poliziotteschi, road movie. Un noir esistenziale e vitalistico [a Puglian Bonnie & Clyde soaked with Scarface, the

Italian crime film and the road movie. A vital and existential noir.]" *"Fine pena mai"*.
12 Hayward, *Cinema Studies*, 218.
13 Ibid., 219.
14 Staiger, "Film Noir as Male Melodrama," 73.
15 Barletti and Conte, "Postfazione."
16 Siracusano, "Diario dal carcere."
17 Dante Alighieri, *The Divine Comedy: Inferno*, 279–80.
18 Schiesari, *The Gendering of Melancholia*, 43; original italics.
19 Ibid., 74.
20 *"Fine pena mai*: Press Book."
21 Schiesari, *The Gendering of Melancholia*, 167.
22 Ibid., 168.
23 Perrone, *Vista d'interni*, 121.
24 Ibid., 16.
25 Ibid., 49.
26 Ibid., 162.
27 Ibid., 61.
28 Blum, *The Other Modernism*, 62.
29 Lacan, *The Four Fundamental Concepts of Psychoanalysis*, 103.
30 Cowie, *Representing the Woman*, 219.
31 Žižek, *Looking Awry*, 133.
32 Doane, *Femmes Fatales*, 2.
33 Silverman, "Fassbinder and Lacan," 59.
34 Ibid., 60.
35 Perrone, *Vista d'interni*, 124.
36 Orsitto, "Martin Scorsese's *Goodfellas*," 147.
37 Perrone, *Vista d'interni*, 35.
38 Ibid., 86.
39 In an interview, Barletti explains that they chose to call the fictional name of town Solino as a homage to the Turkish director Fatih Akin, whose film *Solino* (2002) tells the story of a family who emigrates from Solino to Duisburg, Germany. The scene (and Akin's film) was actually shot in Nardò. "Behind the Scenes."
40 Barletti and Conte, "Postfazione."
41 Schiesari, *The Gendering of Melancholia*, 182.
42 Earlier in the film, Antonio happily watches as Gianfranco goes swimming in the ocean for the first time since his arrest and subsequent imprisonment seven years earlier. We are to assume that Antonio's commemoration of his friend's death is motivated by this earlier memory.

43 "Behind the Scenes," DVD.
44 Perrone, *Vista d'interni*, 43.
45 "Behind the Scenes."
46 Perrone, *Vista d'interni*, 100.
47 Ibid., 155.
48 Modleski, "Clint Eastwood and Male Weepies," 136.
49 "Behind the Scenes," DVD.
50 "Quando il Salento perse la sua verginità."
51 Renga, "Introduction." 4.
52 Schiesari, *The Gendering of Melancholia*, 14.
53 Freud, "Mourning and Melancholia," 244.
54 Perrone, *Vista d'interni*, 122–3.
55 This footage comes from the documentary *Diario di uno scuro* (Diary of a Member of the Sacra Corona Unita, Davide Barletti, Edoardo Cicchetti, and Lorenzo Conte, 2008) that focuses on Daniela Piccinno, who recounts her history with her husband and their two children, details the couple's heavy drug use, and explains his life of crime, involvement with the Mafia, eventual arrests, and periods of incarceration. The documentary also includes interviews with journalists, Perrone's lawyer, and anti-Mafia activists, including Nichi Vendola, the current president of Puglia, among others, who speak to the Sacra Corona Unita's history, structure, and criminal activity.
56 Schiesari, *The Gendering of Melancholia*, 14.

8. Mourning Disavowed

1 Antonello, "Dispatches from Hell," 383.
2 Garrone commented that such a strategy would most likely be unsuccessful, as change would need to come from within (improving social systems, such as education and job opportunities), and not be imposed from the outside, by a state that is historically disinterested in the problem of the Camorra. See Porton, "Inside 'The System.'"
3 For a discussion of the Camorra's recent evolution and expansion, see Felia and Percy Allum, "Revisiting Naples," and Allum, *Camorristi, Politicians and Businessmen*. For a more general history of the Camorra see Behan, *See Naples and Die*; Dickie, *Blood Brotherhoods*; and Sales, *La camorra, le camorre*.
4 Butler, *Frames of War*, 38.
5 Butler, *Precarious Life*, 150.
6 De Lauretis, *Alice Doesn't*, 153.
7 Saviano, *Gomorrah*, 137.

8 An English translation of a selection from Atria's diaries can be found in Pickering-Iazzi, ed. and trans., *Mafia and Outlaw Stories from Italian Life and Literature*, 155–66.
9 For more on the term "submerged centrality," see Principato and Dino, *Mafia donna*, 14. See also Lo Coco, "Lo psichismo mafioso," 213, and Siebert, "Mafia and Anti-Mafia," 49.
10 See Allum, "Doing It for Themselves or Standing In for Their Men?" 10.
11 For a discussion of women and the essential commitment to silence in a Mafia household, see Siebert, "Women and the Mafia."
12 Giorgio Agamben, *Homo Sacer*, 8. Furthermore, Agamben writes, "In the system of the nation-state, the so-called sacred and inalienable rights of man show themselves to lack every protection and reality at the moment in which they can no longer take the form of rights belonging to citizens of a state" (126).
13 Lacan, "The Mirror Stage as Formative of the Function of the I," 4.
14 See Blok, "Mafia and Blood Symbolism."
15 See Antonello, "Dispatches from Hell," 379.
16 Di Forti, quoted in Siebert, *Secrets of Life and Death*, 26. See also di Lorenzo, *La grande madre mafia*, specifically the eponymous chapter, 41–75.
17 Blok, "The Enigma of Senseless Violence," 29.
18 Siebert, *Secrets of Life and Death*, 76. For more on the "price of life" in a Mafia context, see the eponymous section in Siebert, 76–8.
19 Blok, "The Meaning of Senseless Violence," 108.
20 For more on the representation of le Vele and how characters, in particular Don Ciro, inhabit the space, see Small, "No Way Out."
21 Porton, "Inside 'The System,'" 15.
22 See Donnarumma, Policastro, and Taviani, eds, "Ritorno alla realtà?"
23 See Gervasini, "Cinema e gomorre." For a discussion of Saviano's *Gomorrah* as an example of the New Italian Epic, see Ming, *New Italian Epic*, 110–18.
24 Walker, "Trauma Cinema," 214.
25 Santner, "History beyond the Pleasure Principle," 144.
26 Bruder, "Aestheticizing Violence, or How to Do Things with Style."
27 Siebert, *Secrets of Life and Death*, 82.
28 Saviano, *Gomorrah*, 255–7.
29 Ibid., 248.
30 Ibid., 256.
31 Žižek, "From Virtual Reality to the Virtualization of Reality," 291.
32 See, for example, Turan, "*Gomorrah*'s Hazardous-to-Health Gangster Life," and Ebert, "*Gomorrah*."
33 Butler, *Precarious Life*, 148.
34 Ibid., 149.

9. Recasting Rita Atria in Amenta's *La siciliana ribelle*

1 For more on Atria as an emblem for women in their protest against the Mafia, see Pickering-Iazzi, "(En)gendering Testimonial Bodies of Evidence," and Siebert, "Women and the Mafia: The Power of Silence and Memory," 84–6.
2 Pickering-Iazzi, "(En)gendering Testimonial Bodies of Evidence," 22.
3 In Rizza, *Una ragazza contro la mafia*, 174.
4 Ibid., 159.
5 Pickering-Iazzi, "(En)gendering Testimonial Bodies of Evidence," 27.
6 Ibid., 22.
7 All citations from Atria's diaries are taken from Pickering-Iazzi, ed. and trans., *Mafia and Outlaw Stories from Italian Life and Literature*, 157–61.
8 Hirsch, *Afterimage*, 98.
9 Ibid., 99.
10 Ibid., 95.
11 Ibid.
12 Silverman, *Male Subjectivity at the Margins*, 41.
13 Silverman, *The Threshold of the Visible World*, 179.
14 For an analysis of young Rita's relationship with her father and her selective memory of her childhood see the chapter "Le bambine e la mafia" from Santoro's dissertation "I bambini e la mafia."
15 Hirsch, *Afterimage*, 7.
16 Silverman, *Male Subjectivity at the Margins*, 15–16.
17 Pickering-Iazzi, "(En)gendering Testimonial Bodies of Evidence," 28.
18 Ibid., 33.
19 For a discussion of the "Situation" "at the heart of the melodrama," see Singer, *Melodrama and Modernity*, 41. See Singer's chapter "Meanings of Melodrama," in particular pages 37–44, for a useful and comprehensive definition of the genre.
20 See Doane, *The Desire to Desire*, 13.
21 Ibid., 122.
22 Doane, "The Clinical Eye," 153.
23 Ibid., 173.
24 Wade, "Fighting the Mafia through Cinema," 6.
25 Kaplan, "Melodrama, Cinema and Trauma," 204.
26 Lanthier, "*The Sicilian Girl*."
27 Pickering-Iazzi, *Mafia and Outlaw Stories*, 161.
28 See Brooks, *The Melodramatic Imagination*; Vincendeau, "Melodramatic Realism"; Gledhill, "'An Abundance of Understatement'"; and Mercer and Shingler, *Melodrama*.

29 Brooks, *The Melodramatic Imagination*, 14.
30 Gledhill, "The Melodramatic Field," 21.
31 Mulvey, "Notes on Sirk and Melodrama," 40.
32 Ibid., 40.
33 Atria was involved with Calogero Cascio from Partanna, who had ties to the local Mafia, but as soon as Piera Aiello became a collaborator of justice, Cascio left Atria.
34 "Interview with Marco Amenta."
35 LaCapra, *Representing the Holocaust*, 48.
36 And the same has been said of Amenta's earlier documentary on Atria. In her discussion of the documentary *Diario di una siciliana ribelle*, Pickering-Iazzi points out that "the complex layering of acoustic, visual, and verbal images designed to tell the story of Rita Atria's journey from the origins of her birth as a '*figlia di mafiosi*' to a heroic symbol of the law silences the signs of difference." "Re-membering Rita Atria," 457.
37 Kaplan, "Melodrama, Cinema and Trauma," 204.
38 Hirsch, *Afterimage*, 19.
39 Ibid., 15.
40 Ibid., 3.
41 Leake, *After Words*, 3.
42 Pickering-Iazzi, "(En)gendering Testimonial Bodies of Evidence," 34.
43 Kaplan, *Trauma Culture*, 74.
44 Wade, "Fighting the Mafia through Cinema," 6.
45 Doane, *The Desire to Desire*, 136.
46 Kaplan, "Melodrama, Cinema and Trauma," 203.

10. Trauma Postponed

1 Krutnik, *In a Lonely Street*, 86.
2 Woolfolk, "The Horizon of Disenchantment," 118.
3 Palmer, "'Lounge Time' Reconsidered," 63.
4 Ibid., 63.
5 Ibid., 62.
6 Woolfolk, "The Horizon of Disenchantment," 117.
7 Freud, *The Interpretation of Dreams*, 279.
8 Johnston, "Double Indemnity," 91.
9 Krutnik, *In a Lonely Street*, 76; original italics.
10 Freud, *Moses and Monotheism*, 82. See in particular the section "Application" (81–92), where Freud asserts that "the killing of Moses by his Jewish people ... thus becomes an indispensable part of our

construction, an important link between the forgotten event of primaeval times and its later emergence in the form of monotheist religions" (89).
11 Assman, *Religion and Cultural Memory*. She continues: "Freud's examples refer to the traumatization of the perpetrator. The murders of the primal father and of Moses leave traces in the psyche of perpetrators. It is particularly true in their case that their experience is delayed, since at the time of the deed 'they knew not what they did'" (50).
12 Metz, *The Imaginary Signifier*, 53; original italics.
13 Ibid., 51.
14 Ibid., 45.
15 Ibid., 46.
16 Mulvey, "Visual Pleasure and Narrative Cinema," 20. For more on Mulvey's classification of the traditional male hero of classical cinema, see the introductory section of chapter 1.
17 Woolfolk, "The Horizon of Disenchantment," 119.
18 Lacan, *Speech and Language in Psychoanalysis*, 271.
19 Wood, "*Chiaroscuro*," 163.
20 Ibid., 165.
21 Ibid., 158.
22 Žižek, *Enjoy Your Symptom!* 160.
23 Siebert, *Secrets of Life and Death*, 26.
24 Ibid., 69.
25 Di Forti, *Per una psicoanalisi della mafia*, 58.
26 Place, "Women in Film Noir," 60.
27 Ibid., 61.
28 Gledhill, "Klute 1," 31.
29 Wood, "*Chiaroscuro*," 66.
30 Abrams, "A Quiet Life."
31 Wood, "Italian Film Noir," 264
32 Krutnik, *In a Lonely Street*, 164.
33 Staiger, "Film Noir as Male Melodrama."
34 Cowie, "Film Noir and Women," 130.
35 Nowell-Smith, "Minnelli and Melodrama," 115.
36 Ibid., 116.
37 Mulvey, "Notes on Sirk and Melodrama," 40.
38 Cowie, "Film Noir and Women," 130.
39 Nowell-Smith, "Minnelli and Melodrama," 117.
40 Ibid., 116.
41 Ibid., 117.
42 Ibid., 117.
43 Hirsch, *Afterimage*, 21.

44 Ibid., 20
45 Ibid., 21.
46 Nowell-Smith, "Minnelli and Melodrama," 118.
47 Freud, *Moses and Monotheism*, 129.
48 Here I am referring to the song "A Quiet Life," by Teho Teardo, that plays at the film's conclusion, which I cite in full:

> Maybe this time, maybe this time I'll outwit my past
> I throw away the numbers the keys and all the cards
> maybe I can carve out a living in some coop in the outskirts of some city
> I'll extinguish all my recent pasts, become another man again
> And have the quiet life, a quiet life for me, a quiet life
> A quiet life for me, a quiet life for someone, and a quiet life for me.
> I lost my ring, I started once anew, in northern grey, in drizzling rain, in salted slush and bitter hail
> But the order is always merciless, it wants to see me fail
> So the hunter is now the hunted, past voices call my name.
> I renounce my past to live again, a quiet life, a quiet life, a quiet life for me.
> A quiet life for someone, and a quiet life for me.
> I thought I have been given another chance again
> But heaven lies as usual, I repented but in vain
> It tries to cheat me out of my good aim
> Take away what I never really got
> My quiet life no quiet life for me
> No quiet life no quiet life no quiet life for me
> A quiet life for someone no quiet life for me
> Even if I have to stray again
> There is a life for me
> A quiet life a quiet life for me a quiet life.

49 Kehr, "The New Male Melodrama," 43.
50 Ibid., 47.
51 Giesen, "The Trauma of Perpetrators," 114.

Epilogue

1 Main or supporting characters who are murdered: Peppino Impastato and Cesare Manzella (*I cento passi*); Placido Rizzotto (*Placido Rizzotto*); Titta di Girolamo (*Le conseguenze dell'amore*); Leonardo Vitale and Giovanni Battista Vitale (*L'uomo di vetro*); Infantino (*Galantuomini*); Gianfranco and Daniele (*Fine pena mai: Paradiso perduto*); Maria, Marco, and Ciro (*Gomorra*); Don

Michele, Carmelo, and the judge based on Borsellino (*La siciliana ribelle*); Edoardo and Diego (*Una vita tranquilla*). Characters who commit suicide: Rita Atria (*La siciliana ribelle*). Characters who are raped: Lia (*Placido Rizzotto*); Anna Siringo (*L'uomo di vetro*); Lucia Rizzo (*Galantuomini*); the woman who testifies in court (*La siciliana ribelle*). Characters who die in a car accident: Luigi Impastato (*I cento passi*); Sofia (*Le conseguenze dell'amore*). Characters who die from a drug overdose: Fabio (*Galantuomini*).

I do not include in these statistics the murder of several other minor characters such as the many Mafiosi killed in various shootouts in *Gomorra* and *Galantuomini*, the girl murdered by the SS officer in *Placido Rizzotto*, Signor Santangelo who was murdered in Saro's office in *Angela*, the two men murdered by the Mafioso in *Le consegeunze dell'amore*, or the murder of Michael Richter in *Una vita tranquilla*.

2 Considering its strength and influence, it is surprising that as of April 2012 only two feature films have been made on the 'Ndrangheta: *Il brigante Musolino* (*Outlaw Girl*, 1950) and *Il coraggio di parlare* (Leandro Castellani, 1987). There are several television series, made-for-television movies, and documentaries that treat the Mafia of Calabria, however.
3 Kaplan and Wang, "From Traumatic Paralysis to the Force Field of Modernity," 9–10.
4 Ibid., 9.
5 Ibid., 11.
6 Irigaray, *The Sex Which Is Not One*, 24.
7 Santner, "History beyond the Pleasure Principle," 149.
8 Ibid., 147.
9 Ibid., 144.
10 The Tavianis explain that they chose to shoot most of the film in black and white for several reasons, such as underlining "the passing of time." They also point out that "colour is realistic and black and white is unrealistic." "*Caesar Must Die*: A Film by Paolo and Vittorio Taviani, Press Kit."
11 Early on in the film, we learn that Gallo and Striano are imprisoned for Mafia-related activity. Rega is very outspoken about his pre-incarceration life as a Camorrista and published the autobiography *Sumino 'o falco* that chronicles his youth, membership in the Camorra, incarceration, and journey towards spiritual rebirth.
12 "Jail Docu-drama *Caesar Must Die* Wins Berlin Award."
13 Lardera, "Italy Triumphs at Berlinale."
14 "Italian Dealing with Overcrowded Detention Centers."
15 "Pope Visits Prisoners, Says Poor Conditions Amount to 'Double Sentence.'"

16 Collett-White, "Mafioso and Murderer Tackle Shakespeare in New Film."
17 Santner, "History beyond the Pleasure Principle," 144.
18 One reviewer points out that "Shakespeare's themes of power, corruption, murder and vengeance in 'Julius Caesar' naturally resonate with performers who are serving sentences ranging from 14 years to life." Collett-White, "Mafioso and Murderer Tackle Shakespeare in New Film."
19 The expression "quaquaraquà" was first used by Leonardo Sciascia in the novel *Il giorno della civetta* (*The Day of the Owl*, 1961) during a conversation between Captain Bellodi and a Mafia boss named Don Mariano Arena. The expression is now in common usage.
20 Collett-White, "Mafioso and Murderer Tackle Shakespeare in New Film."
21 Glynn, "Writing the Female Self," 15.
22 The Tavianis state that they did "follow the screenplay" for the most part, although they point out that the film does include a few of the actors' "unexpected performances." "*Caesar Must Die*: A Film by Paolo and Vittorio Taviani, Press Kit."
23 Williams, "Film Bodies: Gender, Genre, and Excess," 31.
24 A staging in 2012–13 of *Julius Caesar* at the Donmar Warehouse in London offers an interesting counterpoint to the homosociality at work in *Cesare deve morire*. Phyllida Lloyd's production is set in a woman's prison and features an entirely female cast.
25 Mercer and Shingler, *Melodrama*, 99.
26 We learn at the film's end that two of the inmates are recently published authors: Cosimo Rega (Cassius) published *Sumino 'o falco: Autobiografia di un ergastolano*, while Giovanni Arcuri (Caesar) is the author of *Libero dentro: Brevi osservazioni di vita vissuta* [*Free Inside: Brief Observations on a Life Lived*].

Works Cited

Abrams, Simon. "*A Quiet Life.*" *Slant Magazine,* 22 April 2011. http://www.slantmagazine.com/film/review/a-quiet-life/5450.

Agamben, Giorgio. *Homo Sacer: Sovereign Power and Bare Life.* Trans. Daniel Heller-Roazen. Stanford: Stanford University Press, 1998.

Aiello, Piera, and Umberto Lucentini. *Maladetta mafia: Io, donna, testimone di giustizia con Paolo Borsellino.* Milan: San Paolo, 2012.

Alexander, Jeffrey C. "Toward a Theory of Cultural Trauma." In *Cultural Trauma and Collective Identity,* ed. Jeffrey C. Alexander, et al., 1–30. Berkeley, Los Angeles, London: University of California Press, 2004. http://dx.doi.org/10.1525/california/9780520235946.003.0001.

Alexander, Jeffrey C., et al. *Cultural Trauma and Collective Identity.* Berkeley, Los Angeles, London: University of California Press, 2004. http://dx.doi.org/10.1525/california/9780520235946.001.0001.

Alighieri, Dante. *The Divine Comedy: Inferno.* Trans. Charles S. Singleton. Princeton: Princeton University Press, 1989.

Allum, Felia. *Camorristi, Politicians and Businessmen: The Transformation of Organized Crime in Post-War Naples.* Leeds: Northern Universities Press, 2008.

Allum, Felia. "Doing It for Themselves or Standing In for Their Men? Women in the Neopolitan Camorra (1950–2003)." In *Women and the Mafia: Studies in Organized Crime,* ed. Giovanni Fiandaca, 9–17. New York: Springer-Verlag, 2007. http://dx.doi.org/10.1007/978-0-387-36542-8_2.

Allum, Felia, and Percy Allum. "Revisiting Naples: Clientelism and Organized Crime." *Journal of Modern Italian Studies* 13, no. 3 (2008): 340–65. http://dx.doi.org/10.1080/13545710802218569.

Allum, Felia, and Renate Siebert, eds. *Organized Crime and the Challenge to Democracy.* London, New York: Routledge, 2003.

Anderson, Victoria. "Sins of Permission: The Union of Rape and Marriage in *Die Marquise Von O* and *Breaking the Waves*." In *Rape in Art Cinema*, ed. Dominique Russell, 69–82. New York, London: Continuum, 2010.

Angelone, Anita. "Talking Trash: Documentaries and Italy's 'Garbage Emergency.'" *Studies in Documentary Film* 5, nos. 2–3 (2011): 145–56. http://dx.doi.org/10.1386/sdf.5.2-3.145_1.

Antonello, Pierpaolo. "Dispatches from Hell: Matteo Garrone's *Gomorrah*." In *Mafia Movies: A Reader*, ed. Dana Renga, 377–85. Toronto, Buffalo, London: University of Toronto Press, 2011.

Antonello, Pierpaolo, and Alan O'Leary, eds. *Imagining Terrorism: The Rhetoric and Representation of Political Violence in Italy 1969–2009*. Oxford: Legenda, 2009.

Apollonio, Andrea. *Sacra corona unita: Riciclaggio, contrabbando. Profili penali economici del crimine imprenditoriale*. Rome: Carocci editore, 2010.

Arlacchi, Pino. *Men of Dishonor: Inside the Sicilian Mafia*. New York: William Morrow, 1993.

Assman, Jan. *Religion and Cultural Memory*. Trans. Rodney Livingstone. Stanford: Stanford University Press, 2006.

Babini, Luana. "The Mafia: New Cinematic Perspectives." In *Italian Cinema: New Directions*, ed. William Hope, 229–50. Oxford, Bern: Peter Lang, 2004.

Bach, Steven. *Marlene Dietrich: Life and Legend*. Minneapolis: University of Minnesota Press, 2011.

Bal, Mieke. *A Mieke Bal Reader*. Chicago, London: University of Chicago Press, 2006.

Barletti, Davide, and Lorenzo Conte. "Postfazione." http://www.mannieditori.it/libro/vista-dinterni.

Behan, Tom. *See Naples and Die: The Camorra and Organized Crime*. London: I.B. Tauris Publishers, 2002.

"Behind the Scenes." In "Contenuti extra," *Fine pena mai: Paradiso perduto*, DVD.

Bellavia, Enrico. "Fiamme, misteri, dicerie, depistaggi e sullo sfondo il business dei rifiuti." *La Repubblica*, 31 January 2006. http://ricerca.repubblica.it/repubblica/archivio/repubblica/2006/01/31/fiamme-misteri-dicerie-depistaggi-sullo-sfondo-il.html.

Bergmann, Mayna. "Angela." *Video Business* 26, no. 39 (25 September 2006): 10–11.

Biagi, Enzo. *Il boss è solo*. Milan: Mondadori, 1990.

Blake, Linnie. *The Wounds of Nations*. Manchester, New York: Manchester University Press, 2009.

Blok, Anton. "The Enigma of Senseless Violence." In *Meanings of Violence: A Cross-Cultural Approach*, ed. Göran Aijmer and Jon Abbink, 23–38. Oxford, New York: Berg Books, 2000.
———. *Honour and Violence*. Oxford, Cambridge: Polity Press, 2001.
———. "Mafia and Blood Symbolism." In *Risky Transactions: Trust, Kinship and Ethnicity*, ed. Frank K. Salter, 109–28. New York: Berghahn Books, 2002.
Blum, Cinzia Sartini. *The Other Modernism: F.T. Marinetti's Futurist Fiction of Power*. Berkeley, Los Angeles, London: University of California Press, 1996.
Bolzoni, Attilio, and Giuseppe D'Avanzo. *Il capo dei capi: Vita e carriera criminale di Totò Riina*. Milan: Arnoldo Mondadori Editore, 1993.
Bondanella, Peter. *A History of Italian Cinema*. New York, London: Continuum, 2009.
Bongiovanni, Giorgio. "Le parole di Pippo Fava: 'I mafiosi stanno in Parlamento, sono a volte ministri, sono banchieri.'" *Antimafia duemila*, 5 January 2011. http://www.antimafiaduemila.com/2011011432343/Articoli-vari/parole-di-pippo-fava-i-mafiosi-stanno-in-parlamento-sono-a-volte-ministri-sono-banchieri.html.
Bongiovanni, Giorgio, and Anna Petrozzi. "Leonardo Vitale: La prigione della follia." *l'Unità*, 23 December 2009, 36–7.
Boylan, Amy. "Pasquale Scimeca's *Placido Rizzotto*: A Different View of Corleone." In *Mafia Movies: A Reader*, ed. Dana Renga, 312–19. Toronto, Buffalo, London: University of Toronto Press, 2011.
Brooks, Peter. *The Melodramatic Imagination: Balzac, Henry James, Melodrama and the Mode of Excess*. New Haven: Yale University Press, 1995.
Bruder, Margaret Ervin. "Aestheticizing Violence, or How To Do Things with Style." http://www.gradnet.de/papers/pomo98.papers/mtbruder98.htm.
Bruneli, Michele. "Italy Keeps a Rein on Smallest Mafia Group." *Jane's Intelligence Review*, July, 2009: 40–3.
Butler, Judith. *Bodies That Matter: On the Discursive Limits of "Sex."* New York, London: Routledge, 1993.
———. *Frames of War: When Is Life Grievable*. London, New York: Verso, 2009.
———. *Precarious Life: The Powers of Mourning and Violence*. London, New York: Verso, 2004.
"*Caesar Must Die*: A Film by Paolo and Vittorio Taviani, Press Kit." http://www.filmpressplus.com/wp-content/uploads/dl_docs/CaesarMustDie-Notes.pdf.
Camoletto, Raffaella Ferrero, and Chiara Bertone. "Coming to Be a Man: Pleasure in the Construction of Italian Men's (Hetereo)Sexuality." *Italian*

Studies 65, no. 2 (July 2010): 235–50. http://dx.doi.org/10.1179/0161462 10X12593180182775.
Caprara, Valerio. "Vitale, pentito e martire." *Il mattino*, 16 June 2007. http://www.amicidelcabiria.it/file/film-lunedi/2007-2008/uomoVetro.pdf.
Carella, Antonio. *Nel cuore della luna*. Unpublished screenplay, 1998.
Caruth, Cathy. "Introduction." In *Trauma: Explorations in Memory*, ed. Cathy Caruth, 3–12. Baltimore, London: Johns Hopkins University Press, 1995.
Catacchio, Antonio. "Cosa nostra, Leonardo 'morto che cammina.'" *Il Manifesto*, 29 June 2007. http://www.amicidelcabiria.it/file/film-lunedi/2007-2008/uomoVetro.pdf.
Cavarero, Adriana. *Horrorism: Naming Contemporary Violence*. Trans. William McCuaig. New York, Chichester: Columbia University Press, 2009.
Céline, Louis-Ferdinand. *Journey to the End of the Night*. Trans. Ralph Manheim. New York: New Directions Books, 2006.
Cervantes, Miguel de. "Man of Glass." In *The Portable Cervantes*. Trans. Samuel Putnam. 760–96. New York: The Viking Press, 1951.
Chiarelli, Mara. *Sacra corona unita*. Rome: Editori internazionali Riuniti, 2012.
Clover, Carol J. *Men, Women and Chainsaws: Gender in the Modern Horror Film*. Princeton: Princeton University Press, 1992.
Codelli, Lorenzo, and Paul Thirard. "Entretien avec Paolo Sorrentino: Un Homme et un Hotel." *Positif* 528 (2005): 35–8.
Collett-White, Mike. "Mafioso and Murderer Tackle Shakespeare in New Film." *Reuters*, 19 February 2012. http://in.reuters.com/article/2012/02/11/film-us-berlinale-prison-idINTRE81A0AR20120211.
Consolo, Vincenzo. *Le pietre di Pantalica*. Milan: Mondadori, 1988.
Coulthard, Lisa. "Killing Bill: Rethinking Feminism and Film Violence." In *Interrogating Postfeminism: Gender and the Politics of Popular Culture*, ed. Vyonne Tasker and Diane Negra, 153–75. Durham: Duke University Press, 2007.
Cowie, Elizabeth. "Film Noir and Women." In *Shades of Noir: A Reader*, ed. Joan Copjec, 121–65. London, New York: Verso, 1993.
———. *Representing the Woman: Cinema and Psychoanalysis*. Minneapolis: University of Minnesota Press, 1997.
Creed, Barbara. *The Monstrous Feminine: Film, Feminism, Psychoanalysis*. London, New York: Routledge, 1993.
Custen, George F. "Where Is the Life That Late He Led: Hollywood's Construction of Sexuality in the Life of Cole Porter." In *The Columbia Reader on Lesbians and Gay Men in Media, Society, and Politics*, ed. Larry Gross and James D. Woods, 306–16. New York, Chichester: Columbia University Press, 1999.

dalla Chiesa, Nando. *Le ribelli: Storie di donne che hanno sfidato la mafia per amore*. Milan: Milampo Editore, 2006.
Dall'Orto, Giovanni. "La 'tolleranza repressiva' dell'omosessualità: Quando un atteggiamento legale diviene tradizione." In *Omosessuali e stato*, ed. Arcigay Nazionale, 37–57. Bologna: Centro di documentazione il cassero, 1987.
De Donno, Antonio, V. Santoro, A.P. Rossi, et al. "Manners of Killing and Rituals in Apulian Mafia Murders." *Journal of Forensic Sciences* 54, no. 4 (July 2009): 895–9. http://dx.doi.org/10.1111/j.1556-4029.2009.01068.x. Medline:19486252.
de Lauretis, Teresa. *Alice Doesn't: Feminism, Semiotics, Cinema*. Bloomington, Indianapolis: Indiana University Press, 1984.
———. *Technologies of Gender: Essays on Film, Theory, Fiction*. Bloomington, Indianapolis: Indiana University Press, 1987.
Dentice, Alberto. "Cinema Padrino." *L'Espresso*, 4 March 2008. http://espresso.repubblica.it/dettaglio/Cinema-Padrino/1998347/9.
De Stefano, George. *An Offer We Can't Refuse: The Mafia in the Mind of America*. New York: Faber and Faber, 2006.
———. "Marco Tullio Giordana's *The Hundred Steps*: The Biopic as Political Cinema." In *Mafia Movies: A Reader*, ed. Dana Renga, 320–28. Toronto, Buffalo, London: University of Toronto Press, 2011.
De Toni, Alice. *Dolentissime donne: La rappresentazione giornalistica delle donne di mafia*. Bologna: CLEUB, 2012.
Deutsch, Hélène. *The Psychology of Women: A Psychoanalytic Interpretation*. Vol. 1. New York: Grune & Stratton, 1944.
di Amato, Astolfo. *Criminal Law in Italy*. Alphen aan den Rijn, The Netherlands: Kluwer Law International, 2011.
Dickie, John. *Blood Brotherhoods: The Rise of the Italian Mafias*. London: Sceptre, 2011.
———. *Cosa Nostra: A History of the Sicilian Mafia*. New York: Palgrave Macmillan, 2004.
di Forti, Filippo. *Per una psicoanalisi della mafia*. Verona: Berani, 1982.
di Lorenzo, Silvia. *La grande madre mafia: Psicoanalisi del potere mafioso*. Parma: Pratiche Editrice, 2006.
di Pelo. "*I cento passi*." http://www.mescalina.it/cinema/recensioni/marco-tullio-giordana/i-cento-passi.
Doane, Mary Ann. "The Clinical Eye: Medical Discourses in the 'Woman's Film' of the 1940s." In *The Female Body in Western Culture: Contemporary Perspectives*, ed. Susan Rubin Suleiman, 152–74. Cambridge, MA: Harvard University Press, 1986.

———. *The Desire to Desire: The Woman's Film of the 1940s*. Bloomington, Indianapolis: Indiana University Press, 1987.

———. *Femmes Fatales: Feminism, Film Theory, Psychoanalysis*. New York, London: Routledge, 1991.

———. "The Woman's Film: Possession and Address." In *Revision: Essays in Feminist Film Criticism*, ed. Mary Ann Doane, Patricia Mellencamp, and Linda Williams, 67–82. Los Angeles: University Publications of America, 1984.

Donnarumma, Raffaele, Gilda Policastro, and Giovanna Taviani, eds. "Ritorno alla realtà? Narrativa e cinema alla fine del postmoderno." *Allegoria* 57 (2008): 7–93.

D'Onofrio, Emanuele. "Italian Cinema Revisits the 1970s: Film Music and Youth Identity in De Maria's *Paz*." *Music, Sound and the Moving Image* 1, no. 2 (2007): 161–86. http://dx.doi.org/10.3828/msmi.1.2.4.

———. "Percorsi di identità narrativa nella memoria difficile: La musica in *I cento passi* e *Buongiorno, notte*." *Italianist* 30, no. 2 (2010): 219–44. http://dx.doi.org/10.1179/026143410X12724449730178.

Duggan, Christopher. *Fascism and the Mafia*. New Haven: Yale University Press, 1989.

Dyer, Richard. *White*. New York, London: Routledge, 1997.

Ebert, Roger. "*Gomorrah*." *Chicago Sun Times*, 25 February 2005. http://rogerebert.suntimes.com/apps/pbcs.dll/article?AID=/20090225/REVIEWS/902259991/1023.

Elsaesser, Thomas. "Postmodernism as Mourning Work." *Screen* 42, no. 2 (Summer 2001): 193–201. http://dx.doi.org/10.1093/screen/42.2.193.

Erikson, Kai T. *Everything in Its Path: Destruction of Community in the Buffalo Creek Flood*. New York: Simon and Schuster, 1976.

Escobar, Roberto. "L'uomo di vetro." *Il Sole – 24 Ore*, 30 June 2007. http://www.amicidelcabiria.it/file/film-lunedi/2007-2008/uomoVetro.pdf.

Eyerman, Ron. *Cultural Trauma: Slavery and the Formation of African American Identity*. Cambridge: Cambridge University Press, 2001. http://dx.doi.org/10.1017/CBO9780511488788.

Falcone, Giovanni. *Men of Honour: The Truth about the Mafia*. London: Warner, 1992.

Felman, Shoshana, and Dori Laub. *Testimony: Crises of Witnessing in Literature, Psychoanalysis and History*. New York, London: Routledge, 1992.

Fiandanca, Giovanni, ed. *Women and the Mafia: Female Roles in Organized Crime Structures*. New York: Springer, 2007.

"*Fine pena mai*: Press Book." http://www.mymovies.it/filmclub/2008/02/047/mymovies.pdf.

Fiore, Innocenzo. "La famiglia nel 'pensare Mafioso.'" In *La mafia dentro:*

Psicologia e psicopatologia di un fondamentalismo, ed. Girolamo Lo Verso, 47–65. Milan: Franco Angeli, 2002.

Follain, John. *The Last Godfather: Inside the Mafia's Most Infamous Family*. New York: St Martin's Press, 2008.

Foucault, Michel. "Madness Only Exists in Society." In *Foucault Live (Interviews, 1961–1884)*, ed. Sylvère Lotringer, trans. Lysa Hochroth and John Johnston, 7–9. New York: Semiotext(e), 1996.

———. "Of Other Spaces." Trans. Jay Miskowiec. *Diacritics* 16, no. 1 (Spring 1986): 22–7. http://dx.doi.org/10.2307/464648.

Francesco, Merlo. "Il 'Professor' del crimine che leggeva Kant." *Corriere della sera*, 16 November 1993. http://archiviostorico.corriere.it/1993/novembre/16/Professore_del_crimine_che_leggeva_co_0_9311165838.shtml.

Freud, Sigmund. "'A Child Is Being Beaten': A Contribution to the Study of Sexual Perversions." In *The Standard Edition of the Complete Psychological Works of Sigmund Freud*, vol. 17, trans. and ed. James Strachey, 175–204. London: Hogarth Press, 1968.

———. *Beyond the Pleasure Principle*. In *The Standard Edition of the Complete Psychological Works of Sigmund Freud*, vol. 18, trans. and ed. James Strachey. London: Hogarth Press, 1955.

———. "From the History of Infantile Neurosis." In *The Standard Edition of the Complete Psychological Works of Sigmund Freud*, vol. 17, trans. and ed. James Strachey, 3–123. London: Hogarth Press, 1955.

———. "Inhibitions, Symptoms, and Anxiety." In *The Standard Edition of the Complete Psychological Works of Sigmund Freud*, vol. 20, trans. and ed. James Strachey, 77–175. London: Hogarth Press, 1975.

———. *The Interpretation of Dreams: The Complete and Definitive Text*. Trans. and ed. James Strachey. New York: Basic Books, 2010.

———. "Medusa's Head." In *The Standard Edition of the Complete Psychological Works of Sigmund Freud*, vol. 18, trans. and ed. James Strachey, 273–4. London: Hogarth Press, 1955.

———. *Moses and Monotheism: Three Essays*. In *The Standard Edition of the Complete Psychological Works of Sigmund Freud*, vol. 23, trans. and ed. James Strachey. London: Hogarth Press, 1964.

———. "Mourning and Melancholia." In *The Complete Psychological Works of Sigmund Freud*, vol. 14. trans. and ed. James Strachey, 243–58. London: The Hogarth Press, 1975.

Friedlander, Saul. *When Memory Comes*. Trans. Halen R. Lane. New York: Farrar, Straus, Giroux, 1979.

Frisch, Michael. *A Shared Authority: Essays on the Craft and Meaning of Oral and Public History*. New York: State University of New York Press, 1990.

"Galantuomini," *Multicinema Network Blog*. http://www.stellablog.eu/?page_id=1725.

Galluzzo, Lucio, Franco Nicastro, and Vincenzo Vasile. *Obiettivo Falcone*. Naples: Tullio Pironti Editore, 1992.

Gambetta, Diego. *The Sicilian Mafia: The Business of Private Protection*. Cambridge, MA, London: Harvard University Press, 1993.

Gamble, Sarah. "Postfeminism." In *The Routledge Companion to Feminism and Postfeminism*, ed. Sarah Gamble, 43–54. London, New York: Routledge, 2001.

Gelso, Aldo. *Mafia: Capitalism and Democracy*. Bloomington, IN: Exlibris, 2007.

Gervasini, Mauro. "Cinema e gomorre." *Carmilla: Letteratura, immaginario e cultura di opposizione*. 9 June 2008. http://www.carmillaonline.com/archives/2008/06/002668.html.

Giancristofaro, Raffaella. "*Fine pena mai*: Ascesa e caduta di un affiliato alla Sacra corona unita. Una storia vera, raccontata dal collettivo romano-pugliese Fluid Video Crew." *Rolling Stone Magazine*, March 2008.

Giap Parini, Ercole. "The Strongest Mafia: '*Ndrangheta* Made in Calabria." In *Italy Today: The Sick Man of Europe*, ed. Andrea Mammone and Giuseppe A. Veltri, 173–84. London, New York: Routledge, 2010.

Giesen, Bernhard. "The Trauma of Perpetrators: The Holocaust as the Traumatic Reference of German National Identity." In *Cultural Trauma and Collective Identity*, ed. Jeffrey C. Alexander, et al., 112–54. Berkeley, Los Angeles, London: University of California Press, 2004. http://dx.doi.org/10.1525/california/9780520235946.003.0004.

Giordana, Marco Tullio, Claudio Fava, and Monica Zapelli. *I cento passi*. Milan: Giangiacomo Feltrinelli Editore, 2001.

Girard, René. *Violence and the Sacred*. London, New York: Continuum, 2005.

Gledhill, Christine. "'An Abundance of Understatement': Documentary, Melodrama and Romance." In *Nationalizing Femininity: Culture, Sexuality and British Cinema in the Second World War*, ed. Christine Gledhill and Gillian Swanson, 213–29. Manchester: Manchester University Press, 1996.

———. "*Klute 1*: A Contemporary Film Noir and Feminist Criticism." In *Women in Film Noir*, ed. E. Ann Kaplan, 20–34. London: British Film Institute, 1998.

———. "The Melodramatic Field: An Investigation." In *Home Is Where the Heart Is: Studies in Melodrama and the Woman's Film*, ed. Christine Gledhill, 5–39. London: BFI Books, 1987.

———, ed. *Home Is Where the Heart Is: Studies in Melodrama and the Woman's Film*. London: BFI Books, 1987.

Glynn, Ruth. "Through the Lens of Trauma: The Figure of the Female Terrorist in *Il prigioniero* and *Buongiorno, notte*." In *Imagining Terrorism:*

The Rhetoric and Representation of Political Violence in Italy 1969–2009, ed. Pierpaolo Antonello and Alan O'Leary, 62–76. Oxford: Legenda, 2009.

———. *Women, Terrorism and Trauma in Italian Culture*. New York: Palgrave Macmillan, 2013.

———. "Writing the Terrorist Self: The Unspeakable Alterity of Italy's Female Perpetrators." *Feminist Review* 92, no. 1 (2009): 1–18. http://dx.doi.org/10.1057/fr.2009.6.

Glynn, Ruth, and Giancarlo Lombardi, eds. *Remembering Moro: Historiographical and Cultural Representations of the Moro Affair*. Oxford: Legenda, 2012.

Glynn, Ruth, Giancarlo Lombardi, and Alan O'Leary, eds. *Terrorism, Italian Style: Representations of Political Violence in Contemporary Italian Cinema*. London: IGRS Press, 2012.

Grossman, Julie. *Rethinking the Femme Fatale in Film Noir: Ready for Her Close-Up*. Hampshire: Palgrave Macmillan, 2009. http://dx.doi.org/10.1057/9780230274983.

Hanson, Helen, and Catherine O'Rawe, eds. *The Femme Fatale: Images, Histories, Contexts*. Hampshire: Palgrave Macmillan, 2010. http://dx.doi.org/10.1057/9780230282018.

Haskell, Molly. *From Reverence to Rape: The Treatment of Women in the Movies*. New York, Chicago, San Francisco: Holt, Rinehart and Winston, 1974.

Hayward, Susan. *Cinema Studies: The Key Concepts*. 2nd ed. London, New York: Routledge, 2000.

Herman, Judith. *Trauma and Recovery: The Aftermath of Violence – From Domestic Abuse to Political Terror*. New York: Basic Books, 1997.

Higgins, Lynne A. "Screen/Memory: Rape and Its Alibis in *Last Year at Marienbad*." In *Rape and Representation*, ed. Lynn A. Higgins and Brenda R. Silver, 303–21. New York: Columbia University Press, 1991.

Higgins, Lynne A., and Brenda R. Silver. "Introduction: Rereading Rape." In *Rape and Representation*, ed. Lynn A. Higgins and Brenda R. Silver, 1–11. New York: Columbia University Press, 1991.

———, eds. *Rape and Representation*. New York: Columbia University Press, 1991.

Hipkins, Danielle. "Which Law Is the Father's? Gender and Generic Oscillation in Pietro Germi's *In the Name of the Law*." In *Mafia Movies: A Reader*, ed. Dana Renga, 203–10. Toronto, Buffalo, London: University of Toronto Press, 2011.

———. "Why Italian Film Studies Needs a Second Take on Gender." *Italian Studies* 63, no. 2 (2008): 213–34. http://dx.doi.org/10.1179/007516308X344360.

Hirsch, Joshua. *Afterimage: Film, Trauma and the Holocaust.* Philadelphia: Temple University Press, 2004.
Horeck, Tanya. *Public Rape: Representing Violence in Fiction and Film.* New York, London: Routledge, 2004.
Igartua, Juanjo, and Dario Paez. "Art and Remembering Traumatic Collective Events: The Case of the Spanish Civil War." In *Collective Memory of Political Events: Social Psychological Perspectives,* ed. James W. Pennebaker, Dario Paez, and Bernard Rimé, 79–101. Mahwah, NJ: Lawrence Erlbaum Associates, 1997.
Impastato, Felicia Bartolotta. *La mafia in casa mia: Intervista di Anna Puglisi e Umberto Santino.* Palermo: La luna, 2003.
Impastato, Giuseppe. *Lunga è la notte: Poesie, scritti, documenti.* Ed. Umberto Santino. Palermo: Centro di documentazione Giuseppe Impastato, 2006.
Ingrascì, Ombretta. *Donne d'onore: Storie di mafia al femminile.* Milan: Bruno Mondadori Editore, 2007.
"Interview with Marco Amenta." Press kit to *The Sicilian Girl* from Music Box Films. http://musicbox.ehclients.com/mbf/press-notes/SG_PressNotes071410.pdf.
Iovino, Serenella. "Ecocriticism and a Non-Anthropocentric Humanism." In *Local Natures, Global Responsibilities: Ecocritical Perspectives on the New English Literatures,* ed. Laurenz Volkmann, et al., 29–53. Amsterdam, New York: Rodopi, 2010.
Irigaray, Luce. *The Sex Which Is Not One.* Trans. Catherine Porter. Ithaca: Cornell University Press, 1985.
"Italian Dealing with Overcrowded Detention Centers." *Press TV,* 14 February 2012. http://www.presstv.ir/detail/226654.html.
Jacobs, Lea. *The Wages of Sin: Censorship and the Fallen Women Film, 1928–1942.* Berkeley, Los Angeles, London: University of California Press, 1997.
"Jail Docu-drama *Caesar Must Die* Wins Berlin Award." *BBC News,* 19 February 2012. http://www.bbc.co.uk/news/entertainment-arts-17085227.
Jamieson, Alison. *The Antimafia: Italy's Fight against Organized Crime.* London: Macmillan Press Ltd, 2000.
Johnston, Claire. "Double Indemnity." In *Women in Film Noir,* ed. E. Ann Kaplan, 89–98. London: British Film Institute, 1998.
———. "Women's Cinema as Counter Cinema." In *Feminism and Cultural Studies,* ed. Morag Shiach, 247–58. New York: Oxford University Press, 1999.
Kaes, Anton. *Shell Shock Cinema: Weimar Cinema and the Wounds of War.* Princeton: Princeton University Press, 2009.

Kaplan, E. Ann. "Global Trauma and Public Feelings: Viewing Images of Catastrophe." *Consumption Markets & Culture* 11, no. 1 (2008): 3–24. http://dx.doi.org/10.1080/10253860701799918.

——. "Melodrama, Cinema and Trauma." *Screen* 42, no. 2 (2001): 201–5. http://dx.doi.org/10.1093/screen/42.2.201.

——. *Trauma Culture: The Politics of Terror and Loss in Media and Literature*. New Brunswick, NJ, and London: Rutgers University Press, 2005.

——, ed. *Women in Film Noir*. London: British Film Institute, 1998.

Kaplan, E. Ann, and Ban Wang. "From Traumatic Paralysis to the Force Field of Modernity." In *Trauma and Cinema: Cross-Cultural Explorations*, ed. E. Ann Kaplan and Ban Wang, 1–22. Hong Kong: Hong Kong University Press, 2004.

——, eds. *Trauma and Cinema: Cross-Cultural Explorations*. Hong Kong: Hong Kong University Press, 2004.

Kehr, Dave. "The New Male Melodrama: Today's Sensitive Heroes Can Cook, Clean, and Take Care of Junior While the Women Are out of the Picture." *American Film* 8 (1983): 43–7.

King, Caire Sisco. *Washed in Blood: Male Sacrifice, Trauma and the Cinema*. New Brunswick, NJ: Rutgers University Press, 2011.

Kristeva, Julia. *Black Sun: Depression and Melancholia*. New York, Oxford: Columbia University Press, 1989.

——. *Powers of Horror: An Essay on Abjection*. New York: Columbia University Press, 1982.

——. *Revolt, She Said: An Interview with Philippe Petit*. Trans. Brian O'Keeffe. Los Angeles, New York: Semiotext(e), 2002.

Krutnik, Frank. *In a Lonely Street: Film Noir, Genre, Masculinity*. New York, London: Routledge, 1991.

Lacan, Jacques. *The Four Fundamental Concepts of Psychoanalysis*. Ed. Jacques-Alain Miller. Trans. Alan Sheridan. London: The Hogarth Press, 1977.

——. "The Mirror Stage as Formative of the Function of the I as Revealed in Psychoanalytic Experience." In *Écrits: A Selection*. Trans. Alan Sheridan, 1–7. New York, London: W.W. Norton & Co., 1977.

——. *Speech and Language in Psychoanalysis*. Trans. Anthony Wilden. Baltimore, London: Johns Hopkins University Press, 1981.

LaCapra, Dominik. *History in Transit: Experience, Identity, Critical Theory*. Ithaca: Cornell University Press, 2004.

——. *Representing the Holocaust: History, Theory, Trauma*. Ithaca: Cornell University Press, 1994.

Landesman, Cosmo. "Gomorra." *Times Online*, 12 October 2008. http://entertainment.timesonline.co.uk/tol/arts_and_entertainment/film/film_reviews/article4907928.ece.

Lanthier, Joseph John. "The Sicilian Girl." *Slant Magazine*, 1 August 2010. http://www.slantmagazine.com/film/review/the-sicilian-girl/4921.

Lanza, Angela. *Donne contro la mafia: L'esperienza del digiuno a Palermo*. Rome: Datanews, 1994.

——— . *Ho fame di giustizia: La rivolta delle donne a Palermo contro la mafia*. Marsala: Navarra, 2011.

Lardera, Natasha. "Italy Triumphs at Berlinale." *I-Italy*, 20 February 2012. http://www.i-italy.org/19852/italy-triumphs-berlinale.

Leake, Elizabeth. *After Words: Suicide and Authorship in Twentieth-Century Italy*. Toronto, Buffalo, London: University of Toronto Press, 2011.

Leotta, Alfio. "Do Not Underestimate the Consequences of Love: The Representation of the New Mafia in Contemporary Italian Cinema." *Italica* 88, no. 2 (2011): 286–96.

Leys, Ruth. *Trauma: A Genealogy*. Chicago, London: University of Chicago Press, 2000.

Lo Coco, Gianluca. "Lo psichismo Mafioso: Una bibliografia ragionata." In *La Mafia dentro: Psicologia e psicopatologia di un fondamentalismo*, ed. Girolamo Lo Verso, 195–216. Milan: Franco Angeli, 2002.

Longrigg, Claire. *No Questions Asked: The Secret Life of Women in the Mob*. New York: Hyperion, 2004.

Lo Verso, Girolamo. "Mafia e follia: Il caso Vitale. Uno studio psicodinamico e psicopatologico." *Psicoterapia e Scienze Umane* 3 (1995): 99–121.

——— . "Mafia, psicopatologia, psicoterapia." In *La mafia dentro: Psicologia e psicopatologia di un fondamentalismo*, ed. Girolamo Lo Verso, 129–56. Milan: Franco Angeli, 2002.

——— . "Per uno studio dello psichismo mafioso." In *La mafia dentro: Psicologia e psicopatologia di un fondamentalismo*, ed. Girolamo Lo Verso, 23–36. Milan: Franco Angeli, 2002.

——— , ed. *La mafia dentro: Psicologia e psicopatologia di un fondamentalismo*. Milan: Franco Angeli, 2002.

Lo Verso, Girolamo, and Gianluca Lo Coco. "Working with Patients Involved in the Mafia: Considerations from Italian Psychotherapy Experiences." *Psychoanalytic Psychology* 21, no. 2 (2004): 171–82. http://dx.doi.org/10.1037/0736-9735.21.2.171.

Lowenstein, Adam. *Shocking Representation: Historical Trauma, National Cinema and the Modern Horror Film*. New York: Columbia University Press, 2005.

Lupo, Salvatore. *History of the Mafia*. Trans. A. Shugar. New York: Columbia University Press, 2009.

Madeo, Liliana. *Donne di mafia: Vittime, complici e protagonisti*. Milan: Baldoni & Castoldi, 1997.
Marangi, Marco. "Mafia e legge (del desiderio)." *Cineforum* 43 (2003): 41–4.
Marcus, Millicent. *Filmmaking by the Book: Italian Cinema and Literary Adaptation*. Baltimore: Johns Hopkins University Press, 1993.
———. "In Memoriam: The Neorealist Legacy in the Contemporary Anti-Mafia Film." In *Italian Neorealism and Global Cinema*, ed. Laura E. Rorato and Kristi M. Wilson, 290–306. Detroit: Wayne State University Press, 2007.
———. *Italian Film in the Light of Neorealism*. Princeton: Princeton University Press, 1986.
———. *Italian Film in the Shadow of Auschwitz*. Toronto, Buffalo, London: University of Toronto Press, 2007.
———. "Return of the Referent: Italian Cinema for the New Millennium." *Semiotica* 183.1–4 (2011): 273–82.
Masciopinto, Rosa. *Donne d'onore: Monologo teatrale*. Palermo: Edizioni della battaglia, 1994.
Massari, Monica. *La sacra corona unita: Potere e segreto*. Rome: LaTerza, 1998.
Massari, Monica, and Cataldo Motta. "Women in the Sacra Corona Unita." In *Women and the Mafia: Female Roles in Organized Crime Structures*, ed. Giovanni Fiandanca, 53–66. New York: Springer, 2007.
McIntosh, Shawn, and Marc Leverette, eds. *Zombie Culture: Autopsies of the Living Dead*. Lanham, MD, Toronto, Oxford: Scarecrow Press, 2008.
Mercer, John, and Martin Shingler. *Melodrama: Genre, Style, Sensibility*. London: Wallflower Press, 2004.
Metz, Christian. *The Imaginary Signifier: Psychoanalysis and the Cinema*. Bloomington: Indiana University Press, 1982.
Ming, Wu. *New Italian Epic: Letteratura, sguardo obliquo, ritorno al futuro*. Turin: Einaudi, 2009.
Mitchell, Elvis. "A Sleeping Mafia Wife, Awakened by Some Irresistible Cheekbones." *New York Times*, 4 April 2003. http://movies.nytimes.com/movie/review?_r=2&res=9E04E1DB1638F937A35757C0A9659C8B63.
Modleski, Tania. "Clint Eastwood and Male Weepies." *American Literary History* 22, no. 1 (2009): 136–58. http://dx.doi.org/10.1093/alh/ajp051.
———. *Feminism without Women: Culture and Critique in a "Postfeminst" Age*. New York, London: Routledge, 1991.
———. "Rape versus Mans/laughter: Hitchcock's *Blackmail* and Feminist Interpretation." *PMLA* 102, no. 3 (May 1987): 304–15. http://dx.doi.org/10.2307/462478.
Molino, Walter. *Taci infame: Vite di cronisti dal fronte del sud*. Milan: Il Saggiatore, 2010.

Moore, Michelle E. "If It Was a Rape, Then Why Should She Be a Whore? Rape in Todd Solondz' Films." In *Rape in Art Cinema*, ed. Dominique Russell, 129–42. New York, London: Continuum, 2010.

Morgoglione, Claudio. "La tragedia di un uomo solo diviso tra la mafia e la passione." *La Repubblica*, 21 September 2004. http://www.repubblica.it/2004/i/sezioni/spettacoli_e_cultura/sorrentin/sorrentin/sorrentin.html?ref=search.

Muller, Eddie. "Opening Remarks to *The Woman Men Yearn for*." *Indiewire*, 16 July 2011. http://blogs.indiewire.com/leonardmaltin/san_francisco_silent_film_festival.

Mulvey, Laura. "Afterthoughts on 'Visual Pleasure and Narrative Cinema' Inspired by King Vidor's *Duel in the Sun* (1946)." In *Visual and Other Pleasures*, 29–38. Bloomington, Indianapolis: Indiana University Press, 1989.

———. "Notes on Sirk and Melodrama." In *Visual and Other Pleasures*, 39–44. Bloomington, Indianapolis: Indiana University Press, 1989.

———. *Visual and Other Pleasures*. Bloomington, Indianapolis: Indiana University Press, 1989.

———. "Visual Pleasure and Narrative Cinema." In *Visual and Other Pleasures*, 14–30. Bloomington, Indianapolis: Indiana University Press, 1989.

Neal, Arthur G. *National Trauma and Collective Memory: Major Events in the American Century*. Armonk, NY: M.E. Sharpe, 1998.

———. *National Trauma and Collective Memory*. Armonk, NY, and London: M.E. Sharpe, 2005.

Nepoti, Roberto. "Rizzotto, l'eroe bello contro 'Lo sciancato.'" *La Repubblica*, 22 October 2000. http://www.repubblica.it/online/cinema_recensioni/oro/oro/oro.html?ref=search.

Nowell-Smith, Geoffrey. "Minnelli and Melodrama." *Screen* 18, no. 2 (1977): 113–18. http://dx.doi.org/10.1093/screen/18.2.113.

Occhigrosso, Franco, ed. *Ragazzi della mafia: Storie di criminalità e contesti minorili, voci dal carcere, le reazioni e i sentimenti, i ruoli e le proposte*. Milan: Franco Angeli, 1993.

O'Healy, Áine. "Anthropological Anxieties: Roberta Torre's Critique of Mafia Violence." In *Visions of Struggle in Women's Filmmaking in the Mediterranean*, ed. Flavia Laviosa, 83–101. New York: Palgrave Macmillan, 2010.

O'Healy, Áine. "Politics and Sociosexual (In)Difference from *Roma città aperta* to *The Last Emperor*." *Romance Languages Annual* 6 (1994): 321–7.

O'Leary, Alan. "Power as Such: The Idea of the Mafia in Francesco Rosi's *Illustrious Corpses*." In *Mafia Movies: A Reader*, ed. Dana Renga, 279–86. Toronto, Buffalo, London: University of Toronto Press, 2011.

———. *Tragedia all'italiana: Italian Cinema and Italian Terrorisms, 1970–2010*. Oxford: Peter Lang, 2011.

O'Rawe, Catherine. "'A Past That Will Not Pass': Italian Cinema and the Return to the 1970s." *New Cinemas: Journal of Contemporary Film* 9.2–3 (2011): 101–13.

———. "More More Moro: Music and Montage in *Romanzo criminale*." *Italianist* 29, no. 2 (2009): 214–26. http://dx.doi.org/10.1179/026143409X12488561926388.

———. "Roberta Torre's *Angela*: The Mafia and the Woman's Film." In *Mafia Movies: A Reader*, ed. Dana Renga, 329–37. Toronto, Buffalo, London: University of Toronto Press, 2011.

Orsitto, Fulvio. "Martin Scorsese's *Goodfellas*: Hybrid Storytelling between Realism and Formalism." In *Mafia Movies: A Reader*, ed. Dana Renga, 141–48. Toronto, Buffalo, London: University of Toronto Press, 2011.

Palmer, R. Barton. "'Lounge Time' Reconsidered: Spatial Discontinuity and Temporal Contingency in *Out of the Past*." In *Film Noir Reader 4*, ed. Alain Silver and James Ursini, 53–66. New York: Limelight, 2004.

Palmer, R. "Moral Man in the Dark City: Film Noir, the Postwar Religious Revival, and *The Accused*." In *The Philosophy of Film Noir*, ed. Mark T. Conrad, 187–206. Lexington: University of Kentucky Press, 2007.

Paparcone, Anna. "Echoes of Pierpaolo Pasolini in Contemporary Italian Cinema: The Cases of Marco Tullio Giordana and Aurelio Grimaldi." PhD diss., Cornell University, 2009.

Parlagreco, Salvatore. *L'uomo di vetro: Il caso di Leonardo Vitale, il primo pentito di mafia che non fu creduto*. Milan: Bompiani, 1998.

Pasolini, Pier Paolo. *Roman Poems*. Trans. Lawrence Ferlinghetti and Francesca Valente. San Francisco: City Lights Books, 1986.

———. *Tutte le poesie*. 2 vols. Milan: Arnoldo Mondadori Editore, 2003.

Past, Elena. "'Trash Is Gold': Documenting the Ecomafia and Campania's Waste Crisis." *ISLE: Interdisciplinary Studies in Literature and the Environment* (forthcoming).

Penley, Constance. "Introduction. The Lady Doesn't Vanish: Feminism and Film Theory." In *Feminism and Film Theory*, ed. Constance Penley, 1–24. New York, London: Routledge, 1988.

———, ed. *Feminism and Film Theory*. New York, London: Routledge, 1988.

Perrone, Antonio. *Vista d'interni: Diario di carcere, di "scuri" e seghe, di trip e di sventure*. Lecce: Piero Manni, 2003.

Pickering-Iazzi, Robin. "(En)gendering Testimonial Bodies of Evidence and Italian Antimafia Culture: Rita Atria." *Italian Culture* 28, no. 1 (March 2010): 21–37. http://dx.doi.org/10.1179/016146210X12626054653135.

——. "Re-membering Rita Atria: Gender, Testimony and Witnessing in the Documentary *Diario di una siciliana ribelle*." *Italica* 84.2–3 (2007): 438–60.
——, trans. and ed. *Mafia and Outlaw Stories from Italian Life and Literature*. Toronto, Buffalo, London: Toronto University Press, 2007.
Pitrè, Giuseppe. *Usi e costumi, credenze e pregiudizi del popolo siciliano*. Vol. 2. Palermo: Libreria L. Pedone Lauriel, 1899.
Pizzini-Gambetta, Valeria. "Becoming Visible: Did the Emancipation of Women Reach the Sicilian Mafia." In *Speaking Out and Silencing: Culture, Society and Politics in Italy in the 1970s*, ed. Anna Cento Bull and Adalgisa Giorgio, 201–11. Oxford: Legenda, 2006.
Place, Janey. "Women in Film Noir." In *Women in Film Noir*, ed. E. Ann Kaplan, 47–68. London: British Film Institute, 1998.
"Pope Visits Prisoners, Says Poor Conditions Amount to 'Double Sentence.'" 19 December 2011. http://www.catholicculture.org/news/headlines/index.cfm?storyid=12713.
Porton, Richard. "Inside 'The System': An Interview with Matteo Garrone." *Cineaste* 34, no. 2 (2009): 12–15.
Principato, Teresa. "The Reasoning behind This Research: An Evaluation of the Results." In *Women and the Mafia: Studies in Organized Crime*, ed. Giovanni Fiandaca, 285–302. New York: Springer-Verlag, 2007. http://dx.doi.org/10.1007/978-0-387-36542-8_17
Principato, Teresa, and Alessandra Dino. *Mafia donna: Le vestali del sacro e dell'onore*. Palermo: Flaccovio Editore, 1997.
Projansky, Sarah. *Watching Rape: Film and Television in Postfeminist Culture*. New York, London: New York University Press, 2001.
Puglisi, Anna. *Donne, Mafia e antimafia*. Trapani: Di Girolamo Editore, 2005.
——. *Sole contro la mafia*. Palermo: La luna, 1990.
——. *Storie di donne*. Trapani: Di Girolamo Editore, 2007.
"Quando il Salento perse la sua verginità." *Lecceprima.it*, 4 May 2007. http://www.lecceprima.it/eventi/quando-il-salento-perse-la-sua-verginita.html.
Radstone, Susannah. "Trauma and Screen Studies: Opening the Debate." *Screen* 42, no. 2 (Summer 2001): 188–93. http://dx.doi.org/10.1093/screen/42.2.188.
Read, Jacinda. *The New Avengers: Feminism, Femininity and the Rape Revenge Cycle*. Manchester, New York: Manchester University Press, 2000.
Rega, Cosimo. *Sumino 'o falco: Autobiografia di un ergastolo*. Rome: Robin Edizioni, 2012.
Renga, Dana. "Introduction: The Corleones at Home and Abroad." In *Mafia Movies: A Reader*, ed. Dana Renga, 4–31. Toronto, Buffalo, London: University of Toronto Press, 2011.

———. "Pier Paolo Pasolini and the Memory of Martyrdom in New Italian Cinema." *Italica* 85.2–3 (2008): 197–209.
———. "Screening the Italian Mafia: Bystanders, Perpetrators and Pentite." *Journal for Italian Cinema and Media Studies* 1, no. 1 (2012): 55–70.
———, ed. *Mafia Movies: A Reader*. Toronto, Buffalo, London: University of Toronto Press, 2011.
Reski, Petra. *The Honoured Society: The Secret History of Italy's Most Powerful Mafia*. London: Atlantic, 2012.
Rizza, Sandra. *Una ragazza contro la mafia: Rita Atria, morta per solitudine*. Palermo: La Luna, 1993.
Rodriguez, Hilario J. "Ejercicios deconstructivos." *Dirigido por* 362 (2006): 40–1.
———. "Entravista: Paolo Sorrentino." *Dirigido por* 362 (2006): 42–3.
Romney, Jonathan. "Tragedies of Ridiculous Men." *Sight and Sound* 17, no. 4 (2007): 40–2.
Rooney, David. "Placido Rizzotto." *Variety*, 7 September 2000. http://www.variety.com/review/VE1117788026?refcatid=31.
Rousso, Henry. *The Haunting Past: History, Memory and Justice in Contemporary France*. Trans. Ralph Schoolcraft. Philadelphia: University of Pennsylvania Press, 2002.
———. *The Vichy Syndrome: History and Memory in France since 1944*. Trans. Arthur Goldhammer. Cambridge, MA, and London: Harvard University Press, 1991.
Rousso, Henry, and Eric Conan. *Vichy: Un passé qui ne passe pas*. Paris: Fayard, 1994.
Russell, Dominique, ed. *Rape in Art Cinema*. New York, London: Continuum, 2010.
Sales, Isaia. *La camorra, le camorre*. Rome: Editori Riuniti, 1993.
Santner, Eric. "History beyond the Pleasure Principle: Some Thoughts on the Representation of Trauma." In *Probing the Limits of Representation: Nazism and the Final Solution*, ed. Saul Friedlander, 143–54. Cambridge, London: Harvard University Press, 1992.
Santoro, Lara. "I bambini e la mafia: rappresentazioni letterarie e cinematografiche dell'infanzia nel genere-mafia del XXI secolo." PhD diss., Rutgers University, 2011.
Sarat, Austin, Nadav Davidovitch, and Michael Alberstein, eds. *Trauma and Memory: Reading, Healing and Making Law*. Stanford: Stanford University Press, 2007.
Saviano, Roberto. *Gomorrah: A Personal Journey into the Violent International*

Empire of Naples' Organized Crime System. Trans. Virgina Jewiss. New York: Farrar, Straus and Giroux, 2007.

Schiesari, Juliana. *The Gendering of Melancholia: Feminism, Psychoanalysis, and the Symbolics of Loss in Renaissance Literature.* Ithaca, London: Cornell University Press, 1992.

Schneider, Jane C., and Peter T. Schneider. *Reversible Destiny: Mafia, Anti-Mafia, and the Struggle for Palermo.* Berkeley, Los Angeles, London: University of California Press, 2003.

Sciascia, Leonardo. *Il giorno della civetta.* Turin: Einaudi, 1961.

Sedgwick, Eve Kosofsky. *Between Men: English Literature and Male Homosocial Desire.* New York: Columbia University Press, 1985.

Siebert, Renate. "Mafia and Anti-Mafia. Concepts and Individuals." http://www.essex.ac.uk/ecpr/events/jointsessions/paperarchive/grenoble/ws8/siebert.pdf.

——. "Mafia and Anti-Mafia: The Implications for Everyday Life." In *Organized Crime and the Challenge to Democracy,* ed. Felia Allum and Renate Siebert, 39–54. London, New York: Routledge, 2003.

——. *Secrets of Life and Death: Women and the Mafia.* Trans. Liz Heron. London, New York: Verso, 1996.

——. "Women and the Mafia: The Power of Silence and Memory." In *Gender and Memory,* ed. Selma Leydesdorff, Luisa Passerini, and Paul Thompson, 73–87. New Brunswick: Transaction Publishers, 2009.

Silver, Alain, and James Ursini, eds. *Film Noir Reader 4.* New York: Limelight, 2004.

Silverman, Kaja. *The Acoustic Mirror: The Female Voice in Psychoanalysis and Cinema.* Bloomington, Indianapolis: Indiana University Press, 1988.

——. "Fassbinder and Lacan: A Reconsideration of Gaze, Look, and Image." *Camera Obscura* 7, no. 1 19 (1989): 54–85. http://dx.doi.org/10.1215/02705346-7-1_19-54.

——. *Male Subjectivity at the Margins.* New York: Routledge, 1992.

——. "On Suture." In *Film Theory and Criticism: Introductory Readings,* ed. Leo Braudy and Marshall Cohen, 137–47. New York, Oxford: Oxford University Press, 1999.

——. *The Subject of Semiotics.* New York: Oxford University Press, 1983.

——. *The Threshold of the Visible World.* New York, London: Routledge, 1996.

Singer, Ben. *Melodrama and Modernity: Early Sensational Cinema and Its Context.* New York: Columbia University Press, 2001.

Siracusano, Alfio. "Diario dal carcere." 8 December 2003. http://www.mannieditori.it/rassegna/antonio-perrone-vista-d'interni.

Small, Pauline. "Giordana'a *I cento passi*: Renegotiating the Mafia Codes." *New Cinemas: Journal of Contemporary Film* 3, no. 1 (2005): 41–54. http://dx.doi.org/10.1386/ncin.3.1.41/1.

———. "No Way Out: Set Design in Mafia Films." *Italian Studies* 66, no. 1 (2011): 112–27. http://dx.doi.org/10.1179/007516311X12918079775785.

Smelser, Neil J. "Psychological Trauma and Cultural Trauma." In *Cultural Trauma and Collective Identity*, ed. Jeffrey C. Alexander, et al., 31–59. Berkeley, Los Angeles, London: University of California Press, 2004. http://dx.doi.org/10.1525/california/9780520235946.003.0002.

Smith, Tamsin. "Sicily Offers a Safe Taste of Mafia Life." *BBC News*, 11 June 2004. http://news.bbc.co.uk/2/hi/europe/3790401.stm.

Staiger, Janet. "Film Noir as Male Melodrama: The Politics of Film Genre Labeling." In *The Shifting Definitions of Genre: Essays on Labeling Films, Television Shows, and Media*, ed. Lincoln Geraghty and Mark Jancovich, 71–91. Jefferson, NC: McFarland, 2008.

Stille, Alexander. *Excellent Cadavers: The Mafia and the Death of the First Italian Republic*. New York: Pantheon, 1995.

Sturken, Marita. *Tourists of History: Memory, Kitsch, and Consumerism from Oklahoma City to Ground Zero*. Durham: Duke University Press, 2007.

Takahashi, Kosuke. "Capital Punishment: Japan's Yakuza Vie for Control of Tokyo." *Jane's Intelligence Review*, December 2009: 1–5.

Truzzolillo, Fabio. "The 'Ndrangheta: The Current State of Historical Research." *Modern Italy* 16, no. 3 (2011): 363–83. http://dx.doi.org/10.1080/13532944.2011.554805.

Turan, Kenneth. "*Gomorrah*'s Hazardous-to-Health Gangster Life." *Los Angeles Times*, 19 December 2008. http://articles.latimes.com/2008/dec/19/entertainment/et-gomorrah19.

Turim, Maureen. "The Trauma of History: Flashbacks upon Flashbacks." *Screen* 42, no. 2 (Summer 2001): 205–10. http://dx.doi.org/10.1093/screen/42.2.205.

Uva, Christian, ed. *Schermi di piombo: Il terrorismo nel cinema italiano*. Soveria Manelli: Rubbettino, 2007.

Vincendeau, Ginette. "Melodramatic Realism: On Some French Women's Films in the 1930s." *Screen* 30, no. 3 (1989): 51–65. http://dx.doi.org/10.1093/screen/30.3.51.

Wade, Diana. "Fighting the Mafia through Cinema: An Interview with Marco Amenta." *Cineaste* 36, no. 1 (2010): 4–9.

Walker, Janet. *Trauma Cinema: Documenting Incest and the Holocaust*. Berkeley, Los Angeles, London: University of California Press, 2005.

―――. "Trauma Cinema: False Memories and True Experience." *Screen* 42, no. 2 (Summer 2001): 211–16. http://dx.doi.org/10.1093/screen/42.2.211.
Williams, Linda Ruth. *The Erotic Thriller in Contemporary Cinema*. Bloomington, Indianapolis: Indiana University Press, 2005.
―――. "Film Bodies: Gender, Genre, and Excess." In *Genre, Gender, Race, and World Cinema: An Anthology*, ed. Julie F. Codell, 23–37. Malden, MA, and Oxford: Blackwell Publishing, 2007.
Wittman, Laura. "Pasolini's 'Inner Enemy' and the Revisionist Mafia Movie." Paper presented at the Annual Meeting of the American Association for Italian Studies, Ottawa, Ontario, 30 April–2 May 2004.
Wood, Mary P. "*Chiaroscuro*: The Half-Glimpsed *Femme Fatale* of Italian Film Noir." In *The Femme Fatale: Images, Histories, Contexts*, ed. Helen Hanson and Catherine O'Rawe, 157–69. Hampshire: Palgrave Macmillan, 2010.
―――. *Italian Cinema*. Oxford, New York: Berg, 2005.
―――. "Italian Film Noir." In *European Film Noir*, ed. Andrew Spicer, 236–72. Manchester, New York: Manchester University Press, 2007.
―――. "Lipstick and Chocolate: Paolo Sorrentino's *The Consequences of Love*." In *Mafia Movies: A Reader*, ed. Dana Renga, 354–62. Toronto, Buffalo, London: University of Toronto Press, 2011.
Woolfolk, Alan. "The Horizon of Disenchantment: Film Noir, Camus, and the Vicissitudes of Descent." In *The Philosophy of Film Noir*, ed. Mark T. Conrad, 107–23. Lexington: University of Kentucky Press, 2007.
Young, Alison. *The Scene of Violence: Cinema, Crime, Affect*. New York, Abingdon: Routledge, 2010.
Yuval-Davis, Nira. *Gender and Nation*. London, Thousand Oaks, New Delhi: Sage Publications, 1997.
Zagarrio, Vito. "Incontro con Pasquale Scimeca." *La rivista cinema* 60, March–April 2001. http://www.bibliotecadelcinema.it/incontri/inc_scimeca.htm.
Zermo, Tony. "A 87 anni è morto il questore Angelo Mangano, arrestò Liggio." *Città Nuove Corleone*, 3 April 2005. http://www.cittanuove-corleone.it/E'%20morto%20il%20questore%20Mangano.html.
Žižek, Slavoj. *Enjoy Your Symptom! Jacques Lacan in Hollywood and Out*. New York: Routledge, 2001.
―――. "From Virtual Reality to the Virtualization of Reality." In *Electronic Culture: Technology and Visual Representation*, ed. Timothy Druckery, 290–5. New York: Aperture, 1996.
―――. *Interrogating the Real*. Trans. Rex Butler and Scott Stephens. London, New York: Continuum, 2006.
―――. "Introduction: Alfred Hitchcock, or, The Form and Its Historical Mediation." In *Everything You Always Wanted to Know about Lacan (But Were*

Afraid to Ask Hitchcock), ed. Slavoj Žižek, 1–12. London, New York: Verso, 1992.

——— . *Looking Awry: An Introduction to Jacques Lacan through Popular Culture.* Boston: Massachusetts Institute of Technology Press, 1991.

——— . *The Plague of Fantasies*. London: Verso, 1997.

——— . *The Sublime Object of Ideology*. London: Verso, 1989.

Index

41bis, 116–17, 121, 132
416bis, 185

abjection, 62–4; female as abject, 24, 67–70, 76, 79, 91
A ciascuno il suo (Petri), 18
Agamben, Giorgio, 138, 215n12
Agrisano, Nicola, 193n11
Aiello, Piera, 150, 156, 164, 217n33
Alexander, Jeffrey C., 3, 8–10, 15, 192n6, 192n20, 193n23
Alighieri, Dante, 119–20, 123
Alla luce del sole (Faenza), 141
All That Heaven Allows (Sirk), 113–14
Allum, Felia, 138
Amenta, Marco, 18, 52, 151–2, 156–9, 161, 163–4, 217n36
Angela (Torre), 19, 51–64, 101, 114, 131, 133, 183, 197n7, 203n1, 204n15, 205n34, 220n1
anti-bribe campaigns, 10
Antigone, 79, 160–1
anti-Mafia campaigns, 11, 16–17, 36, 151, 154, 163, 214n55
anti-Mafia martyr narrative, 21–35, 36–8, 48–50, 52, 80–2, 88, 96–8, 149, 150–8, 160, 162–4, 181–3, 197n7, 201n2
anti-Mafia martyrs, 5, 10–11, 14, 16, 18, 22, 36, 42, 49, 51, 82, 97, 149, 151, 157
Antonioni, Michelangelo, 75, 147
Arcuri, Giovanni, 187, 221n26
Assman, Jan, 168–9, 218n11
Atria, Nicola, 150, 152
Atria, Rita, 18, 52, 138, 150–3, 155–64, 196n2, 216n1, 217n33, 217n36
Atria, Vito, 150, 152, 155

Babini, Luana, 41, 197n4
Badalamenti, Gaetano (Tano), 21, 25, 51
Bal, Mieke, 94–5
bambina deve prendere aria, La (Prudente), 192n11
Barletti, Davide, 19, 116, 119–20, 122, 132–3, 186, 213n39, 214n55
Benigni, Roberto, 18
Bergmann, Mayna, 204n14
Berlusconi, Silvio (as recent prime minister), 10
Bertolucci, Bernardo, 199n30
Bertone, Chiara, 198n17

Biagi, Enzo, 43
biopic, the, 13–14, 22, 52, 97–8, 182, 185, 197n4; homosexuality and, 98
Biùtiful cauntri (Calabria and D'Ambrosio), 192n11
Blake, Linnie, 194–5n46
Blok, Anton, 138, 141–3
blood: as abject, 63, 71, 84–5, 208n13
blood brotherhoods, 17, 23, 139, 168, 173–4
Blum, Cinzia Sartini, 123
Bolzoni, Attilio, 202n29
Bondanella, Peter, 197n4
Bonetti, Juan, 187
Bongiovanni, Giorgio, 202n26
Bonnie and Clyde (Penn), 124
Borsellino, Paolo, 10–11, 97, 116–17, 150–2, 154, 157, 160, 163, 201n2, 220n1
Boylan, Amy, 38, 40, 48, 201n11, 201n13
Brooks, Peter, 159
Bruder, Margaret Ervin, 144–5
Brusca, Giovanni, 36
buddy movie, 188
Buffalo Creek Flood, 7
Buscetta, Tommaso, 80–1
Buscetta theorem, 80, 208n1
Butler, Judith: *Bodies That Matter*, 23–4; *Frames of War*, 137; *Precarious Life*, 15–16, 134, 137, 148–9

Cadaveri eccellenti (Rosi), 18
caduta degli dei, La (Visconti), 198n30
Calabria, 5, 166, 191n2, 210n1, 220n2
Calabria, Esmeralda, 192n11
Calvino, Italo, 40
Camoletto, Raffaella Ferrero, 198n17
Camorra, 5–6, 116, 134–9, 141, 147–9, 166, 167, 171, 182, 184–5, 191n2, 196n72, 214n2, 214n3, 220n11
camorrista, Il (Tornatore), 18, 146
Campania, 5–6, 134–5, 139, 147, 166, 171, 175, 191n2
Campania In-Felix (Corsale), 193n11
Carella, Antonio, 34, 200n56
Caro diario (Moretti), 147
Caruth, Cathy, 7
Castelvolturno, 5
castration anxiety, 58, 70–1, 90, 107, 126, 172, 204n17, 211n28
Cavalli, Fabio, 187
Cavani, Liliana, 199n30
Cavarero, Adriana, 17, 107, 115
Céline, Louis-Ferdinand, 65, 68–9, 205n7, 206n8, 207n32
cento passi, I (Giordana), 19, 21–36, 39, 44, 51, 82, 98, 131, 183, 196n1, 197n4, 197n6, 197n7, 198n8, 200n51, 200n56, 208n7, 220n1
Certi bambini (the Frazzi brothers), 134
Cervantes, Miguel de, 28, 82, 88
Cesare deve morire (Paolo and Vittorio Taviani), 181–9, 221n24
Chase, David, 37
Cinisi, 21, 25–8, 35, 201n2
classical (realist) cinema, 13–14, 22, 30, 35, 38, 58, 67, 83, 92–3, 110, 118, 126, 158, 161–2, 164, 178, 182–3; traditional male protagonist of, 22, 38, 40–1, 59–60, 83, 92–3, 113, 118, 146, 170, 176–7, 197n5, 218n16
Clover, Carol J., 110, 212n40
Codelli, Lorenzo, 207n38
collaborators of justice. *See* pentiti
collective identity, 7–9, 15, 17, 25, 130–1, 133, 159, 193n25, 194n34
Collett-White, Mike, 221n18

conformista, Il (Bertolucci), 199n30
conseguenze dell'amore, Le (Sorrentino), 19, 65–79, 114, 183, 220n1
Consolo, Vincenzo, 192n8
Conte, Lorenzo, 19, 116, 119–20, 122, 127–8, 130–3
conversion hysteria, 177–9
Coppola, Francis Ford, 36, 37–8, 55, 87, 146, 151
Corben, Billy, 46
Corleonesi, the, 37, 41, 49
Corsale, Ivana, 193n11
Cosa Nostra, 5–6, 10, 21, 37, 52, 54, 66–7, 72, 75, 80, 84–5, 101, 116, 135, 138, 182, 191n2, 196n72; initiation into, 85; women excluded from, 56–7
Coulthard, Lisa, 102, 112
Cowie, Elizabeth, 176
Creed, Barbara, 24
Crialese, Emanuele, 175
Crow, The (Proyas), 146
Cupellini, Claudio, 19, 165

dalla Chiesa, Nando, 199n47
Dall'Orto, Giovanni, 23
D'Ambrosio, Andrea, 192n11
Damiani, Damiano, 18
D'Avanzo, Giuseppe, 202n29
da Volpedo, Pellizza, 48
death drive, 75–6, 137, 141, 174
de Lauretis, Teresa: *Alice Doesn't*, 25, 35, 40–1; *Technologies of Gender*, 50, 83, 137
della Chiesa, Carlo Alberto, 49
Democrazia proletaria, 22
Dentice, Alberto, 211n23
De Palma, Brian, 126, 146
De Stefano, George, 33, 37, 197n4
Deutsch, Hélène, 45

Diario di una siciliana ribelle (Amenta), 52, 151, 217n36
Dickie, John, 28, 42, 192n7, 208n1
di Matteo, Giuseppe, 10
Dimenticare Palermo (Rosi), 18
Dino, Alessandra, 196n69, 215n9
di Robilant, Alessandro, 52
divo, Il (Sorrentino), 144
Divorzio all'italiana (Germi), 57
Doane, Mary Ann, 72; "The Clinical Eye," 158; *The Desire to Desire*, 70, 100–1, 104, 157, 164, 211n21; *Femmes Fatales*, 71–2, 107–8, 125; "The Woman's Film," 51, 59–60
docu-drama, 184
dolce vita, La (Fellini), 147
dominant fiction, 13, 15, 19–20, 48–50, 77, 155–6, 163–4
"donna angelicata," the, 123
"donna integrante," the, 71
Donne di mafia (Ferrara), 52
Donnie Brasco (Newell), 146
D'Onofrio, Emanuele, 22, 198n8
Don Quixote (Cervantes), 28
drug trade, 5, 10, 105, 138, 142, 147–8, 182, 185
Duisburg murders, the, 166, 213n39
Dyer, Richard, 210n64

Eastwood, Clint, 118
eclisse, L' (Antonioni), 75
eco-Mafia, 10, 136, 167, 171, 182; documentaries on, 192n11
ego ideal, the 16, 20, 39, 51, 59, 83, 105, 145, 152, 170–2, 174, 179, 197n5
Elsaesser, Thomas, 12–13
Erikson, Kai T., 7–8
eroe Borghese, Un (Placido), 18, 52
excellent cadavers, 37

Excellent Cadavers (Tognazzi), 18, 52
extortion, 5–6, 10–11, 146
Eyerman, Ron, 9

Faenza, Roberto, 141
Falcone, Giovanni, 10–11, 36, 80, 97, 116–17, 151, 154, 201n2
Fall, the, 106–7
family: agnatic vs. affinal, 27, 139
fascism, 26, 40
Fava, Claudio, 200n56
Fellini, Federico, 147
Felman, Shoshana, 12
femme fatale, the, 18, 67, 70–2, 75–6, 79, 100, 107–8, 115, 124–6, 165, 173–5, 206n18
Ferrara, Giuseppe, 52
fetishism, 70–1
filicide, 140, 167
film noir, 13, 18, 65–7, 71–2, 76–9, 165–7, 167, 170, 171, 173–6, 181–2, 206n18, 213n11; Italian political film noir, 173, 175; Mafia noir, 65–7; noir redemption film, 66; nurturing (safe) woman in, 174; spider woman in, 174; trauma in, 167–8
Fine pena mai: Paradiso perduto (Barletti and Conte), 19, 116–33, 183, 186, 188, 213n11, 220n1
Finocchiaro, Donatella, 59, 101, 197n7, 204n21
Fiore, Innocenzo, 31
First World War, 4, 12
flashback: classical, 102–4, 153–5; modernist, 14; post-traumatic, 154–6, 177–9; realist, 178–9
Follain, John, 202n31
Fortapàsc (Risi), 131, 185
Foucault, Michel: "Madness Only Exists in Society," 81–2; "Of Other Spaces," 85, 208nn17–19
Francesco, Merlo, 43
Frasca, Antonio, 187
Frazzi, Andrea, 134
Frazzi, Antonio, 134
Freud, Sigmund, 33, 45, 122, 177, 193n16, 211n21; "'A Child Is Being Beaten,'" 103–4; *Beyond the Pleasure Principle*, 7; "From the History of Infantile Neurosis," 89–91; "Inhibitions, Symptoms, Anxiety," 72; *The Interpretation of Dreams*, 217n7; "Medusa's Head," 107, 211n28; *Moses and Monotheism*, 168–9, 178–9, 218n10, 218n11; mourning and melancholia, 15–16, 62–3, 131–2
Friedlander, Saul, 9, 193n20
Frisch, Michael, 14–15

Galantuomini (Winspeare), 19, 99–115, 131, 133, 183, 198n7, 220n1
Gallo, Enzo, 185–8
Galluzzo, Lucio, 208n10, 209n30
Gamble, Sarah, 108
Garrone, Matteo, 19, 126, 134–6, 139–40, 144, 146–7, 149, 185, 214n2
gattopardo, Il (Visconti), 17–18
Gelso, Aldo, 208n25
gender, 103; in Italian Mafia cinema, 4, 15, 18, 22–3, 131, 158, 181–2, 206n14; in mainstream cinema, 38, 40, 53, 176; as metaphor, 40; and nation, 17; normative gender in the Mafia, 23–7, 34–5, 37, 55, 60, 63, 140–1, 157; traumas relating to, 13
Germany: as setting for Mafia movie, 166

Germi, Pietro, 18, 57
Gervasini, Mauro, 144
giallo, the 47–8
Giancristofaro, Raffaella, 213
Giesen, Bernhard, 11, 165, 179
Giordana, Marco Tullio, 19, 21–2, 25, 29–30, 33–5, 36, 39, 51, 82, 98, 220n51
giorno della civetta, Il (Damiani), 18
giorno della civetta, Il (Sciascia), 221n19
giorno di San Sebastiano, Il (Scimeca), 44–5, 202n37
Girard, René, 97
giudice ragazzo, Il (di Robilant), 52
Giuliano, Salvatore, 201n2
Gledhill, Christine, 159, 174
Glynn, Ruth, 187–8, 192n5
Godfather, The (Coppola), 37–8, 55, 146
Godfather, The (Puzo), 87
Godfather: Part II, The (Coppola), 146
Gomorrah (Garrone), 6, 19, 126, 134–49, 182–3, 185, 220n1
Gomorrah (Saviano), 5–6, 134–7, 145–7
Goodfellas (Scorsese), 126, 145
grief: unresolved, 15–16, 49, 52, 62, 145, 182
Grossman, Julie, 207n26

Hanno tutti ragione (Sorrentino), 206n8
Hanson, Helen, 206n18
Haskell, Molly, 38
Hawks, Howard, 146
Heimat (Reitz), 144
"Herculaneum" (Massive Attack), 147
Herman, Judith, 6, 14

heterotopias, 85–6; of deviation, 86; the Mafia as, 85
Higgins, Lynne A., 36, 41–2, 110
Hipkins, Danielle, 18, 70, 196n75, 206n14
Hirsch, Joshua, 13–14, 154–6, 162, 178
Hitchcock, Alfred, 93
Holocaust, the 12, 144, 161
Holocaust (TV mini-series), 144
Homo Sacer, 138
homosexuality, 90–2, 200n53, 200n56, 209n30; as abjected, 23–4; elided or repressed from narrative, 4, 18, 19, 22–4, 33–5, 44, 82, 98, 181
homosocial desire, 23–4, 127, 198n17
honour, 10, 17–18, 28–9, 31–2, 37–8, 44, 57, 63, 78–9, 84–6, 106, 153, 155, 160, 184
honour, shame, vendetta (cycle of), 37–8, 44–5, 202n36
Horeck, Tanya, 42, 46–7
horror films, 12, 24, 194n46

Igartua, Juanjo, 194n27
imaginary, the 170, 173
imbalsamatore, L' (Garrone), 146
Impastato, Felicia Bartolatto, 34, 199
Impastato, Giovanni, 34, 199
Impastato Giuseppe (Peppino), 21–2, 33–4, 40, 51, 82, 97–8, 149, 160, 164, 196n2, 201n2, 206n56
Impastato, Luigi, 21, 26
Incerti, Stefano, 19, 80–2, 86, 98
Inferno (Dante), 120–1
"L'infinito" (Leopardi), 26–7
Ingrascì, Ombretta, 31–2, 199n45, 204n11
In nome della legge (Germi), 18
internal exile (confino), 26

Iovino, Seranella, 192–3n11
Irigaray, Luce, 183
Irréversible (Noé), 46
Italian American Defense
  Association, 36

Jacobs, Lea, 58, 157
Johnny Stecchino (Benigni), 18
Johnston, Claire, 119, 168
jouissance, 31, 35, 69, 73, 76
Journey to the End of the Night
  (Céline), 63, 68–9, 206n8
Julius Caesar (Shakespeare), 184–9,
  221n18, 221n24

Kaplan, E. Ann: "From Traumatic
  Paralysis to the Force Field of
  Modernity," 182–3; "Melodrama,
  Cinema and Trauma," 3, 13, 150,
  158, 161–2, 164; *Trauma and Cinema*, 194n46; *Trauma Culture*, 9–11,
  13, 163–4, 193n13
Kehr, Dave, 179
Kristeva, Julia: *Black Sun*, 71; *Powers
  of Horror*, 62–3, 65, 67, 69, 73–4;
  Revolt, She Said, 16, 195n67
Krutnik, Frank, 168, 176

Lacan, Jacques 38, 76, 79, 116,
  207n46; *The Four Fundamental
  Concepts of Psychoanalysis*, 124;
  "The Mirror Stage as Formative
  of the Function of the I," 24, 86,
  139, 171; *Speech and Language in
  Psychoanalysis*, 172
LaCapra, Dominik, 161
amico di famiglia, L' (Sorrentino),
  205n5, 206n8
Lampedusian gesture, 48
Landesman, Cosmo, 3

la Torre, Pio, 36, 48–9
Lattuada, Alberto, 18
Laub, Dori, 12
Leake, Elizabeth, 162
Leggio, Luciano, 38, 42–5, 49, 51,
  202n29, 202n31
Leopardi, Giacomo, 26–7
Leotta, Alfio, 205n1
Leys, Ruth, 7
Libera Terra, 36, 201n2
*Libero dentro: Brevi osservazioni di vita
  vissuta*, 221n26
Lilith, 106
Lo Cascio, Luigi, 22, 197n7
Lo Coco, Gianluca, 85, 215n9
Lo Verso, Girolamo, 81, 85, 199n45,
  209n30, 210n65
Lowenstein, Adam, 194–5n46
Lucky Luciano (Rosi), 18, 146
lupara bianca, 38, 44, 79, 136, 143
Lupo, Salvatore, 208n1

MacGuffin, the, 38; woman as, 91–5,
  209n59
Mafia: as heteronormative, 17,
  23–4, 34, 85–6; as homosocial, 17,
  23–4, 39, 173; Mafia families vs.
  blood family, 27, 53, 63–4, 102, 137,
  139, 141–2, 168, 177–8,
  203n4; as "men only society,"
  4, 17, 27, 55, 57, 111, 191n1; as
  "piovra" (octopus), 4, 10; the price
  of life in, 136, 142; and superego,
  31, 69; as traumatizing, 4–7,
  10–11, 13, 16, 19, 35, 77, 79, 105–6,
  115, 137, 163, 167, 181, 184, 189,
  192n6
the "mafia dentro," 158, 161
Mafia women, 4, 10, 14, 16–17,
  24, 31–2, 51–7, 99–102, 111, 114,

136–8, 162, 196n72, 204n9, 211n10, 215n11; as men's property, 57
Mafiosi (men of honour), 6, 10, 17, 26–7, 28, 38, 67, 84–6, 99, 101, 119, 137, 150–1, 174, 187; normative behaviour of, 17, 23–5, 39, 85; obsessed with Mafia movies, 136, 145–6; as represented as redeemed, 48, 183, 188–9; as represented as sympathetic, 131, 182–3, 186, 187–9
Mafioso, Il (Lattuada), 18
male melodrama, 116, 118–20, 165, 175–6, 179, 181, 183, 188–9
mammasantissima (the "holy holy mother"), 17, 31, 141, 172–5
"Man of Glass" (Cervantes), 88
mani sulla città, Le (Rosi), 18
Manzella, Cesare, 21
Marcus, Millicent, 12, 21–2, 28, 35, 40, 197n6
Marra, Vincenzo, 135
martyrdom, 11, 18–19, 22–5, 32, 35–6, 38, 40–2, 49–52, 82, 96–8, 128, 149–51, 154, 157, 160, 181–3, 197n4
masculinity: crisis of, 74, 159, 171, 176
Massari, Monica, 211n10
Massive Attack, 147
master narrative, 9, 10, 12, 113, 163–4, 183
matricide, 137, 141
Maxi-trails, 80, 97
Medea, 107
Medusa, 107, 115, 211n28
meglio gioventù, La (Giordana), 29
melancholia, 15, 118, 122; and abjection, 63; cultural, 16; Freud on, 15–16, 62, 122, 131–2; male melancholic, 118–19, 128; national, 4, 15, 134, 150, 162–3, 181
melodrama, 3, 13, 52, 57–60, 62, 64, 99–100, 102, 111, 113–14, 116, 134, 150, 153–60, 162–5, 165, 167, 176–7, 179, 181–3, 197n7, 204n15, 216n19; post-mafia melodrama, 157–60
memorials: to anti-Mafia martyrs, 11, 197n4, 201n11; collective, 40, 50, 164
men of honour. *See* Mafiosi
mental illness: as constructed, 81–2, 87–9
Mercer, John, 188
Metz, Christian, 41, 46, 118, 170
Ming, Wu, 215n23
Milton, John, 132
Mimi metallurgico, ferito nell'onore (Wertmuller), 18
mirror stage (phase), the, 24–5, 31, 86, 139, 170–1
Mitchell, Elvis, 204n15
Modleski, Tania: "Clint Eastwood and Male Weepies," 116, 118, 129; *Feminism without Women*, 212n47; "Rape versus Mans/laughter," 45
monotheism, 168–9, 178, 218n10
Moore, Michelle E., 212n40
montagna di balle, Una (Agrisano), 193n11
Moretti, Nanni, 147
Mori, Cesare, 39
Motta, Cataldo, 211n10
mourning, 4, 6, 7, 15, 97, 131–2, 136, 143–5, 181–2, 187; collective, 19; disavowed, 4, 15, 16, 79, 136–7, 147–9, 184; Freud on, 16–17, 62; national 11, 12, 16, 184

252 Index

Mulvey, Laura: "Afterthoughts on 'Visual Pleasure and Narrative Cinema,'" 58–9, 197n5, 204n17, 204n20; "Notes on Sirk and Melodrama," 99–101, 113–14, 159–60, 176; "Visual Pleasure and Narrative Cinema," 22, 51–2, 58, 170, 218n16

name of the father (law of the father), 3, 17, 24, 72, 103, 140–1, 164, 176
Naples, 5, 135
narrative fetishism, 142–5, 184; vs. mourning, 144–5
Navarra, Michele, 41, 51
Nazism, 40–1
'Ndrangheta, 5, 116, 138, 166, 191n2, 196n72, 210n1, 220n2
Neal, Arthur G., 192n6, 194n34
Nel cuore della luna (Carella), 34, 200n56
neorealism, 39–40, 197n4
Newell, Mike, 146
New Italian Epic, 144
Nicastro, Franco, 208n10, 209n30
Night and Fog (Resnais), 10, 161
Noé, Gaspar, 46
Novecento (Bertolucci), 199n30
Nowell-Smith, Geoffrey, 176–8
nuclear war, 12
Nuovomondo (Crialese), 175

objet petit a, 38, 70, 93, 124
Oedipal conflicts, 19, 27–33, 82, 89–90, 98, 137, 167–73, 178–80
Oedipal narrative, 13, 25–6, 29, 35, 38, 91, 93, 107–8, 137, 154–5, 165–72, 176–80, 198n30
Oedipal nostalgia, 58–60

Oedipus complex, 19, 25–34, 72, 80, 95, 155, 159–60, 168, 172, 178, 209n30; positive Oedipus complex, 155
Oedipus Rex (Pasolini), 29
O'Healy, Áine, 53, 61, 201n14, 203n1
O'Leary, Alan, 23, 85
omertà, 3, 17, 27, 48–50, 52–3, 57–8, 80–1, 92, 97, 130–1, 140, 215n11
O'Rawe, Catherine, 22, 53–4, 57–8, 63, 197n6, 204n21, 206n18
Orsitto, Fulvio, 126–7

Paez, Dario, 194n27
Palermo, 5, 49, 51, 81, 83, 192n7, 192n8, 201n2
Palmer, R. Barton, 66, 167
Pankeieff, Sergei (the Wolf-Man), 90–1
Paparcone, Anna, 200n53
Paradise Lost (Milton), 132
Parlagreco, Salvatore, 80–1, 84–5, 87–9, 201n65
parricide, 28, 72, 140, 167, 168, 177–80
Partanna, 150–2, 154, 217n33
Partisan Resistance, 32, 38–40, 198n30
Pasqualino settebellezze (Wertmuller), 199n30
Pasolini, Pier Paolo, 21, 27–33, 32–4, 147, 200n50, 200n51
Pasolini, Susanna, 33
Past, Elena, 192–3n11
penal code 587: the "crime of honour," 57
Penley, Constance, 103
Penn, Arthur, 124
pentitismo, 16

pentito (collaborator of justice), the, 5, 16–17, 52, 80–1, 86, 96, 132, 150, 154, 157–8, 161, 164, 208n1, 217n33
Perrone, Alessio, 118, 132
Perrone, Antonio, 117–20, 122–3, 125–7, 129, 132–3, 196n2, 212n2, 214n55
Perrone, Ruben, 122–3, 132
Petrarch, Francesco, 119, 122–3
Petri, Elio, 18
Piccinno, Daniela, 118, 132–3, 214n55
Pickering-Iazzi, Robin, 151–2, 156–7, 162, 216n1, 217n36
Pio la Torre Cooperative, 26
Pitrè, Giuseppe, 27
Pizzini Gambetta, Valeria, 54, 204n9
Placido, Michele, 18, 52
Placido Rizzotto (Scimeca), 19, 21, 36–51, 92, 97, 131, 183, 202n37, 208n7, 220n1
political thriller (film), 13
Portella della ginestra massacre, 36, 201n2
portiere di note, Il (Cavani), 199n30
Porton, Richard, 214n2
post-feminism, 101–2, 108, 112, 114
post-Mafia, 11, 112, 131, 158
post-traumatic cinema, 162
post-traumatic consciousness, 11, 13–14, 162, 184
post-traumatic incubation period, 7
post-traumatic memory, 178
pre-symbolic, the, 24, 63
primal scene, 45–7, 89–91
Principato, Teresa, 57, 196n69, 215n9
prison system in Italy, 116–18, 120, 125, 132, 185–8
Projansky, Sarah, 102, 113–14
prostitution, 10, 28, 85, 88–9, 182
Proyas, Alex, 146

Prudente, Barbara Rossi, 192n11
public rape, 39–42
Puglia, 5, 100–7, 114, 119, 124, 128, 131, 133, 191n2, 214n55
Puglisi, Giuseppe, 141
Pulp Fiction (Tarantino), 146
Purgatory (Dante), 120–1

"quaquaraquà," 187, 221n19
"Il quarto stato" (da Volpedo), 48
"A Quiet Life" (Teardo), 216n48

racketeering, 182
Radstone, Susannah, 195n47
rape, 16, 19, 28, 38, 100–2, 107, 112, 155, 157, 182, 220n1; fantasies of, 45; gang rape, 94; invented, 95; Philomena (rape of), 49, 95
rape narrative, 36, 41–8, 50, 82, 92–5, 98, 114, 131, 202n37, 212n34
rape revenge narrative, 102, 108–13, 212n40; post-feminist, 102, 111
Raw Deal: A Question of Consent (Corben), 46
Read, Jacinda, 111
Rebibbia prison, 184, 186–7
Rega, Cosimo, 185, 187–8, 220–1n11, 221n26
Reitz, Edgar, 144
Renga, Dana, 192n9, 200n50
repressive tolerance, 23
Resnais, Alain, 10, 161
return of the repressed, 177–9
Riina, Toto, 36
Risi, Marco, 131, 185
Rizzotto, Placido, 36–8, 40, 42–4, 49, 51, 97, 149, 160, 164, 196n2
Romney, Jonathan, 205n5
Rooney, David, 41
Rorschach test, 91

254 Index

Rosi, Francesco, 18, 146
Rousso, Henry, 12, 193n25, 195n56

Sacra Corona Unita, 5, 99–106, 114–15, 117–18, 120, 124–6, 128–32, 138, 182, 191n2, 196n72, 210n9, 214n55; as believed to be defeated, 105–6, 114–15, 130–1
Salvatore Giuliano (Rosi), 18
Sandokan, 146
Santner, Eric, 12, 144, 183–4, 187, 194n42
Santoro, Lara, 216n14
Saviano, Roberto, 5, 134–7, 145–7
Scampia, 134–5, 137, 143, 148
scapegoat, the, 97, 114, 131; women as scapegoated, 4, 20, 38, 63
Scarface (De Palma), 126, 129, 146
Scarface (Hawks), 146
Schiavone, Walter, 146
Schiesari, Juliana, 116, 118–19, 122, 128, 133
Sciascia, Leonardo, 221n19
Scimeca, Pasquale, 19, 21, 36, 38–9, 42, 44–6, 48, 51, 92, 97
scissionista, 136, 139, 185
scopophilia, 46, 58, 170
Scorsese, Martin, 126–7
scrota, La (Tognazzi), 18, 52
Secondagliano, 134
Second World War, 4, 12, 198n30, 201n2; Italian Jews sent to concentration camps, 4
Sedgwick, Eve Kosofsky, 23
sexual normativity, 15, 17, 23–4, 26–7, 34–5, 72, 85, 95, 98, 113, 115, 156, 176, 183
Shakespeare, William, 53, 82, 184, 186–7, 221n18

Shingler, Martin, 188
Siani, Giancarlo, 185
siciliana ribelle, La (Amenta), 18, 150–64, 183, 220n1
Sicily, 18, 35, 66, 75, 150–1, 153
Siebert, Renate: "Mafia and Anti-Mafia: Concepts and Individuals," 5; "Mafia and Anti-Mafia: The Implications for Everyday Life," 24; *The Secrets of Life and Death*, 3, 17, 23–4, 27, 43–4, 57, 142, 145, 190n1, 203n4, 215n11, 215n18
Silver, Brenda R., 42, 110
Silverman, Kaja: *The Acoustic Mirror*, 92–3; "Fassbinder and Lacan," 126; *Male Subjectivity at the Margins*, 10, 15, 20, 34, 47, 50, 92–3, 155; "The Subject of Semiotics," 24; "On Suture," 31; *The Threshold of the Visible World*, 19–20, 156
Singer, Ben, 216n19
Sirk, Douglas, 100, 113
Small, Pauline, 197n4, 207n45, 215n20
Smelser, Neil J., 193n16
Sopranos, The (Chase), 37
Sorrentino, Paolo, 19, 65, 68, 72, 144, 205n5, 206n8, 206n14, 207n38
Staiger, Janet, 120, 176
Stelley, Santiago, 193n11
strada, La (Fellini), 147
strategia del ragno, La (Bertolucci), 199n30
Striano, Salvatore, 185, 187, 220n11
Sturken, Marita, 193n13
submerged centrality, 17, 138, 196n69
Sud Side Story (Torre), 53
suicide, 16, 19, 52, 87, 95, 120, 129, 151–2, 160–4; ethical suicide, 76–9

Sumino 'o falco (Rega), 220n11, 221n26
"Supplica a mia madre," (Pasolini), 27–32
suture, 30–2, 63
symbolic, the, 24, 31, 58, 62–3, 73, 76–7, 79, 86, 93, 131, 168, 170–2, 174, 176, 183

Tano da morire (Torre), 53
Tarantino, Quentin, 146
Taviani, Paolo, 181, 184–6, 220n10, 221n22
Taviani, Vittorio, 181, 184–7, 220n10, 221n22
Teardo, Teho, 219n48
Terracciano, Bernardino, 146
terrorism, 5, 147–8; 9/11, 12, 15, 145, 148–9, 181, 184, 193n13; in Italy (the "anni di piombo"), 4–5, 11–12, 20, 181, 184, 192n5
Thirard, Paul, 207n38
Tognazzi, Ricky, 18, 52
Tornatore, Giuseppe, 18, 146
Torre, Roberta, 19, 51–3, 55–6, 58, 60–1, 64, 101, 133, 203n1
Toxic: Napoli (Stelley), 193n11
trauma, 182, 187; cinema of, 182–3; collective, cultural, historical, or national, 5–12, 14–15, 20, 161, 163, 167–8, 178–81, 192n6, 194n34; individual or personal trauma, 7–8, 13, 19, 49–50, 82, 91, 94–5, 98, 107, 109–10, 112, 152–3, 156, 162, 167–8, 172; Italian Mafia as latent trauma, 181–2; Mafia-related, 4, 11–14, 16, 20, 22, 62, 64, 79, 102, 154, 163, 167–8, 181; Mafia-related trauma as disavowed or postponed (delayed), 64, 115, 167–8, 181, 184, 187–9; Mafia-related trauma as disregarded, downplayed, or neutralized, 4, 35, 115, 133, 137, 154, 159, 161, 184; perpetrator trauma, 10, 165, 168–9, 178–80, 187–9, 218n11; primal trauma (murder of primordial father), 168–9, 178, 218n10; as repressed, 16, 112, 167–9, 178–80, 187
trauma discourse and narrative, 4, 7–9, 11–12, 14, 90, 154, 168, 181, 184
trauma theory, 3–4, 6, 8, 12–13, 193n16, 194n27, 194n46; deferred action, 7, 9; fright (Freud), 7; grief work (*Trauerarbeit*), 12, 15, 181, 187; latency period, 6–7, 11–12; *Nachträglichkeit* (belatedness), 7, 90; working through, 7–9, 12, 14–16, 62, 169, 184
traumatic consciousness, 14
traumatic memory, 9, 16, 90, 153–7, 193n16
Turim, Maureen, 13–14, 144

Ucciardone Prison, 39, 208n10
Ulysses, 120–1, 133
uomo di vetro, L' (Incerti), 19, 80–98, 131, 183, 220n1
uomo di vetro, L' (Parlagreco), 80–1, 84–5, 87–91

Vasile, Vincenzo, 208n10, 209n30
Vassallo, Angelo, 5
Vele, le, 137–8, 140–1, 143–7, 215n20
vendetta (revenge), 17, 24, 31–2, 37–8, 41, 44, 142, 151–2, 157, 160, 184, 187
Vento di terra (Marra), 135

Visconti, Luchino, 17, 198n30
Vista d'interni (Perrone), 119–23, 127–9, 132–3
Vitale, Giovanni Battista, 84
Vitale, Leonardo, 80–98, 160, 196n2, 208n10, 209n30, 210n65
Vitale, Maria, 81, 89, 91
Vitale, Rosalia, 81, 91
Vitale, Salvatore, 95
vita tranquilla, Una (Cupellini), 19, 165–80, 183, 187, 220n1
voyeurism: 29, 31, 41, 46–7, 58, 119, 170, 183

Walker, Janet, 14
Wang, Ban, 182–3
weepie, the, 204n15; male weepie, 116, 118, 129, 188
Wertmuller, Lina, 18, 199n30
western, the, 58
Williams, Linda Ruth, 93–4, 188
Winspeare, Edoardo, 19, 99, 105–6, 114, 131, 201n9, 210n2, 211n23
witnessing, cinema of, 155–6, 161–2, 182–3
Wittman, Laura, 27
Wood, Mary P., 18, 23, 66, 77, 165, 173, 175–6, 206n12
Woolfolk, Alan, 167
Wolf-Man, the (Sergei Pankeieff), 90–1
woman: as animalized, 141; as castrating, 73, 108, 125, 131; as fetish object, 58, 70–1, 119, 204n17, 206m14; as othered, 168; and precariousness, 17, 49, 101, 137–8, 142, 149, 162, 182; as projection of male fantasy, 19, 38, 71, 75–6, 119, 125–6, 173; as scapegoated, 4, 20, 36–8, 63, 131; as symbolizing lack, 41, 92–3, 119, 124, 173, 204n17; as "symptom of man," 67, 70–2, 76, 79, 108, 173, 207n46
woman's film, 13, 51, 53, 57–60, 100–2, 104, 118, 157–60, 181–2, 211n21; fallen women's film, 58, 64; with a medical discourse, 60, 158
women's movement in Italy, 203n1

Yakuza, the, 105
Young, Alison, 109–11
Yuval-Davis, Nira, 17

Zagarrio, Vito, 44–5, 202–3n37
Zapelli, Monica, 200n56
Žižek, Slavoj: *Enjoy Your Symptom!* 76–7, 79, 173; "From Virtual Reality to the Virtualization of Reality," 147; *Interrogating the Real*, 71–2, 76; "Introduction: Alfred Hitchcock," 93; *Looking Awry*, 76–7, 124; *The Plague of Fantasies*, 70; *The Sublime Object of Ideology*, 37–8
"Zobeide" (Calvino, *Invisible Cities*), 40–1
zombie films, 12

www.ingramcontent.com/pod-product-compliance
Lightning Source LLC
Chambersburg PA
CBHW030312080526
44584CB00012B/535